DATE DUE

Pluralizing Journalism Education

PLURALIZING JOURNALISM EDUCATION

A Multicultural Handbook

Edited by Carolyn Martindale

Greenwood Press
Westport, Connecticut • London

LIBRARY OF CONGRESS CATALOGING-IN-PUBLICATION DATA

Pluralizing journalism education : a multicultural handbook / edited
   by Carolyn Martindale.
        p. ; cm.
     Includes bibliographical references and index.
     ISBN 0-313-28592-6
        1. Journalism—Study and teaching.   I. Martindale, Carolyn, 1938–
PN4785.P58   1993
070.4′071′1—dc20   92-35923

British Library Cataloguing in Publication Data is available.

Library of Congress Catalog Card Number: 92-35923
ISBN: 0-313-28592-6

First published in 1993

Greenwood Press, 88 Post Road West, Westport, CT 06881
An imprint of Greenwood Publishing Group, Inc.

Printed in the United States of America

The paper used in this book complies with the
Permanent Paper Standard issued by the National
Information Standards Organization (Z39.48–1984).

10 9 8 7 6 5 4 3 2 1

CONTENTS

PREFACE

This book is the work of many minds and an astonishing degree of enthusiasm by its contributors. Ever since I conceived the idea several years ago, I have been encouraged at each step of the way. My university granted me a sabbatical to work on the book, Greenwood Press expressed interest in seeing the prospectus, and everyone I approached for a contribution to the book not only agreed, but did so with enthusiasm and genuine pleasure. And they have come through with an exceptionally rich and multifaceted selection of ideas and suggestions from their own pioneering experiences. The contributors even agreed to donate their honoraria to establish a new award to encourage development of multicultural curricular materials. Our editors at Greenwood have been unfailingly enthusiastic and supportive. From the beginning it has been a book that was meant to be written.

The idea for the book was born in 1990 at a convention of the Association for Education in Journalism and Mass Communication (AEJMC), a leading national organization of college communications educators. The council that accredits journalism and mass communication programs passed in 1984 a standard for accreditation, called Standard 12, that required such programs to show evidence that they were attempting to recruit minority journalism students and faculty and make efforts to include multicultural perspectives in their curricula. Since then enough programs had come up for reaccreditation that the lack of available information about pluralizing was being felt. During the 1990 convention member after member spoke up at general sessions saying that they wanted to pluralize their faculty, student body and curricula, but did not know how to begin.

For years, I, along with many other educators, had been giving sparsely attended workshops at AEJMC and writing articles about ways to bring multiculturalism into journalism and mass communication programs. It occurred to me at the convention that many people held scattered segments of knowledge about these topics, while a lot other people were crying for that information. What was needed was a way of bringing them together. Thus this book.

An additional facet of the book—suggestions for ways to pluralize the coverage and staffs of the student press and other media—grew out of my experiences as a college publications adviser. Again, for several years I had been giving workshops on this topic at conventions of college media advisers and the student press, and these workshops were jammed. Clearly many advisers and students recognized the need to make the student media more inclusive and were eager to find ways to do it.

We hope the book will generate the same excitement about multicultural education that we have felt, and an eagerness to try some of the suggested ideas. They can only enrich you, your teaching and your communications program.

I salute the efforts of all those who have been working quietly for years to bring a pluralistic perspective to their teaching, and apologize that I didn't learn of them in time to ask to include their ideas in this book. The information offered here is just a beginning, an initial sampling of the many techniques we can use to make our journalism and mass communication programs more inclusive. The entries represent some of the best ideas to have been developed so far, but many other excellent techniques must surely exist, and others will be developed.

This book, it is hoped, will offer a way to get started for those faculty and administrators who want to do more to work diversity into their programs. Ideally it also will offer additional insights and ideas to those educators who have been working on their own for years to make their teaching and their communications programs more inclusive.

Because an underlying theme of the book is appreciating and valuing diversity, I wanted to leave the contributors free to use whatever terms they preferred to describe various racial and ethnic groups. It seemed clear that no editor who valued pluralism would force homogeneity onto the contributing authors' word choices. As a result, the reader will find a wide array of terms for various groups, including AHANA or ALANA, an acronym for African, Hispanic or Latino, Asian and Native American; Chicano for Mexican American; and people of color. We have chosen to capitalize Black and White when using those words to refer to races, just as we would capitalize Negro or Caucasian.

Contributors to this book include African Americans, Hispanics, Asian Americans and White Americans; they work at universities from New York to Florida, from the Midwest and the Southwest, from California to Washington state. They range from persons with many years of experience in journalism education, including several deans, to persons not long out of graduate school. Many are former newspaper reporters; one is a Pulitzer winner. Others have spent most of their careers in the academic world, and several have published books on multicultural topics.

Because many of the authors share a background in newspaper journalism, numerous suggestions focus on courses that teach print journalism, but most of the teaching ideas presented also will work well in broadcast classes, in advertising and public relations, and in other aspects of the communications field. In fact, the curriculum ideas can be adapted to many disciplines, while the suggestions for recruiting and retaining minority students and faculty can be used by any department or college.

In order to make the book as useful as possible, we have included numerous bibliographies. In addition to the bibliographies at the end of most chapters, Parts II, III and IV end with bibliographies on recruiting and retaining minority students and faculty, pluralizing the curriculum and pluralizing student media, respectively. The bibliography at the end of Part III includes audiovisual materials, articles on pluralizing the curriculum, resources for sensitizing faculty, and histories of racial and ethnic groups, as well as the major resources on the different groups covered.

Some organizations and their acronyms receive frequent mention. In addition to AEJMC, the American Society of Newspaper Editors (ASNE) and the recently renamed American Newspaper Publishers' Association, both leading organizations in their field, appear often. Also mentioned is the Task Force on Minorities in the Newspaper Business, a group formed by the above two organizations to encourage the employment of more minority journalists.

A few words seem appropriate about the growing protest against multiculturalism in education. During the past several years scores of articles have appeared in the national media describing the various persons and movements protesting the idea of multiculturalism. During that same period of time very little has appeared about people protesting the tremendous growth of overt racism in this country, although racism is clearly a vicious philosophy, while multiculturalism simply seems wrong-headed to its critics.

It is easy to object to the excesses of those who wish to teach that everything that has come from Whites, from males, from Western Europe is evil and should be eliminated. But short of that stance, there is plenty of opportunity for including a greater variety of peoples, perspectives and histories in our teaching. Why should that effort be suspect? Why is it being leaped upon as though it must be stamped out of existence before it even has a chance to be tried? At the vast majority of our institutions of higher education, not the Harvards and Michigans but the thousands of smaller universities and community colleges, multiculturalism has hardly even been heard of, let alone instituted.

The acquittal of the police who beat Rodney King and the recent Los

Angeles riots illustrate clearly the yawning gulf in understanding between classes and races in the United States. Clearly our nation needs mass media communicators who can help people see across that gulf and begin to understand each other. It is up to university journalism and mass communication programs to try to prepare students to communicate across cultures.

In a February 3, 1992, *Time* essay on diversity and multiculturalism, Robert Hughes expressed clearly several of the strongest arguments for broadening our—and our students'—perspectives. In a global economy and in the absence of a cold war, he wrote, the future leadership of America

will rest with people who can think and act with informed grace across ethnic, cultural, linguistic lines. And the first step in becoming such a person lies in acknowledging that we are not one big world family, or ever likely to be; that the differences among races, nations, cultures and their various histories are at least as profound and as durable as the similarities; that these differences are not divagations from a European norm but structures eminently worth knowing about for their own sake. In the world that is coming, if you can't navigate difference, you've had it.

It is hoped that this book will help us navigate those differences, and with "informed grace."

I INTRODUCTION

1 A RATIONALE FOR PLURALIZING JOURNALISM EDUCATION

John F. Greenman

In connection with a recent project for the American Society of Newspaper Editors (ASNE), I was looking for examples of how diversity training was being used in the United States. One example was a daycare center in suburban Boston that is teaching three-year-olds how to resist prejudice and value diversity.[1] The case of the daycare center reminded me of the importance of reaching people early, an often-discussed concern in newsrooms when the issue of diversity is on the table.

One reason this book is important is its potential for reaching people at the earliest point in their journalism education—college. No time is quite as crucial when viewed from the editor's perspective of what needs to be done to diversify newsrooms.

I came to this view over the last few years as, along with other editors and researchers, I grappled with the question, To what extent can the colleges help newsrooms become racially diverse?

Admittedly, this question is self-serving. Colleges are independent institutions. Whatever they do to encourage diversity ought to reflect their values and further their goals. Yet, college is the gate through which virtually all journalists pass. The college journalism experience—especially work on the college newspaper—is meaningful in terms of diversity in several ways.[2]

The most significant is socialization. For many journalists, the college newspaper is the seminal newspaper experience. The socialization issue is one of imprint. Imagine the imprint on the White student if that college newsroom is racially homogeneous. Then consider the imprint on the student of color who, for one reason or another, is excluded.

From a vocational standpoint, we know that newspapers weight college newspaper experience heavily when deciding who will get internships and entry-level jobs. Minority students who don't work on college newspapers—and they won't unless those newspapers encourage diversity—are at a disadvantage.

Finally, in terms of learning, college newspapers are typically the best laboratory available to college journalism students. They are "the heart of journalism education," says John David Reed, chairman of the department of journalism at Eastern Illinois University.[3] Minority students who are not involved with the college newspaper miss this experience and probably can't find a comparable one.

If college journalism programs are to reach students of color early, they will have to invest in recruiting and retention. There is reason to believe that the people who lead these programs are eager to do so. More than four years ago, nearly two-thirds of the journalism deans, directors and department heads responding to an ASNE survey said that recruiting and retention of minority students is the "most important" recruiting and retention issue they face. Since then, several useful how-to guides have been published, and the issue is a regular panel topic when journalism educators meet. And there is good evidence that vigorous recruiting pays off with improved numbers.[4]

Recruiting and retaining faculty of color are similarly important. It's hard to imagine a racially homogeneous faculty teaching credibly about diversity in newsrooms and in story content, much less succeeding with recruiting and retention of minority students. But for the most part, that is the condition of college journalism faculties. Progress is being made, abetted by pressure from accrediting standards, but it is halting and painful.

In addition, it is important that all journalism students get training in how to cover different racial and ethnic groups with accuracy and sensitivity. They also have to learn how to work well with people of different backgrounds. Part of this knowledge can be imparted through course work, and journalism faculty of any color can do much to infuse into their curricula information about the contributions of people of color and women to American society and to journalism history.

The test of all such efforts will be what the student takes from the experience. The best college journalism programs will be those whose graduates have visited the rich diversity of American life, who trust and value differences among co-workers, and who know that reporting that embraces inclusiveness is the fairest and most accurate.

I commend this book to you selfishly; if colleges do a better job of fostering diversity, the pool of talent available for work on commercial daily newspapers will be enlarged and improved. A lot has been written about that pool of talent, mostly from the perspective of the percentage of minorities working in the newsrooms of commercial dailies. One set of numbers is numbingly familiar: minorities comprise about 25 percent of the U.S. population, but hold fewer than 9 percent of the jobs in U.S. newsrooms—nowhere near parity.[5]

Another set of numbers is less familiar: in 1991, according to the American Society of Newspaper Editors, minorities comprised 22.5 percent of entry-level newsroom hires.[6] These numbers are important because they signal that at the entry level—at the crucial opening of the funnel—commercial dailies are approaching parity.

With parity, the discussion will shift from the issue of who is represented in newsrooms to how newsrooms value differences among their members. Unless newsrooms are prepared to value differences, to make what R. Roosevelt Thomas, Jr., calls the transition from affirmative action to affirming diversity, the effort to reach parity will be wasted.[7]

This book will reach journalism educators in different stages of consciousness about diversity. Those who are familiar with the research on changes in the make-up of the U.S. population will welcome it as an additional tool for teaching and administering for diversity.

Other journalism educators, like many editors of commercial dailies, will ask why they need to learn to teach and administer for diversity. "I know how to teach and administer already," they will say. True, perhaps, but maybe not well enough to prepare the workforce that will be in place at the turn of the century. By then, according to the Hudson Institute:

• Only 15 percent of the new entrants to the workforce will be native White males;

• 61 percent of the new workers will be women;

• 29 percent will be minorities.[8]

Journalism educators who don't think their classrooms will change will be as surprised in 10 years as were editors of 20 years ago who didn't think their readership would change.

As the population changes, journalism educators will have to choose between two alternatives. They can resist change and try to preserve the face of the classroom and the curriculum as it is today. This means having an ever-smaller pool of talent to teach. Or educators can adapt to the change, learning to teach and administer for diversity.

This book goes a long way toward explaining what that means and how it gets done. Its chapters contain advice ranging from how to find potential journalism students among students of color to how to retain faculty of color, and from teaching ideas for pluralizing the journalism curriculum to means of encouraging diversity in student media.

Journalism educators who follow the advice will, through the journalists who emerge from their classrooms, show the way to some of their recalcitrant colleagues who edit commercial dailies.

As an editor who values diversity, I hope they will.

NOTES

1. Laura Batten, "Teaching the Very Young to Battle Prejudice," Boston *Globe*, 28 April 1991, p. A19.

2. This analysis has appeared in different form in articles the author has co-written with Barbara Hipsman and Stanley Wearden, associate professors in the School of Journalism and Mass Communication at Kent State University. See "College Newspaper Staffs Are Diversifying, but Most Top Editors Still Are White," *ASNE Bulletin*, April 1990, pp. 13–17; "Racial Diversity in College Newsrooms," *Newspaper Research Journal* 11 (Summer 1990), 80–95; and "The College Newsroom: Still White at the Top," *College Media Review* 29 (Summer 1990), 5–7.

3. Greenman, Hipsman and Wearden, "College Newspaper Staffs Are Diversifying," p. 15.

4. Barbara J. Hipsman and Stanley T. Wearden, "Peering Down the Pipeline: Minority Editors at College Newspapers Are Increasing—but to Only a Handful," *ASNE Bulletin*, April 1991, p. 28.

5. Cornelius F. Foote, Jr., "Level of Minorities in the Newsroom at 8.72 Percent," *ASNE Bulletin*, April 1991, p. 21.

6. Ibid., p. 22.

7. R. Roosevelt Thomas, Jr., "From Affirmative Action to Affirming Diversity," *Harvard Business Review*, March-April 1990, pp. 107–117.

8. Hudson Institute, *Workforce 2000: Work and Workers for the 21st Century* (Washington DC: U.S. Department of Labor, 1987).

2 PHILOSOPHICAL AND ECONOMIC ARGUMENTS FOR MEDIA DIVERSITY

Ted Pease

There are really only two reasons why the news media, and those who read newspapers and watch TV, should worry about demographic changes and the media's employment and coverage of racial and ethnic "minorities"—non-White Americans—in the United States.

These demographic changes mean that more different kinds of citizens need to participate in the marketplace of ideas on which this country's democratic system is based. In a democracy, everyone must be allowed to participate in both the information marketplace and the political arena if the system is to survive. That's the first reason. The second one is economic: It is in the self-interest of any business to tailor products to reach new consumers and consumer needs. Both reasons should be painfully obvious, but apparently haven't been to U.S. newspapers and other mass media, which have been slow in employing and serving America's rapidly diversifying population.

How slow is slow? As Chuck Stone of the Philadelphia *Daily News*, founding president of the National Association of Black Journalists, wrote in 1988, "Since the Kerner Commission, the number of minority journalists has inched up with all the speed of a one-legged tortoise climbing a hill in a hailstorm."[1]

When the Kerner Commission chastised the newspaper business in 1968 for its failure to inform society about issues in Black America, more than 99 percent of U.S. newspaper reporters and editors were White.[2] Now, almost a quarter-century later, the proportion of racial minorities in the population still outstrips the proportion of minorities in newspaper newsrooms by three to one. At the end of 1990, 8.72 percent of newsroom professionals—reporters, copy editors, desk editors, photographers, graphic artists, and so on—were minorities.[3] The country, however, is more than 24 percent non-White and is projected to be 32 percent minority by the year 2010; by the middle of the next century, Whites no longer will be the numerical majority in this country.[4] But where will the news organizations that cover America be?

It is not only fatally shortsighted but morally wrong for the press that covers the United States not to reflect more accurately the make-up of its population. Furthermore, it is economic stupidity in a nation where 87 percent of the population growth between now and the year 2000 will be among people of color.[5] Even now, in 1992, 119 different languages are spoken in New York City, and the non-Anglo populations in the states of Texas and California are approaching 50 percent.[6] The country is changing all around us; the news media face both the moral obligation and the economic necessity of changing as well or risking loss of their influence as purveyors in the marketplace of ideas.

As great as the economic risk to the media is, however, the greater risk is to ourselves—a population uninformed, ill-informed or misinformed by a mass media that can view the nation—view us—only myopically and incompletely.

Some in this country consider racism to be even more prevalent at the start of the 1990s than in the 1960s, when the Rev. Martin Luther King, Jr., and the civil rights movement forced the nation to acknowledge the injustice of a society that systematically excludes citizens because of race or ethnic background. Much has changed since the 1960s, but people of color still are largely excluded from both newsrooms and news content, or are included only as second-class citizens. Although most large U.S. newspapers circulate in urban areas with non-White populations of 50 percent and higher, few cover adequately those increasingly pluralistic neighborhoods. In fact, a variety of scholarly studies of news media performance show that coverage of minorities by those large metropolitan newspapers tends to account for only about 3 percent of their total news coverage.[7] Further, more than half of White journalists and more than 70 percent of minority journalists, responding to a national 1991 study, said that their own newspaper covered minority communities only marginally or poorly.[8]

From these examples, it is apparent that the news industry, whether intentionally or not, still excludes people from the media mainstream because of their race or cultural perspective. The news industry is not keeping up with demographic change in this country, either in terms of employing people of diverse backgrounds as information-gatherers and gatekeepers, or in terms of providing content and coverage of people who are not White.

Which brings us to the question: Why should we care?

WHY WE CARE

As suggested, two basic reasons to worry about diversity in the newsrooms or in news content are philosophical and practical. The U.S. news media should pay greater attention to employing and covering people of color because it is right and just under the democratic ideals on which this nation was founded, and because any industry that ignores the nation's rapid demographic shifts may not survive in the changing marketplace.

The United States, despite (or perhaps because of) its demographic vitality, nevertheless remains inherently racist in its institutions and resists acknowledging the implications of multicultural change in the workplace and the marketplace. The news media, ever reflective of what they perceive as the expedient social ground swell, may give lip service to issues of racial diversity in the nation and the individual markets they serve, but they lack the moral strength and the economic vision to understand that times—and the society— are changing.

There is no more comprehensive or far-reaching change in U.S. society in the 1990s than its growing multiculturalism and racial diversity. The result of the news media's tendency to bury their collective head in the sand on this point is that the "mainstream" news organizations in this country have abandoned their moral imperative to represent the society they serve. Simultaneously, they are losing their economic ability to survive in an increasingly diverse culture whose needs they fail to fulfill.

So how can the collective consciousness of the U.S. news media be raised, prompting the media to fulfill their moral obligation to permit the kind of robust and wide-open debate on which the marketplace of ideas and participatory democracy were built? It is worthwhile to recall the Hutchins Commission report of 1947, which provided a practical, eloquent five-point defense against attempts to restrict the media's right to supply goods to the marketplace of ideas.

THE MORAL ARGUMENT

The Hutchins Commission, formally known as the Commission on Freedom of the Press, was convened by the news industry itself in 1947. Concerned that U.S. society might rescind the press' First Amendment "franchise" to operate in the marketplace of ideas, *Time* magazine's Henry Luce convened the blue-ribbon panel to evaluate the roles and responsibilities of the press in a free society. The commission's charge was to evaluate, in the context of constitutionally mandated First Amendment freedoms of expression, the press' responsibilities in the U.S. marketplace of ideas.

Robert M. Hutchins, the University of Chicago chancellor who chaired the commission, understood his task this way: "The tremendous influence of the modern press makes it imperative that the great agencies of mass communication show hospitality to ideas which their owners do not share. Otherwise, these ideas will not have a fair chance."[9]

The commission said that freedom of the press was in danger in 1947 for three reasons: (1) As the media's reach had grown, the diversity of ideas and opinions expressed through the media had declined; (2) those who could express ideas in the press had "not provided a service adequate to the needs of society"; and (3) press performance had so outraged, disenfranchised and disappointed segments of society that there was a threat that the media might lose their franchise under the First Amendment to participate in the free and open marketplace of ideas.[10]

In the 1940s, the press feared government limitations because of short-comings in press performance. In the 1990s, however, it is clear that the media's loss of franchise in the American marketplace of ideas is market-based and self-inflicted; poor service to a changing marketplace has resulted in information consumers abandoning existing "mainstream" news media for other information sources that serve them better.

The Hutchins Commission guidelines for responsible press performance in a free society are:

1. The media should provide "a truthful, comprehensive and intelligent account of the day's events in a context which gives them meaning."
2. The media should be "a forum for exchange of comment and criticism" on matters of public importance.
3. The media should present "a representative picture of the constituent groups in the society."
4. The media should undertake the "presentation and clarification of the goals and values of the society."
5. The media must provide to the public "full access to the day's intelligence."[11]

In the civil rights context, the third point may be the most crucial; how well have the media, then or today, represented the constituent groups in the society?

By the 1960s, it was clear that press adherence to these principles was a matter of lip service, convenience or both. Most White Americans were caught by surprise by the racial violence that spread across the country in the mid–1960s. The Kerner Commission, convened by President Lyndon B. Johnson in 1967 to evaluate what had occurred, reported that the environment in which most Black Americans lived was "totally unknown to most white Americans."[12] Had the media provided a truthful, comprehensive and intelligent account of the day's events in Black America, in a context that gave them meaning? Had they offered access to all segments of society for comment and criticism on matters of public importance? How well had the media offered a representative picture of all the constituent groups of society, helped the nation clarify its goals and values, or provided full coverage of news in all parts of the nation? The answers were largely negative. "Far too often," the Kerner Commission found, "the press acts and talks about Negroes as if Negroes do not read newspapers or watch television, give birth, marry, die or go to PTA meetings."[13]

The media had failed both Negro Americans, by ignoring issues in their communities, and White Americans, who lacked the information they needed to make judgments about their society, the Kerner Commission said. Its statement on the media presents a clear, concise summation of the role and responsibilities of the press in a free and diverse society:

Our . . . fundamental criticism is that the news media have failed to analyze and report adequately on racial problems in the United States and, as a related matter, to meet the Negro's legitimate expectations in journalism. By and large, news organizations have failed to communicate to both their black and white audiences a sense of the problems America faces and the sources of potential solutions. The media report and write from the standpoint of a white man's world. The ills of the ghetto, the difficulties of life there, the Negro's burning sense of grievance, are seldom conveyed. Slights and indignities are part of the Negro's daily life, and many of them come from what he now calls the "white press"—a press that repeatedly, if unconsciously, reflects the biases, the paternalism, the indifference of white America. This may be understandable, but it is not excusable in an institution that has the mission to inform and educate the whole of our society.[14]

In the 1990s, the media have made little real progress in terms of giving media consumers—White and non-White alike—a "representative picture of the constituent groups of society," which is an integral responsibility of a free press in an open marketplace of ideas. Philosophically, efforts to increase diversity in news content must be, as President Lyndon B. Johnson said in his charge to the Kerner Commission, "fired by conscience."[15] If we are to exist in a pluralistic society governed by democratic precepts, we must know ourselves and our own values and goals for the society.

THE ECONOMIC SELF-INTEREST ARGUMENT

If the moral argument pales, then it is both logical and perhaps expedient to invoke economic self-interest. As the United States emerges from the 1980s, a decade characterized by self-interest, the philosophical imperative to make room in the marketplace of ideas for all newcomers in society might seem passé. There is reason to wonder if the precepts that formed the marketplace of ideas in the first place as an integral part of this nation even survived the "Me Generation."

Despite newspapers' difficulties, because of language and cultural barriers, in attracting readers among immigrant groups, readership studies have shown that ethnic and racial minorities are at least as loyal newspaper readers as

Whites. Further, readership depends much more on education and economic variables than on race, and non-White Americans are consistently gaining ground in college graduation rates and income.[16]

If the news media continue to do such a poor job of serving the needs of minority consumers in terms of tone and content, how long are those consumers likely to remain loyal? And how long will advertisers stay with media that are unable to deliver audiences among the only growing segments of the population—African Americans, Asian Americans and Hispanics? Stated more positively, the media must be able to see the large body of unserved and disenfranchised potential consumers out there in growing minority communities. Making the news product fill those consumers' needs is not just good economic sense, but the key to economic survival in an increasingly multicultural U.S. melting pot.

As the latest U.S. census figures show, the melting pot is becoming much more ethnically and racially diverse. David Lawrence, Jr., publisher of the Miami *Herald* and former president of the American Society of Newspaper Editors, notes: "Much of the energy behind minority hiring and advancement in our business has been the moral obligation to do what is right and fair. Rightly so. [But] what is right and fair is also smart business."[17]

In 1989 the industry's Task Force on Minorities in the Newspaper Business made the case for linking the moral obligation for inclusivity with the economic opportunities of diversity. If the moral obligation to cover and involve all segments of society in the marketplace of ideas is not enough for a media owner, then the economic and demographic realities should be. As noted above, the vast majority of U.S. population growth through the turn of the century will be among minorities. The media companies that beat the odds of declining readership markets will tap those growing population segments.

Newspaper readership and voter turnout are both declining. In the late 1980s, 60 percent of adults in this country read a daily newspaper, down from 80 percent in 1960; only half of registered voters cast votes in the 1988 presidential election compared to 64 percent in 1960. Is there a relation between information and political participation?

More than 60 percent of White adults read newspapers every day, as do 51 percent of Blacks, 52 percent of Hispanics, and 42 percent of Asian Americans. The readership gap between Whites and non-Whites is narrowing: Black readership has declined half as much as White readership since the mid–1970s.

Although language barriers are a problem among some Hispanics and Asians, once language problems are overcome, these groups are as likely as Whites to read newspapers; in various studies, Black readers show greater loyalty than White readers to their newspapers.[18]

What all this means from a market perspective is that non-White groups quickly are becoming larger segments of the U.S. market for both newspapers and other news media, and for goods and services.

Between 1990 and 2000, more than 63 percent of the new U.S. workforce—wage earners and consumers—will be women; 56 percent will be minorities. News organizations that fail to hold those wage earners by delivering content and coverage that satisfy their needs will lose them as well as the advertisers seeking to reach those increasingly affluent audiences. For news organizations unable to reach, attract and hold the increasingly diverse people of America, the dawning of the next century may coincide with their own final days.

The news media—and the society they seek to serve—must come to the realization that there are compelling philosophical and pragmatic reasons to be concerned with the increasing ethnic and racial diversity of this country. How can an information medium remain a true mass medium central to the health of a democratic society when its content is increasingly unimportant to the lives of the fastest-growing parts of that society? And once the realization of these stark facts has sunk in, the news media must act to reach and hold these growing audiences, not just for purposes of economic gain, but because communication between and among the segments of an increasingly diverse society serves, as the Hutchins Commission members said, to establish and clarify the goals and values of the society.

Without such internal communication and debate among all segments and facets of society, the media's franchise to inform society slips away, not by government edict but by neglect. Those poorer for it are not just the news media, but the society that can no longer depend on them for information and tough scrutiny of issues of pressing concern. As the workforce and the population change, news media that fail to keep up with changes may go the way of the dodo.

It is a frustrating contradiction about the news business that we who cover society can know so well the culture's ills and yet be so slow to recognize those same sicknesses when they are our own. The news industry, so self-righteous in defending its place in the democratic marketplace of ideas as essential to the Republic, has proven itself, like the dominant White society it reflects, self-serving and shortsighted in recognizing the inevitable trends and directions of social change.

Editors, publishers and news directors may justify their lack of thoughtful coverage of issues reflecting the increasingly pluralistic nature of the society by saying that they're giving readers and viewers what they want. But even people living in homogeneous communities where racial diversity means the big city (not *my* neighborhood) are a part of a larger national and global community of many different kinds of people not like themselves. Sooner or later those people will venture beyond their own monochromatic communities, either by bus or by thought, and find that they need to know about people not like themselves if they are to participate fully in the 21st century.

The aims of this book on pluralizing journalism education are to help our classrooms and newsrooms become more multicultural, in both attitude and action, and to raise the consciousness of educators and communication professionals alike about the issues surrounding the mass media in a racially and ethnically pluralistic America.

Journalism classrooms are, in some demographic and attitudinal ways, microcosms of media newsrooms. Despite lofty rhetoric about recruiting a more diverse student body, many of our schools and departments of mass communication have been no more successful than the news media themselves in pluralizing student bodies or course content. Although some ideas in this handbook may be old hat to those programs that have been successful in recruiting students of color, other parts may offer suggestions for improvement and change.

For programs that have relatively few non-White students, this book can prove invaluable. About one-third of the chapters deal specifically with ways to recruit, nurture, mentor and retain minority students and faculty. Clearly, any gains that we in the academy make in terms of student and faculty diversity will translate directly into greater newsroom and news content diversity in the media.

All journalism and mass communication programs should benefit from the chapters dealing with specific suggestions for diversifying curriculum content. As the nation moves inexorably toward a society in which no single racial or ethnic group is a numerical majority, all our students will need information on covering and living in a truly multiethnic world. Suggestions are offered here for providing such information by infusing material dealing with ethnicity and multiculturalism into existing skills and theory courses and through creation of freestanding courses on diversity and gender.

Going a step further, we can help demonstrate the values of multicultural news coverage and news staffs through the student media at our universities. The last chapters in the book suggest ways that both media advisers and faculty members who are not directly involved with the student media can encourage diversity.

The tasks of recruiting and retaining minority students and faculty, of infusing information about covering a multicultural society into our curricula, of pluralizing our student media, all present a substantial challenge to journalism educators. But in the academy, as in the newsroom, the challenges of diversity must be met. We must show our students, of all backgrounds, how and why multiculturalism matters and why they should care.

NOTES

1. Chuck Stone, "Journalism Schools' Students and Faculty in the Year of Kerner Plus 20," in *Kerner Plus 20* (Washington, DC: National Association of Black Journalists, 1988), p. 7.

2. *Report of the National Advisory Commission on Civil Disorders* (Washington, DC: U.S. Government Printing Office, 1968).

3. See American Society of Newspaper Editors Minorities Committee, "1990 Annual Employment Survey," 5 April 1991.

4. U.S. Bureau of Census, *Statistical Abstract of the United States* (Washington, DC: U.S. Department of Commerce, 1990). See also *Cornerstone for Growth: How Minorities Are Vital to the Future of Newspapers* (Reston, VA: Task Force on Minorities in the Newspaper Business, 1989).

5. *Cornerstone for Growth*, p. 6.

6. Bureau of Census and Jean Gaddy Wilson, "How to Map Directions for Your Media Future," Media Leaders Lecture Series address, St. Michael's College, Colchester, VT, 16 October 1991.

7. See, for example, Carolyn Martindale, "Coverage of Black Americans in Four Major Newspapers, 1950–1989," *Newspaper Research Journal* 11 (Summer 1990), 96–112; Carolyn Martindale, "Changes in Newspaper Images of Black Americans," *Newspaper Research Journal* 11 (Winter 1990), 40–50; Carolyn Martindale, "Coverage of Black Americans in Five Newspapers since 1950," *Journalism Quarterly* 62 (Summer 1985), 321–328; Edward C. Pease, "Kerner Plus 20: Minority News Coverage in the Columbus *Dispatch*," *Newspaper Research Journal* 10 (Spring 1989), 17–37; Ted Pease, "Ducking the Diversity Issue: Newspapers' Real Failure Is Performance," *Newspaper Research Journal* 11 (Summer 1990), 24–37; Paula B. Johnson, David O. Sears and John B. McConahay, "Black Invisibility: The Press and the Los Angeles Riot," *American Journal of Sociology* 76 (January 1971), 707, 712; Thom Lieb, "Protest at the *Post*: Coverage of Blacks in the Washington *Post* Sunday Magazine," paper presented at the national convention of the Association for Education in Journalism and Mass Communication, Portland, OR, July 1988.

8. Edward C. Pease, "Still the Invisible People: Job Satisfaction of Minority Journalists at U.S. Daily Newspapers," doctoral dissertation, E. W. Scripps School of Journalism, Ohio University, June 1991, p. 242. See also Ted Pease and J. Frazier Smith, "The Newsroom Barometer: Job Satisfaction and Racial Diversity at U.S. Daily Newspapers," *Ohio Journalism Monographs*, No. 1, July 1991, p. 25.

9. Robert M. Hutchins, Foreword to Commission on Freedom of the Press, *A Free and Responsible Press: A General Report on Mass Communication: Newspapers, Radio, Motion Pictures, Magazines and Books* (Chicago: University of Chicago Press, 1947), p. viii.

10. Ibid., pp. 1–2.

11. Ibid., pp. 20–29.

12. *Report of the National Advisory Commission*, p. 1.

13. Ibid., p. 10.

14. Ibid., p. 203.

15. Ibid., Lyndon B. Johnson, "Address to the Nation," p. iii.

16. *Cornerstone for Growth*, pp. 13–18.

17. David Lawrence, Jr., Preface to *Cornerstone for Growth*, p. 4.

18. *Cornerstone for Growth*. See also Ted Pease, "Cornerstone for Growth: Why Minorities Are Vital to the Future of Newspapers," *Newspaper Research Journal* 10 (Spring 1989), 1–22.

3 HISTORY OF STANDARD 12: ESTABLISHING REQUIREMENTS FOR PLURALIZING EDUCATION

Robert M. Ruggles

The movement toward pluralizing journalism education has its origins in at least four historic documents: the 1968 Kerner Commission report, two 1978 resolutions by educational and professional groups, and, in 1984, Standard 12.

The first document, the 1968 Kerner Commission report, was issued in the aftermath of unprecedented urban unrest in the 1960s, most of which occurred within and severely damaged minority communities. That report roundly condemned the news media for ignoring the problems, hopes, dreams and aspirations of the people in those communities and suggested directly that coverage was flawed by the absence of media staff members from minority communities.[1]

The report was followed by a flurry of hirings of minority reporters, some good, some wholly unqualified and left to fail without proper training by their employers. Ten years would pass before the newspaper industry would attempt to lead an organized effort to improve representation of minorities in the media.

The second document was the 1978 resolution of the American Society of Newspaper Editors (ASNE), salient parts of which follow:

1. The commitment to recruit, train and hire minorities needs urgently to be rekindled. This is simply the right thing to do. It is also in the newspaper industry's economic self-interest.

2. There should be at least an annual accounting by ASNE of minority employment, including not just total jobs but types of positions held.

3. There should be special emphasis on increasing the number of minority newsroom executives.

4. Smaller papers should especially be encouraged to add minority members to their staffs.

5. Leaders among minority journalists have urged the industry to set a goal of minority employment before the year 2000 equivalent to the percentage of minority persons within the national population.[2]

AEJ RESOLUTION

Hard on the heels of the ASNE resolution came the third document, a resolution from the 1978 convention of the Association for Education in Journalism (AEJ, later to become the Association for Education in Journalism and Mass Communication, or AEJMC). AEJMC, the professional organization for journalism educators, has 2,800 members.[3] In part, that resolution urged that the AEJ membership:

1. Rededicate itself to the principle of affirmative action for minorities and women, with reliance on goals rather than quotas.

2. Endorse, and cooperate in working to achieve, the general goal of the ASNE to achieve, before the year 2000, minority employment at all levels on newspapers at least equal to the proportion of minorities in the population.

3. Urge other segments of the media to adopt similar goals.

4. Establish a comparable goal for the faculties of schools and departments of journalism.[4]

The resolution went on to urge the AEJ's Minorities and Communication (MAC) division to provide leadership in a series of tasks which, in my opinion, should have been undertaken by *all* members of AEJ and other journalism faculty around the country. Constituting a checklist of what remains to be done, the resolution still provides a blueprint for action for any communications program interested in recruiting and retaining minority journalism students. It includes:

(a.) Recruiting minority young people for journalism education through summer or year-round programs and workshops for high school students; providing pre-college skills programs as needed.

(b.) Creating minority newspaper internships, particularly with small and medium-sized media where newspersons have traditionally entered the profession.

(c.) Conducting job-getting skills sessions for students to make them more proficient in writing resumes, in informing themselves about media organizations to which they're applying, and in being interviewed by prospective employers.

(d.) Providing academic and career counseling throughout college to help students develop backgrounds necessary to fully take advantage of the diverse employment opportunities in journalism and communications.

(e.) Developing programs patterned after the Summer Program for Minority Journalists as well as management programs to help working minority journalists qualify for executive positions.

(f.) Providing instruction about minority media so as to stimulate interest among students in working for such media.

(g.) Discussing with media managers their minority employment practices and conducting seminars with editors and minority students concerning employment prospects and means to expand minority employment, and involving minority journalists in various campus visitation programs.

(h.) Expanding efforts to encourage media organizations for minorities and women to join AEJ and to become involved in the accreditation process.

(i.) Originating ways to recognize, reward and encourage media reporting of the nature of minority subcultures, community contributions of minorities and minority problems such as unemployment and educational deprivation.[5]

The ASNE followed through on its plan to conduct an annual survey of minority representation in newsrooms, still done to this day, and it is laying plans to publish the names of newspapers with good and not-so-good minority employment records as this is written. In short, the ASNE has attempted to turn its resolution into positive action.

STANDARD 12 ORIGINS

The AEJ resolution, however, offered no way to transfer sentiment into concrete action. That was remedied by the adoption in 1984 of the fourth document, Standard 12, entitled "Minority and Female Representation," by the Accrediting Council on Education in Journalism and Mass Communications (ACEJMC), the body that sets standards for and accredits journalism and mass communication programs at the university level.

That standard had its genesis during the Accrediting Council's rewriting of its standards, a process that began in 1983 under the leadership of Dr. James Carey, then dean of the University of Illinois College of Communication,[6] and extended into 1984 as the various council constituencies considered the new language. In Section D of the revised materials appeared a subsection newly titled "Affirmative Action and Non-Discrimination."

That subsection's promise was undercut, however, by its last paragraph, which stated: "At the same time, diversity should not be a defense for incompetency. The public as well as professional interest calls for a broad evaluation of performance based upon acceptable minimum standards."[7]

Actually, the offending wording had been contained in the booklet *Preparing for Journalism and Mass Communication Accreditation—Standards, Policies and Procedures* since at least 1979. By 1983–84's "Accredited Journalism and

Mass Communications Education," ACEJMC's brochure listing accredited programs and accreditation standards, a fuller recognition of diversity had begun to creep into the wording:

Consistent with and implicit in this broad goal is recognition that diversity within the student body, the faculty and staff is essential to a full education and to meet the needs of a pluralistic profession and society.

Thus, the unit shall demonstrate a commitment to expanding opportunities for the study of journalism and mass communications and entry into the profession by numbers of groups which in the past (whether through discrimination or outmoded societal expectations) have not had adequate educational opportunities.[8]

But the offending paragraph followed this effort at promoting diversity in journalism education.

I was not alone in being offended by the insensitivity of that statement. Other educators also felt that the Accrediting Council seemed to be about to go on record again intimating that only minorities could be incompetent. At this time (mid–1984), having just been appointed chair of AEJMC's Minorities Task Force, I was as interested as other journalism educators in the proposed new accrediting rules. The MAC division, then headed by Dr. Lawrence Kaggwa of Howard University, also was interested in the new language and especially in that part we considered offensive.

At the same time, both Kaggwa and I were aware of the slow pace of progress toward the ASNE year 2000 goal. We believed that ASNE's goal would never be approached unless more minority students became interested in journalism careers, entered college journalism programs and were graduated from them. In short, the journalism education community somehow had to put muscle into the 1978 AEJMC resolution.

We also believed that the Kerner Commission's stinging indictment of the American media's indifference toward minority hopes and dreams made the integration and diversification of college journalism classrooms imperative. We believed then, and still do, that Whites and minorities have a great deal to learn from each other, and that such learning can lead to better understanding.

The AEJMC Minorities Task Force included, in addition to me, Dr. Pam McAllister Johnson, publisher of the Ithaca *Journal* and a former journalism educator; Ken Bunting, then of the Los Angeles *Times* and now an assistant managing editor of the Fort Worth *Star-Telegram*; Dr. Félix Gutiérrez of the University of Southern California journalism school and now a Freedom Forum vice president; Linda Scanlan, a journalism professor at Norfolk State University; and Don Flores of the Dallas *Times-Herald*, now publisher of the Iowa City *Press-Citizen*.

The task force and Kaggwa met in New York City in early October 1984 to craft recommendations to the Accrediting Council. In addition to recommending changes in offensive language in the new draft standards, the group wrote a proposed Standard 12 for the Accrediting Council to consider. These recommendations, approved by the task force and the MAC division executive committee, were mailed to all members of the Accrediting Council in mid-October.

Kaggwa and I appeared before the Accrediting Council at its October meeting, and after long and sometimes spirited debate, Standard 12, along with additional language speaking to the concerns of women and minorities, was adopted on October 20, 1984, to be published in the 1985–86 academic year accreditation booklets.

THE STANDARD

We had gone to the council primarily to get the concerns of minorities formally recognized. We found ready allies among the women members of the council, such as Dr. Terry Hynes of California State University at Fullerton, who believed, quite correctly, that the concerns of women should also be addressed in Standard 12. These concerns were included in the final language of the standard.

The standard that resulted was expanded and revised by the Accrediting Council early in 1992 after input by AEJMC and the Association of Schools of Journalism and Mass Communication. Excerpts from the standard follow.

12. MINORITY AND FEMALE REPRESENTATION

Standard: Units must make effective efforts to recruit, advise, and retain minority students and minority and women faculty members for their intended career paths. They also must include in their courses information about the major contributions made by minorities and women to the disciplines covered in the unit.

In course offerings across the curriculum, units also must help prepare students to understand, cover, communicate with, and relate to a multi-cultural, multi-ethnic, multi-racial, and otherwise diverse society.

The unit's curriculum must reflect—and student interviews and classroom activity and course syllabi should verify—that the curricula components of Standard 12 are achieved. The contributions of women and minorities to journalism and mass communications must be integrated throughout the unit's program. . . . Units are encouraged to take innovative and creative approaches to exposing students to minority voices and issues.

• • • • •

Explanation: Racial and ethnic minorities constitute an increasing percentage of the population, but they are vastly underrepresented in American journalism and mass communications student bodies and faculties and among practitioners. Women comprise a majority of the population, but they are underrepresented on journalism and mass communications faculties. Aggressive efforts by journalism and mass communications educators can help correct this imbalance.

Preparing students to work in occupations protected by the First Amendment carries with it a basic obligation to see that the total environment—the faculty, the student body, and course content—is strongly supportive of the need for America's journalism and mass communications industries to reflect a better representation of the populations that they serve.

Evidence: Units must present written plans of their own on which to base their efforts to recruit, retain and advance women and minorities into the unit's faculty and . . . student bodies. . . . The plans should be concrete, with measurable goals, and they should operate regardless of whether the university has its own plan. . . .

Units' plans should document the number and percent of minority students currently enrolled and enrollment for the previous two years. They also should detail the units' efforts to recruit and retain minority students, and the number and percent of those students who were graduated at each commencement for the last three years.

Units' plans must ensure that searches are conducted in a fashion so that minorities and women are considered for employment as faculty members. . . .

• • • • •

For compliance with this standard, units must show that they have made substantial, good-faith efforts to find and recruit minority and women faculty and enhance their opportunities to earn promotion and tenure. . . .

• • • • •

If units hire adjunct faculty members, a diligent effort must be made to hire minority and women professionals.[9]

A structured, rather detailed reporting form for Standard 12 was added to the school accreditation previsit reporting forms in 1988 by council action.

The 1989–90 accreditation booklet informed units seeking accreditation or re-accreditation in fall 1990 or afterward that results toward fulfillment of Standard 12 must be demonstrable. The council gave college and university journalism units several years (from 1985–86 to 1990–91) to prepare to meet fully the requirements of Standard 12.

Despite the preparation time provided, Standard 12 remains problematical for many journalism and mass communication units. Part of the problem may be that for the first time since before the era of *All the President's Men*, journalism educators are being asked to recruit students, this time from among minority groups who by the year 2080 will make up at least 44 percent of our population. Many of today's journalism educators never have had to recruit students and therefore don't know how. Others dismiss the need to recruit as not being part of their responsibilities.

One purpose of this book is to suggest techniques for recruiting minority students into college journalism programs and for retaining them. Also provided are ideas for finding and retaining minority and female faculty members.

The book goes beyond these topics to address another area of the Standard 12 mandate, pluralizing the curriculum. Numerous ideas are offered here for assignments and resources to enable faculty members to infuse into their courses information about the contributions of women and people of color. Another section of the book outlines ideas for encouraging student media to pluralize their coverage and their staffs.

These materials will provide a variety of useful suggestions to help journalism and mass communication programs fulfill the purposes of Standard 12: bringing students and faculty of color into university journalism programs and later into the communications industry, and better preparing *all* journalism students for, in the Accrediting Council's words, "professional work in a diverse society."[10]

NOTES

1. *Report of the National Advisory Commission on Civil Disorders* (Washington, D.C.: U.S. Government Printing Office, 1968).

2. ASNE (American Society of Newspaper Editors) *Bulletin*, May/June 1978, p. 11.

3. *AEJMC* (Association for Education in Journalism and Mass Communication) *News*, January 1992, p. 1.

4. *Journalism Quarterly* 55 (Winter 1978), 869–870.

5. Ibid.

6. AEJMC press release, June 1984, p. 2.

7. "Accredited Journalism and Mass Communications Education," supplement to *AEJMC News*, June 1984, p. 9.

8. "Accredited Journalism and Mass Communications Education, 1983–84," ACEJMC brochure, p. 6.

9. "Accredited Journalism and Mass Communications Education, 1991–92," ACEJMC brochure, p. 15, and "Standard 12 (Revised 2 May 1992)," Attachment A.

10. "Standard 12 (Revised 2 May 1992)."

II RECRUITING AND RETAINING STUDENTS AND FACULTY OF COLOR

The foregoing chapters have stated in a variety of ways the crucial importance of finding and retaining students and faculty of color in our universities' journalism and mass communication programs. Part II provides a myriad of suggestions for how to accomplish those goals. Chapter 4 offers ideas for reaching out to high school students through journalism workshops held on campus. Subsequent chapters present ways to recruit, retain and mentor journalism students of color. Finding and keeping minority faculty are addressed, and faculty of color are advised how to avoid the service pitfall on their track toward promotion and tenure. Part II concludes with a bibliography on recruiting and retaining journalism students and faculty of color.

4 FINDING POTENTIAL MINORITY JOURNALISM STUDENTS

Virginia Escalante

Walk into most newsrooms in the nation and they will be, with few exceptions, overwhelmingly White. Walk into journalism classrooms on most college campuses and the student make-up will, in most cases, be overwhelmingly White. Despite the blame placed on the newspaper industry for its failure to recruit, train and retain minorities, journalism schools have contributed to and continue to perpetuate this condition. Not surprisingly, the elitism or White domination that marks the classroom is consequently reflected in the newsroom. The correlation between journalism schools and the newspaper industry they feed is undeniable; critical changes cannot be made in one unless fundamental action is undertaken in the other.

Thus, if journalism schools are to address the racial shortcomings in the profession they serve and the subsequent lack of multicultural perspectives in the news, then they must first integrate their own classrooms. If journalism departments are to diversify their enrollment, then they must do so through early outreach efforts, beginning at the junior and senior high school level, long before students arrive at the university.

These endeavors must go beyond routine Career Day visits in which journalism faculty devote an hour or so to talking about their profession or the one-day workshops in which they do more of the same. The key to recruiting minority students is to offer them a well-organized and challenging opportunity for learning about and falling in love with journalism. After all, when they are asked how they became interested in newspapers, most reporters will recall that they got hooked when they were young and worked on school publications before they ever went to college. This can also happen with minority youngsters when they have the same kind of realistic experience, are inspired by others with whom they can identify, and become aware of the possibilities in the field.

One of the most effective ways to accomplish these goals is through an intensive, two-week summer workshop in which students learn by doing. By producing a laboratory newspaper, they acquire skills in photography, reporting, writing, editing, design and paste-up. Conducted in a university setting where a multiracial mix of faculty and newspaper professionals act as teachers and role models, this type of project familiarizes minority youth with the academic environment, with journalism department offerings and with the craft. It accomplishes these goals through an experience that ultimately demystifies what might seem foreign or out of reach for some.

Such a project builds students' confidence in their abilities, because journalism skills are not difficult—but instead are fun—to learn. The program offers them a chance to create their own product, over which they have control and in which they can take pride. Because the newspaper is produced within a short time, students do not have to wait long to see concrete results. Yet the excitement never ends. At one workshop, for example, the teen and preteen youngsters were so eager to see what they had produced that they could not wait for the instructor to find scissors to cut the tie on the newspaper bundles. Instead, one youngster grabbed a bundle and attacked the cord with her teeth.

Hundreds of journalism schools have yet to embrace the workshop concept, but not because the idea is something new awaiting further development. In fact, the Dow Jones Newspaper Fund, based in Princeton, New Jersey, whose purpose is to encourage young people to consider journalism careers, has been doing it since 1968. The fund has sponsored training for more than 5,000 youngsters through its summer High School Journalism Workshops for Minorities.

In 1991 the Dow Jones Newspaper Fund awarded $90,650 in workshop grants, while newspapers, foundations and other organizations provided nearly $250,000, according to its annual report. That year, the fund and 170 newspapers sponsored 27 workshops for 457 students in 17 states and the District of Columbia. Its National Directory of High School Journalism Workshops for Minorities listed a total of 68 workshops held throughout the country that summer. The directory grew out of a survey designed to identify cities that sponsored such projects as well as others where programs might be needed.

Considering the number of colleges in this nation and the unmet need in the industry, more universities need to launch similar endeavors if parity in newspaper hiring is to be reached by the year 2000, as proposed by the American Society of Newspaper Editors. Thus, with its history, experience, information and expertise, the Dow Jones Newspaper Fund represents the most logical resource to which journalism departments can turn when they first decide to do more to recruit potential minority journalists. The ground-work has already been laid.

The Dow Jones Newspaper Fund issues formats and guidelines for funding proposals, setting budgets, planning the workshop, selecting faculty and staff, conducting the workshop, and recruiting, screening and selecting partici-pants.[1] It has also designed a daily schedule conducive to reaching workshop goals, thus saving journalism schools embarking on this route weeks of or-ganizational time.

Because the Dow Jones Fund grants are limited to a maximum of $4,500, workshops require additional financial and staff support from newspapers. Indeed, commercial newspapers *should* bear part of the responsibility if they are committed to integrating the field and convincing minorities that they are indeed wanted in the media. When it awards grants, the fund also requires the involvement of newspaper executives in planning the workshop along with ethnic reporters and editors who serve as teachers and speakers—and who can demonstrate to minority youth that newspaper careers are attainable for people like them.

FINDING POTENTIAL STUDENTS

The first step in finding prospective journalism students is to launch a series of visits to local high schools with minority student enrollments. De-pending on the number of schools in the area, these visits can be scheduled weekly and can be made by one or several members of journalism depart-ments. In Arizona, for example, the workshop director visited three schools in Tucson's south side within two afternoons, spending an hour at each site. Journalism department administrators and faculty can arrange discussions about their mission with principals and guidance counselors and with jour-nalism, English, or other teachers who double as high school newspaper advisers and who are interested in opportunities colleges are willing to offer their students.

When university educators go out to the schools instead of waiting for the schools to come to them, their actions demonstrate commitment and pave the way for creating strong networks. Later, when it is time to send out the call for workshop applications, the contacts they have made will be instru-mental in identifying and recommending students who may be eligible for the workshop, reducing the need for rounds of personal visits and facilitating recruiting efforts in following years. Journalism faculty can also conduct shorter workshops or classroom visits at the schools in preparation for the more intensive summer workshop. Such guest appearances are a good way to spot youngsters who may benefit from the summer workshop.

It is also important to coordinate these efforts with university recruiters who travel throughout the state and are able to find other students within geographic regions that journalism departments are trying to reach. At the

University of Arizona in Tucson, for example, recruiters from the Office of Minority Student Affairs distributed workshop announcements and applications in rural towns in southern Arizona where they helped students to complete and return the applications to the journalism department. Several teenagers who participated in the workshop came from schools with limited resources and expertise. They were able to improve their high school newspapers the following fall, and are now attending college, majoring in journalism.

Organization and fundraising for the workshops begin early in the fall. The latter can be accomplished with the help of university development officers skilled in writing proposals and locating funding sources. Autumn is also the time to organize advisory boards composed of newspaper executives and to obtain service commitments from them. They can and do release professionals who help teach students photography, reporting, writing, editing and design, and acquaint them as well with the demands of the profession.

In Arizona, for example, a Chicano photographer from the Arizona *Daily Star* teaches students how to load a camera, shoot, develop and print pictures in what is one of the most exciting parts of the workshop and one which presents students with journalistic options other than reporting. One workshop student, when he returned to his high school in the fall, set up a photo lab, taught other students photography, and helped a new and inexperienced journalism adviser run the school newspaper.

Other minority editors and reporters from the Tucson area have served as writing coaches, guest speakers and participants on panels where they discuss their work, career preparation, problems and rewards of the profession. Some of the editors, for example, have reprinted editorials from the workshop newspaper on their Op Ed pages and have hired students as stringers and ultimately as reporters, fulfilling an objective of the workshops.

INVOLVING PARENTS

Because the vision of these workshops reaches beyond summer to the day minority youngsters actually enroll in journalism departments and the day they graduate from universities, program organizers need to remember that parental support plays a major role in teenagers' educational achievement. The interview segment provides a good opportunity for workshop directors to involve parents.

For example, because interviews were held in the early evening or on Saturdays, parents in Arizona who accompanied their children were encouraged to attend the interview instead of remaining in the waiting area. (Of course, the students were asked for their permission first.) Thus the parents learned as much as their sons and daughters about the need for more minority representation in the newsroom, the nature of the training, and the value of the workshop. During the discussions, the director thanked the parents for coming, encouraged them to call if they had questions, and mentioned that students whose efforts received parental support did much better in school than those who did not. When graduation ceremonies were held at a lunchtime banquet, the parents of all but one of the students attended. Later, several called for information when their youngsters were in the process of applying for college.

As a culminating step, some workshops also ask college officials or recruiters to explain entrance requirements, admission procedures and available financial assistance so that students will know what they can do to prepare for the day they enroll in journalism school. More important, providing parents with personal contacts within journalism or other departments makes universities more accessible to the communities they serve.

One of the dangers in recruiting minority youngsters for print media is that they may come to college but go into other fields. Or they may become disillusioned and leave because many journalism departments do not make journalism courses available to first-year students or do not provide publication opportunities until students are sophomores, thus losing students in their freshman year. Clearly, if journalism schools want to make their recruiting pay off within their field, then they need to address these major problems.

In an era when high school journalism is perceived as a frills course, journalism departments can take additional steps to encourage junior and senior high schools to either preserve newspaper production courses or make journalistic writing an integral part of English classes. College journalism departments can offer workshops for teachers in heavily minority schools where journalism may not be an option.

Here, too, the Dow Jones Newspaper Fund can be of invaluable help for all of the schools—elementary to university level—involved in such a project. The Newspaper Fund has articulated the rationale for and designed a curriculum to emphasize journalistic writing in its *Teacher's Guide to Intensive Journalistic Writing Courses*. The book offers sample syllabi, reading lists, bibliographies and actual student writing examples.[2] Primarily for English teachers, it presents techniques applicable for all students, even those who need remedial courses. Such students often get excited about writing when the journalistic emphasis is used. In addition, the fund sponsors a two-week writing institute which focuses on that writing concept and out of which the guide grew. Teachers who attend receive graduate college credit and may also apply for teacher fellowships offered by the fund.[3]

The American Newspaper Publishers Association Foundation (recently renamed the Newspaper Association of America) and the International Reading Association have produced an equally useful teaching tool, *Creating a Classroom Newspaper: Teacher's Guide for Newspaper in Education Week* (1988). This step-by-step publication explains the process, provides assignments and culminates in the production of a newspaper, eliminating the need for teachers to spend time creating the unit, working out lesson plans, or taking basic journalism courses for which they may not have time or money. All they have to do is review and follow the guide, which can be adapted to any age or class level.[4]

In persuading school administrators and teachers to adopt more journalistically oriented activities, programs or classes, university educators may want to point out that, according to journalism educator and author Jack Dvorak, students who work on newspapers or other school publications score higher on writing proficiency tests and tend to be better writers. "Certainly, the influence of participation in high school publications can be seen in the higher percentage of those students who indicate an interest in pursuing publications and media activities in college," he said.[5]

If journalism education is to increase the number of minority voices in the media, then it must give minority young people the same kinds of opportunities that have led other young, nonethnic people into the world of newspapers and into careers in the newsroom. It is time for schools and departments of journalism to reach out into their communities to seek young people to whom to offer these opportunities.

NOTES

1. *The Dow Jones Newspaper Fund High School Journalism Workshop for Minorities, Guidelines for Proposals for Grants,* Dow Jones Newspaper Fund, Inc., P.O. Box 300, Princeton, NJ 08543–0300. Telephone 609–452–2820.

2. *Teacher's Guide to Intensive Journalistic Writing Courses,* available for $10 from the Dow Jones Newspaper Fund.

3. To apply for teacher fellowships for the Intensive Journalistic Writing Institute, request a nomination form from the Dow Jones Newspaper Fund.

4. *Creating a Classroom Newspaper: Teacher's Guide for Newspaper in Education Week,* Order Department, International Reading Association, 800 Barksdale Road, P.O. Box 8139, Newark, DE 19714–8139.

5. Jack Dvorak, "High School Publications Experience as a Factor in College-Level Writing," *Journalism Quarterly* 65 (Summer 1988), 398.

5 RECRUITING STUDENTS

Robert M. Ruggles

Successful recruiting of minority or other students is partly the exercise of common sense and partly clever and consistent use of available tools. Recruiting minority students today almost inevitably must begin at the middle school level or earlier, for two reasons. First, minority students still are underrepresented in secondary education's college preparatory track, so they need to be reached early and made aware that the college prep track will open the way not only to journalism or mass communication careers but also to other fields about which they may have dreamed.

Some journalism educators worry that minority students inevitably will come to college unprepared for college work. To be sure, that is true in some cases, and mechanisms must be set up to assist those students. No one should assume, however, that all minority students will need remediation. Moreover, the possibility that minority students may have received a poor education in early grades underscores the need to reach these students early so that they can pursue the college prep track.

Second, many minority students are not yet aware that the communications fields are open to them. As a result, some degree of career education must be undertaken for those students before high school, when many make up their minds what occupation or profession to pursue, so that journalism and mass communication will not be overlooked.

A University of Arizona report notes that "Decisions at the high school level are crucial, because a majority of students have a fairly firm idea of their career preference and program of study before entering college. Minorities, especially Blacks, report more certainty than Caucasians about these choices."[1]

A student's personal preference has the greatest influence on his or her choice of a program of study and career. Next in importance are parental and family influence, peer influence, adult role models, high school counselors and academic preparation.[2]

Journalism educators entering seriously into the minority recruiting fray today need to understand that they face enormous competition from the sciences, engineering, business and other fields, so they should rely heavily on what they do best: communicating.

Robert Sevier, director of market research at Stamats Communications, says that administrators should recognize that today's student prospects

face an increasingly large number of aggressive college recruiters;

rely on emotions as well as logic in choosing a college;

reject mass messages and expect, even demand, personalized messages;

use a variety of resources ranging from search mailings and publications to videotapes as sources of information about a college; and

want/require different types of messages at different stages of the admissions process.[3]

GOOD MATERIALS ARE ESSENTIAL

The pool of minority students attending college has grown in the recent past. In 1985, 34.4 percent of White high school graduates aged 18 to 24 went on to college, contrasted with 26.1 percent of Black graduates and 29 percent of Latinos. Five years later, the American Council on Education reported statistics of 39.4 percent, 33 percent and 29 percent, respectively.[4]

But as the pool has grown, so has the sophistication level of prospective college-level minority students. They want colorful, informative brochures, perhaps even videotapes, which describe in detail the college or university, the particular program in which they are interested, housing, scholarships, other financial aid and on-campus support mechanisms available to them.

Any journalism or mass communication program hoping to capture the interest of today's minority students must be equipped with good informational materials about itself and its university. These need not be expensive, but they must stand out in the flood of presentations most college-bound minority students are exposed to these days.

Further, many journalism and mass communication programs will find that they must do some career education while recruiting minority students. They should maintain a stock of career publications available from the communication industry's professional organizations, such as the Society of Professional Journalists, the American Society of Newspaper Editors, the American Newspaper Publishers Association (renamed the Newspaper Association of America), its foundation, the Dow Jones Newspaper Fund, the Radio Television News Directors Association, the Public Relations Society of America, the National Association of Black Journalists, and the American Advertising Federation.

Several have publications targeting minorities. At least one has a videotape directed to minority students that can be used on special occasions. Single copies of career brochures usually are free, but multiple copies for distribution in career awareness programs generally can be bought for reasonable prices.

Two especially good career education efforts are a videotape called *Minorities: Making a Difference in Journalism*, produced by KETC–9, St. Louis, Missouri, and underwritten in part by the National Association of Black Journalists, the Washington *Post* and the Corporation for Public Broadcasting, and a Dow Jones Newspaper Fund career brochure, *Journalism Career Guide for Minorities*.

There are essentially two ways to recruit minority students: the "go get 'em" approach and the "armchair" approach; but, in truth, the most successful recruiting is a combination.

THE GO GET 'EM APPROACH

This approach requires some homework first. The administrator or designee of the journalism school or program (hereafter to be called the unit) will need to determine within the unit's service area

which middle and high schools enroll the largest numbers of minorities;

who the media teachers are and if any of the schools have newspapers, radio or closed circuit TV operations;

who the high school and middle school career/guidance counselors are;

whether there are magnet journalism/mass communication/communication high schools in the unit's service area and who their teachers are;

whether there are chapters of any of the minority media professional organizations, such as the National Association of Black Journalists (NABJ), the Asian American Journalists Association, the National Association of Hispanic Journalists, or the Native American Press Association, in the cities the unit serves;

whether the unit has minority graduates working in the target area; and

if the answer to the latter is no, whether there are university minority graduates from other disciplines in the area.

The idea is to get a fix on target audiences and the resources available to help recruit them.

Once the middle and high schools with the highest minority enrollments are determined, the unit head or designee must provide the counselors and media teachers, especially those in magnet schools, with current and complete information about the unit's journalism and mass communication programs. Personal visits by the unit head or another representative serve to attach a face to the program and generally facilitate two-way communication so essential to the minority recruitment process. The teachers and counselors need to have confidence in the university program, and that is often conferred slowly.

A similar approach to the boards of directors of the local or regional minority journalism organizations may lead to programs co-sponsored by the organizations and the unit for the benefit of minority secondary school students. NABJ members may be able to help identify African American students interested in journalism, for example, and help to recruit them for the unit. Joint sponsorship of workshops, special seminars or journalism/mass communication career fairs will expose minority high school students to life in the media and perhaps lead more minority students to major in journalism or mass communication.

If the unit has minority graduates already, they should be asked to help in the recruiting effort. Most will be willing. If the unit has no minority graduates, it is worth the effort to try to enlist the help of minority graduates of the university in other disciplines to boost the minority recruitment effort.

Remember, it is necessary to keep all contacts, from members of minority journalist organizations to teachers and counselors, well informed about the unit. Put them on regular mailing lists for publications and news releases.

On-campus experiences for minority students can also be important to the successful recruiting process. Many universities, sometimes in league with minority journalist organizations, offer two-week summer workshops for minority students. The Dow Jones Newspaper Fund is nationally recognized for its leadership in co-sponsoring such workshops each summer. Other co-sponsors are the involved universities, area newspapers and professional journalism organizations. These workshops naturally focus on newspapers and are directed toward juniors and seniors in high school. For best results, involve good minority role models as instructors.

Other workshops, perhaps directed to minority students interested in broadcasting or advertising, can also serve to introduce minority high school students to college campuses and to collegiate-level journalism and mass communication programs.

Some journalism units stage an annual Journalism Day and invite regional high school students and their teachers to campus. These events usually include exposing the students to dynamic role model professionals, tours of the campus and journalism/mass communication facilities, a luncheon with a major media luminary as a speaker, and several how-to sessions taught by good role model professionals or university faculty.

In connection with these special events, trinkets may be useful. These include specially manufactured pencils, pens, key chains, tee shirts, book covers or tablets. With the exception of tee shirts, these items are relatively inexpensive, but the long-term promotional and goodwill value to the journalism unit can be substantial as the materials find their way back to the high schools from which the students came. Obviously, these promotional materials must have the journalism/mass communication unit's ID prominently featured on them.

In all recruiting efforts, the unit head needs to be prominently featured, for in many ways he or she *is* the journalism/mass communication program to prospective minority recruits and their parents. It is reassuring to them if the unit administrator is deeply involved in the recruiting. For extra impact, reserved for the very top students the unit is trying to recruit, ask the university president to call the students personally. It makes a big impression on the whole family when the president is on the phone asking to speak to a family member.

In an ideal world, of course, each unit would be able to hire a full-time recruiter. Few budgets can tolerate that, however. But surely on every faculty at least one other person besides the unit administrator has an interest in minority student recruiting and could be given some release time to work with the administrator.

THE ARMCHAIR APPROACH

This method is popular and generally effective because of the tremendous help available, at a cost, from the College Board's Student Search Service (SSS) and American College Test's (ACT) Educational Opportunity Service (EOS). Also helpful are the National Merit Scholarship Corporation's list of annual semifinalists in the National Achievement Scholarship Program for Outstanding Negro Students and the College Board's roster of semifinalists in the National Hispanic Scholars Program.

The College Board's SSS program offers college journalism and mass communication units six separate opportunities annually to get the names and addresses of high school students taking the Scholastic Aptitude Test (SAT) who indicate a preference for communications-related areas of college study. The unit specifies which criteria SSS is to use, such as sex, grade level, range of SAT scores, intended major, geographic location, ethnic background and grade point average.[5]

For example, if a unit desired to have a summer SAT search, it would complete the necessary forms and send them in advance to a regional office of the College Board. (The College Board is headquartered in Washington, DC, but has regional offices nationwide.) It would receive in return a list of names and addresses, determined by the criteria it specified, of juniors who took the SAT between January and June, enabling the unit to reach students as they begin their senior year.[6] Reports can be received on gummed four-up labels, Cheshire four-up labels (non–heat sensitive) or magnetic tape.

SSS offers additional criteria options, too, such as criteria relating to religion, class rank, sports interests, extracurricular activities and the like.

Costs include a participation fee and per name fees, so the total expense is determined by the size of the list developed through use of the unit's specified criteria.

The College Board says that an estimated 2.5 million students participated in 1991's Student Search Service program.[7]

The Student Search Service also publishes a semiannual magazine, *Admissions Strategist*, which features articles about recruitment.

Like the Student Search Service, ACT's Educational Opportunity Service offers six opportunities during the year for journalism and mass communication units to get prospective student names.[8] Over 500,000 names are available from EOS annually of students who have taken the ACT. The ACT Assessment that EOS provides gives results from 11th and 12th grade students who took the ACT during a given year.

The P-ACT+ is given to high school sophomores each fall; thus units can get a head start on recruiting before students make their career decisions. Some 280,000 sophomores tested in fall 1990.[9]

Like units using SSS, EOS participants select specific criteria: ACT score (composite and/or any of the four subtests), high school grade average, college major or occupational choice, and additional criteria, including financial aid, religion, educational plans, racial/ethnic group and so on. (ACT is headquartered in Iowa City, Iowa, and, like the College Board, has regional offices.)

EOS output can be supplied on gummed mailing labels, Cheshire mailing labels, magnetic tape, rosters (alphabetical by student name, alphabetical with high school code, alphabetical with a five-digit ZIP code or alphabetical within college major) or EOS mailers. EOS mailers contain the requesting unit's "program description, selection criteria, return address, and student's addresses" computer-printed on postcard stock.[10] Each person identified using the requesting unit's criteria receives an EOS mailer, which also includes a business reply card students can use to request information from the unit.

Again, cost is determined by the type of initial output selected and a fee per label produced or record selected, based on the specified criteria. Whatever output is chosen, however, it is probably smart to get an extra copy or two if follow-up contacts between the unit and prospective students are desired.

Also available for recruitment use is the annual list of National Achievement Scholarship Program semifinalists, generally issued in September of each year by the National Merit Scholarship Corporation. This list of high-achieving African American students is generally sent to the news media first and to universities a bit later. Students are listed alphabetically by high school and by state. Codes identify the student's major and career or occupational objective. The main campus scholarship office at each university also receives a roster of the students with home addresses.

Harvard University generally has led in recruiting National Achievement Scholars but is being pressed by Florida A&M University (FAMU), a public historically Black institution in Tallahassee. In fall 1991 Harvard recruited 64 such scholars, FAMU 62.[11] Four of the 62 at FAMU chose journalism, bringing to 14 the number of National Achievement or National Merit Scholars selecting that field at FAMU since 1986–87.

Since 1982–83 the College Board, in cooperation with the Andrew W. Mellon Foundation, has operated the National Hispanic Scholar Awards Program. For 1992, 3,200 seniors were invited by the College Board to enter the competition for scholarships in the program, which was funded by the Mellon Foundation.[12] The lists did not identify students by interest area, however. Still, university faculty and administrators could be sure the lists contained names of academically well-prepared Hispanic high school students.

How to deal with the list? Smart unit administrators would send only a letter and one or two general university informational brochures to each student, enclosing a return card for those interested in journalism or mass communication studies. FAMU's School of Journalism, Media and Graphic Arts did that in 1991–92 and received 25 responses from students who then were sent full information packages. In this way expensive recruiting materials are conserved.

Unfortunately, the 10-year funding of this program by the Mellon Foundation expires after 1992–93, and the College Board is considering the need to continue furnishing rosters to interested universities if no National Hispanic Scholarship program is in place.[13]

The aforementioned services are available to journalism and mass communication unit administrators at reasonable cost. The key to success in using them, however, is what material is sent to the students initially and in follow-up efforts. Personally signed, friendly, information-packed letters from unit administrators are critical to the initial mailing. Also necessary are attractive brochures or information sheets about the unit, the university, housing, financial aid and costs. Admission and scholarship application forms also should be enclosed.

Follow-up mailings can include newsy letters from the unit head, copies of student newspapers, alumni newsletters, information about campus organizations—religious or otherwise—and criteria for working on student media.

If a student a unit has recruited is admitted to the unit's university, unit recruiters must arrange for the admissions office to contact the unit about the admission right away. Admitted students don't necessarily show up, so some telephone contact is desirable between the unit head and each newly admitted minority student. Why? To make sure no major obstacles prevent the student from attending the university. Often the unit head or designated assistant can trouble-shoot problems which, if left unaddressed, might result in no-shows.

For additional ideas and recruitment strategies, unit heads can subscribe to *Recruitment and Retention*, 2718 Dryden Drive, Madison, Wisconsin 53704–3086. It is a monthly publication.

Unit heads should not forget to recruit among the inevitably large pool of freshman students on their own campuses who have not yet officially declared majors. These students usually are enrolled administratively in a unit called something like university college, general studies or lower division studies.

FINANCIAL AID

Many minority students will need one or more forms of financial aid to attend college. Minority student recruiting is much easier if the unit has a good scholarship program and the unit head is fully informed about other financial aid available at the university level from federal and state sources. Such terms as Pell Grants, Guaranteed Student Loans, Work-Study, Supplemental Educational Opportunity Grants and the like should be part of the unit head's lexicon. Administrators must also be knowledgeable about national sources of financial help for minority students (national scholarship programs of the Scripps Howard Foundation, the Freedom Forum, Knight-Ridder, Inc., the minority professional journalism organizations, the American Society of Newspaper Editors, the Radio and Television News Directors Association, for example).

The unit administrator should advise all minority students to apply for financial aid using special application forms available each January for the next academic year. The importance of accuracy and completeness should be stressed to avoid unnecessary delays. Aid applications should be submitted not later than April 1 each year.

Administrators *and* prospective minority journalism and mass communication majors may benefit from *Financial Aid for Minorities in Journalism and Mass Communication*, a brochure published annually and available for $4.95 from Garrett Park Press, Garrett Park, Maryland 20896.

Recruiting is hard and time-consuming work, but journalism educators must do a better job of getting minorities into the pipeline toward the media if there ever is to be more than token representation of minorities in the media. (Additional suggestions for recruiting minority students can be found in Chapter 23.)

Retaining minority students once they are in college journalism/mass communication programs is the other part of the picture, of course, and no less a challenge than recruiting. One experienced recruiter summed up retention:

"Whatever it took to get 'em it'll take to keep 'em." There is no substitute for hard work and special effort.

NOTES

Some of the material in this chapter was digested from "Recruiting and Retaining Black Students for Journalism and Mass Communication Education," by Diane Hall, Barbara Hines and Robert M. Ruggles, published in July 1989 as a special issue of *Insights*, the journal of the Association of Schools of Journalism and Mass Communications (ASJMC). Limited quantities of the issue are available from ASJMC, 1621 College St., University of South Carolina, Columbia, SC 29208–0251 (telephone 803–777–2005). Another issue of *Insights* on "Pluralism and Diversity" that includes useful information on minority student recruitment and retention was published in the winter of 1990–91 and is available in limited quantities from the same address.

1. Judee K. Burgoon, Michael Burgoon, David Buller, David Coker and Deborah Coker, "Minorities and Journalism: Career Orientations among High School Students," *Journalism Quarterly* 64 (Summer-Autumn 1987), 434–443.

2. Judee K. Burgoon, Michael Burgoon and David Buller, "Why Minorities Do Not Choose Journalism: Academic and Career Orientations among Students," report of the Associated Press Managing Editors' Minorities Committee, APME Annual Convention, Miami, FL, November 1984.

3. Robert Sevier, "Hooked on You," *Currents* 14 (September 1988), 22–25.

4. American Council on Education, "Tenth Annual Report on Minorities in Higher Education," quoted in a Los Angeles *Times* story in the Tallahassee *Democrat*, 20 January 1992, p. 1.

5. The College Board, "Discover How We Can Help You Recruit Students," (Washington, DC: College Entrance Examination Board, 1991), p. 3.

6. Ibid., p. 4.

7. Ibid., p. 1.

8. ACT's Educational Opportunity Service, 1990–91 brochure, "Your Source for Qualified Student Names and Addresses" (Iowa City, IA: American College Testing Program, 1990), p. 3.

9. Linda Banken, coordinator, EOS, in a letter to university participants, February 1991.

10. ACT's Educational Opportunity Service, 1990–91 brochure, p. 6.

11. Tallahassee *Democrat*, 2 December 1991, p. 1.

12. Evelyn Davila, director, National Hispanic Scholar Awards Program, the College Board, phone conversation with the author, 23 January 1991.

13. Ibid.

6   MENTORING MINORITY STUDENTS

Barbara J. Hipsman

Perhaps the slogan for the 1990s in journalism education should be "Reach Out; Don't Single Out." As the communications industry struggles to bring more minorities into its population, media executives plead with educators to send them more minority applicants. And maybe there are more minorities to be drawn into the profession than we, as a mostly White journalism faculty, have recognized.

Certainly, the percentages of minority students working on college papers at accredited journalism schools—nearly 17 percent, or 749, in 1990—would lead us to believe that talented students are coming through the ranks.[1] The question may be, Can we convince enough students of color to continue their career tracks into the newsrooms of America? Will educators' efforts help newsrooms reach parity with the percentage of minorities in the general population—nearly a quarter of the U.S. population?

To get enough students of color really fired up about a communications career, perhaps it is time to reach out to a number of students, to double our efforts, rather than to single out one or two students to help through the maze of academics, resumes, internships and job-hunting.

Perhaps we need to light not a small flame, but bonfires of interest, seeking out and nurturing more minority students. One way to do this is to organize campus-based, minority-oriented publications. In a 1990 study of college publications for the American Society of Newspaper Editors, a significant positive relationship was observed between the existence of a minority publication and the number of minority students writing for the mainstream campus newspaper.[2] Of the 92 accredited schools studied, 52 percent, or 48 schools, reported non-White–oriented publications on campus. Statistically, the campuses that had a minority publication were more likely to have students of color in the top five positions on the staff of the mainstream paper.

The study supported the notion that when students of color see others like themselves working on a publication, they are more likely to be interested in working there as well. It would be a plus if all schools could concentrate on pluralizing the mainstream campus media, or at least on opening doors to discussion about multicultural representation and coverage. But students of color, like many young writers, may find that large newsroom intimidating. By starting at a publication where most staffers are of color, the new staffers likely will build better self-esteem. Also, the publication may be so good that students do not need to move to the mainstream newspaper to obtain the clippings needed to get a commercial media job.

MINORITY JOURNALISM ORGANIZATIONS

At some schools students or faculty have started communications clubs for students of color to provide a common ground for group counseling or programming. New members can be assigned "peer mentors," students who are a little further along in the program. The peers can provide valuable course and instructor selection information.

These groups also can provide a fertile ground for professional mentoring, as their meetings are natural lightning rods for speakers. Students of color meeting with professionals who are also minorities in the newsroom can ask professionally related questions they might not ask the adviser or faculty. The interaction provides a good kickoff point for future discussions. This kind of mentoring also allows the students of color to see the faculty member as a positive force, someone who will help them find a niche in the industry.

Helping students feel comfortable working in publications and in a language-based curriculum is a decided problem for faculty whose job includes protecting the language. As "language cops" it is difficult to play the part of mentors, a role that requires high-level trust. As a mentor, the teacher/adviser must clearly explain the absolute need for excellent language skills in the communications industry. While the conversation would be the same with any student, it could prove to be a "just trust me!" juncture in the mentoring between faculty member and the student of color. To tell students that they need to control the language is a very personal step, requiring the advisees to search their gut feelings. Are they willing to make improved language a goal?

BUILDING TRUST

Alvin S. Bynum, in *Black Student/White Counselor: Developing Effective Relationships*, deals with counseling the African American population at predominantly White institutions. He clearly articulates the need for counselors and advisers to develop trust carefully.[3] Bynum argues that it is "extremely difficult for young blacks today to trust whites who sit in positions of apparent or perceived authority."

"It does not matter how sincere the white counselor is in the relationship," Bynum continues. "A statement of 'you just have to trust me' goes nowhere with the young black person because he or she knows that there are other options available—including: 'No, I do not!' Frequently, the route chosen is avoidance—that client will not likely reappear for advice from the same counselor."[4]

Bynum, dean of the University Division at Indiana University–Purdue University at Indianapolis, suggests that in mentoring any student, but especially students of color, the counselor must start with trust-building, being sure to give the advisee adequate and up-to-date information. Bynum suggests that if a White adviser or mentor is to be successful with an African American client, "he or she must be determined to communicate" and must accept that some distrust may exist at the start of the relationship.[5]

"Each individual client must be accepted by the counselor as a person of worth, with a culture, values, goals and hopes for the future," Bynum says. He adds that the client must be allowed to make his or her own decision. When the counseling process is successful, it "will serve to build a positive self-identity and lead the client into the posture of trusting. As self-determination is fostered, the black client will exhibit changes in feelings and attitudes which can be readily observed. Helping the client to experience successes, no matter how small, will get him or her moving in a positive way towards academic achievement and all it implies."[6]

WORKING WITH ADVISEES

In the university setting, so alien to any new student, it is important to see that students receive the correct information from advisers and that they know specifically where to turn. This may mean the faculty member walking the student down to the academic or club bulletin board the teacher is referring to, or physically pointing the way to the dean's office or calling ahead to make the needed appointment. Also, faculty should leave the door open with each referral or contact with the comment, "If the dean's assistant can't help you or you have more questions about the process, please come back or call me. Here's my number." Part of this process is letting the student take control and make the final moves needed to get the right answers, but also allowing for a fallback, a safe place for the student to come to ask the questions again.

Some of those questions won't be asked if the student doesn't make that first contact or isn't assigned to the faculty member as an advisee. While most schools assign advisers, a student is probably able to seek advice from any faculty. Perhaps one faculty member may feel more open to counseling students of color than a colleague is. Without making an evaluation of the colleague's worth as a counselor, the interested faculty member can still greet the student and make a specific point of asking when he or she will take the faculty member's writing class or sign up for an internship. Just knowing the student's name without a specific introduction is usually enough to open the door to the faculty member's office as a student-friendly advising stop. A student might throw up a natural barrier at that point, wondering just why the teacher knows his or her name, but continued greetings may warm the relationship.

The adviser can start introducing the student to the campus media. This may involve actually walking the student to the media offices and making the contacts in person. Or it may mean encouraging the editor to make sure one staff member is assigned to work with all new writers, not just students of color. That person should make sure the newcomers feel comfortable and that their stories get into the publication or on the air.

For any young students who have not developed sufficient skills to hit the front pages or the nightly news, the right place may be in "the shop" or behind the cameras. There students can watch what goes on, get paid (at some universities) and learn the media organization literally from the inside out. They'll generally build self-esteem, too, as they become respected for their skills in, say, computer design or with the editing equipment. Such experience may give them a leg up on the competition in the main newsroom when they want to move in that direction. For some who were leaders on high school publications, this interim job helps them feel as if they are part of the power structure instead of a little fish in a big sea.

JOB SEARCHES

Finding a career niche can be overwhelming for any student. While younger students concentrate on "finding" themselves more in the social arena, junior and senior students as well as graduate students need more career mentoring. In a way, that mentoring should come easier to the adviser who has started trust-building early in the student's academic career.

Getting students through the campus media and into professional media outlets presents another step in the mentoring process. It has to be preceded by the faculty getting to know the area media exceptionally well, finding out whether special internship slots have been set aside for minorities and how to apply. Inviting editors or news directors to campus to speak with potential interns or clerks is the best approach. Short of that, faculty should meet with the executives one-on-one, or as a group, to establish their credentials as "screeners." Journalism programs change over the years; faculties change; students change—and so does the power structure of the local media. Faculty members shouldn't assume that media executives are familiar with the faculty and communications program. Faculty should ask how previous interns or school contacts worked out and what kind of worker the news directors or managing editors are looking for now. The faculty probably can predict the answers, but asking the questions shows they are concerned. And they *are* concerned, or they wouldn't have tried to get the two groups together.

Once the relationships have been set up, faculty can begin asking for short-term internships/clerkships, one-month work programs to show students the inside of a newsroom or studio. These special jobs may have to be unpaid due to union rules or may have to be very short, say a day or two or even an afternoon of shadowing a professional. But they provide an excellent introduction for the student, plus a way to bolster the trust the faculty member has been building as a mentor and to show the news outlet that the journalism program has some excellent students available.

RESUME WRITING

The next step in student mentoring is usually the building of a resume, a step considered overwhelming by most students, as it represents the first time they have to evaluate themselves as an employer might. Resume-writing also is a critical opportunity to build self-esteem. Knowing how to help students word their resume to present themselves in a positive light can build yet another bridge between faculty and student. The adviser should be prepared to start with the basics, asking the students to write down all jobs they've held and then working with them to describe what their duties were in a way that will make them see the job positively, building their self-esteem.

Occasionally during these sessions, advisers should be prepared to admit that writing that first resume wasn't all clear sailing for them either. Honestly sharing past experiences and fears can help build trust as well.

Perhaps the hardest connection is putting the student in the right place at the right time for the right internship or job. If a prominent professional of color will be appearing on campus, the faculty member should make a point of inviting one or two advisees to the class or lecture, with permission, of course. And the faculty member should make sure to attend also, so that the advisee sees that the faculty member is interested as well. Afterwards, the faculty member can make the introductions with the comment that the student "is interested in XXX and XXX, and I know you are as well." Or the student and the professional can be connected through home towns or whatever hook is available.

The faculty member may have better luck if he or she calls the professional before the session, too. The teacher should let the professional know that the faculty member has a special student to introduce. The faculty member should ask if the professional would be open to a meeting over coffee with the student at a place near the newspaper or station. And then the faculty member can make the suggestion to the student.

Making those first connections on behalf of students can be difficult, but seeing themselves as part of a mostly White newsroom can be even more difficult for students of color. Giving students a ready-made role model can help.

What does all of this take? Time—something faculty never have enough of in any given day, week, month or year. But faculty can think of their investment of time as an investment in the future of the profession. As the profession cries out for help in finding the workers of the future, we should look again at how we can help. It's our profession as well.

NOTES

1. Barbara J. Hipsman and Stanley T. Wearden, "Peering Down the Pipeline: Minority Editors of College Newspapers Are Increasing—But to Only a Handful," American Society of Newspaper Editors *Bulletin*, April 1991, pp. 27–28.

2. Ibid.

3. Alvin S. Bynum, *Black Student/White Counselor: Developing Effective Relationships* (Indianapolis: Alexandria Books, 1987).

4. Ibid., p. 26.

5. Ibid, p. 69.

6. Ibid.

7 STRATEGIES FOR ENHANCING CULTURAL DIVERSITY ON JOURNALISM AND MASS COMMUNICATION FACULTIES

Orlando L. Taylor

The United States is undergoing rapid and significant changes in its racial, cultural and linguistic composition. *Time* magazine, in its April 9, 1990, cover story, "Beyond the Melting Pot," summarized these changes as follows:

Someday soon, surely much sooner than most people who filled out their Census forms last week realize, White Americans will become a minority group. Long before that day arrives, the presumption that the "typical" U.S. citizen is someone who traces his or her descent in a direct line to Europe will be part of the past. . . . Already 1 American in 4 defines himself or herself as Hispanic or non-White. If current trends in immigration and birth rates persist, the Hispanic population will have further increased an estimated 21%, the Asian presence about 22%, Blacks almost 12% and Whites a little more than 2% when the 20th century ends. By 2020, a date no further into the future than John F. Kennedy's election is in the past, the number of U.S. residents who are Hispanic or non-White will have more than doubled, to nearly 115 million, while the White population will not be increasing at all. By 2056, when someone born today will be 66 years old, the "average" U.S. resident, as defined by census statistics, will trace his or her descent to Africa, Asia, the Hispanic world, the Pacific Islands, Arabia—almost anywhere but White Europe.[1]

In this "New America," in which White Americans will eventually become a minority group, the topic of diversity will impact upon virtually every aspect of life.

Within the fields of journalism and mass communication, the topic of diversity has received considerable attention during the past decade. For example, the newspaper industry has set the modest goal of achieving parity in the presence of minorities (people of color) within its newsrooms by the year 2000. The Accrediting Council on Education in Journalism and Mass Communication (ACEJMC) has included faculty and curriculum diversity as one of its standards for awarding accreditation to institutions.

Despite ACEJMC standards, the professoriat in journalism and mass communication education—as well as the leadership in academic administration—is characterized today by an obvious *lack* of diversity. Except for the people of color on journalism and mass communication faculties at historically Black colleges and universities (which enroll approximately 40 percent of all African American journalism/mass communication students), the number of non-Whites holding faculty positions, chairs, directorships and deanships on most university and college journalism/mass communication faculties is embarrassingly small. The figures are even worse when one considers the number of people of color in tenure track positions and those who actually hold tenure.

DIVERSITY ESSENTIAL

Most advocates for increased diversity on college and university faculties argue that diversity is important for both equity and intellectual reasons. The equity reasons revolve around the notion that the workforce in all disciplines should be reflective of the American people. The intellectual reasons typically speak to the desirability of building faculties which, because of the cultural background and experiences of their members, can bring increased diversity into the curriculum. They also can bring more validity to the preparation of *all* journalism and mass communication students, regardless of color.

Racism aside, there may be many legitimate reasons why journalism and mass communication faculties continue to remain overwhelmingly White—and indeed less diverse than the media industries that professors frequently criticize. Among these legitimate reasons are lack of competitive salaries, absence of an academic tradition in journalism and mass communication education among people of color, and a small pool of potential applicants with the traditional faculty credentials of a terminal professional or doctoral degree.

The issue of academic degrees cannot be minimized. In 1990, for example, African Americans, the nation's largest minority group, were awarded only 828 Ph.D. degrees, approximately 2 percent of the total granted in all fields. This number represents a decline from the number of Ph.D.s awarded to African Americans a decade earlier.[2] In 1990 only 12.3 percent of all master's degrees in journalism and mass communication were awarded to people of color, down from 19 percent in 1988. Doctoral degree recipients among people of color in these same fields during this period dropped from 21.6 percent to 18 percent. Of the 47 African American students enrolled in doctoral programs in journalism and mass communication in 1990, 23 (49 percent) were enrolled at Howard University, the historically Black university located in the nation's capital.[3]

Despite the inadequate numbers of people of color in graduate programs in journalism and mass communication fields, colleges and universities can achieve increased cultural diversity on their faculties by using creative alternatives that in no way compromise academic standards. Obviously, one of the alternatives is to give credit for professional experience in lieu of advanced graduate or terminal professional degrees. This has been an established tradition at many institutions of higher learning for many years, especially for hiring faculty to teach skills courses. This single step is sufficient to greatly increase the pool of qualified applicants of color, since approximately 8 percent of the current newspaper workforce are people of color.

Besides establishing a "professional track," however, journalism/mass communication programs can take a variety of other approaches to increase the diversity of their faculties. Before discussing these, however, it is absolutely essential to state as a prerequisite that units and institutions seeking to increase diversity must have a strong and unequivocal commitment to the notion of diversity. This commitment should permeate the policies, practices, climate and offerings of the entire institution. The unit/institutional leadership must place priority on building sensitivity to and knowledge of diversity issues among the faculty and staff. Curricular offerings must reflect the interests of culturally diverse students. Course offerings should reflect the notion that most truths thought to be known by humankind are merely reflections of truth viewed through the prism of culture.

In addition to being committed to diversity, units and institutions should prepare a diversity strategic plan. This plan should, at a minimum, include goals, objectives and evaluation strategies. The plan should be developed collegially by the faculty, staff, students, administrative leaders and alumni.

Ideally, the search for and the hiring, retention, promotion and tenuring of faculty of color should be conducted within the context of a total institutional/unit diversity philosophy and program. Academic leaders and their faculties must set the tone, establish the policies and implement carefully planned programs in order to enhance the success of the diversity agenda.

A PLAN TO ACHIEVE A CULTURALLY DIVERSE FACULTY

University faculty and administrators offer a variety of reasons—some real, others mere excuses—for their inability to achieve cultural diversity on their faculties:

"We can't find any."
"Minorities wouldn't live in the community in which my institution is located."
"We have very few minority students at our institution."

"We announce our positions everywhere. Minorities simply don't apply."

"Qualified minorities have so many higher-paying opportunities outside of academia that they simply don't wish to seek low-paying faculty positions offered by colleges and universities."

"Minorities have little interest in research and publication activity; thus they will have difficulty getting promotion and tenure."

Statements like these represent some of the common beliefs (myths) about why the statistics on the recruitment, retention, promotion and tenuring of faculty of color in journalism/mass communication remain unacceptably low. Indeed, at a recent meeting of the Accrediting Council on Education in Journalism and Mass Communication (ACEJMC), statements such as these were made by several institutions to explain why they had failed to meet the diversity standard (Standard 12) established by ACEJMC for accreditation.

Although some of the above claims may be true in some cases, an institution can take proactive steps to increase the number of people of color who are hired, retained, promoted and tenured on journalism/mass communication faculties. The following suggestions, admittedly anecdotal, are presented for consideration. Four categories of suggestions are offered, with comments as appropriate. They include: enhancing the pool; conducting the interview; preparing for a culturally diverse faculty; and enhancing retention, promotion and tenure.

ENHANCING THE POOL

Clearly faculty diversity cannot be accomplished if the pool of candidates for faculty positions is not diverse. Consequently, the first and in many ways the most important consideration to be addressed is improving the candidate pool. The pool for *every* faculty appointment should be designed to include competitive candidates of color. Institutions or units should make certain that "competitive" is always defined in such a way that it is not virtually impossible for people of color to be selected. For example, if a criterion for a faculty appointment is previous teaching experience in an accredited journalism program, the number of competitive candidates of color will be minuscule, given the dismal history of affirmative action hiring practices in journalism/mass communication education.

In enriching the pool of candidates, institutions or units must make certain that the enrichment is not a mere cosmetic act, either in fact or appearance, for obtaining minority applicants. In such cases, people of color feel used. Over time, a negative reputation becomes attached to an institution or unit that makes insincere efforts toward building a culturally diverse faculty. If this occurs, the institution or unit is almost doomed to fail in its diversity efforts, no matter how serious or committed it might later become.

The following strategies are suggested to enhance the pool of applicants:

Personalize Recruitment. Units should not rely solely on advertisements and flyers for recruiting faculty of color. The personal touch is important, indeed essential. Most groups of color depend heavily on the quality of interpersonal relationships. They like to get a feel for the persons with whom they will be working. This cannot be obtained from a job announcement or advertisement in a professional publication. Wherever possible, make face-to-face contact with potential candidates of color *prior* to the application process. If this is not possible, try to have a telephone conference with potential candidates in order to give them a notion of the interpersonal (and intergroup) dynamics of the leader, the faculty, the unit and the institution generally.

Build a Personal Network with People of Color. Develop personal relationships with people of color in the professional and academic communities in journalism and mass communication. Give these persons opportunities to know the institution, the unit, the faculty and the leaders. When faculty positions arise, contact these individuals directly to inform them of the openings and to seek referrals. This process may be the most effective way to enrich the pool of potential applicants from culturally diverse populations.

Learn Important Humanistic and Social Factors for People of Color. Institutions and units traditionally focus on such factors as salary, rank, duties, facilities, student/faculty profiles, curricular/degree offerings and organizational structure in attempting to encourage individuals to apply for faculty positions. While persons of color want to obtain such information in considering employment, they may often consider other humanistic and social factors to be of equal or greater importance.

These factors typically include such topics as the size of the minority student body and faculty within the institution or unit; affirmative action policies, practices and results; racial/ethnic attitudes within the institution and the surrounding community; demographics of the community; and social, cultural and religious outlets within the community that cater to persons of color. Information pertaining to these topics, particularly when it is positive, can greatly assist enhancement of the applicant pool.

Avoid Tokenism. Institutions and units must aggressively seek diversity for *every* available faculty position, especially after one person of color has already been hired. Persons of color frequently feel isolated in settings in which they are "the only one." Their retention on the faculty may be difficult, if not impossible, unless enough people of color are hired on the faculty to give the campus community a sense that diversity is an institutionalized reality.

Advertise in Publications That Target People of Color. Paid advertisements in traditional education publications, such as the *Chronicle of Higher Education*, are useful in announcing faculty positions to the general academic and professional communities. However, advertisements in publications that target persons of color are more likely to be effective for this segment of the population, particularly if the advertisements include information on some of the humanistic and social topics discussed above. Such publications might include, for example, *Black Issues in Higher Education* and publications of such professional organizations as the National Association of Black Journalists, the Asian American Journalists Association, the National Association of Hispanic Journalists, the Native American Press Association and the National Black Media Coalition. These publications typically have very large academically and professionally oriented constituencies, some of whom might be interested in considering an academic career in higher education.

Recruit at Student and Professional Events That Target People of Color. In addition to the annual meetings and special events of national, regional or local organizations that target people of color, direct face-to-face recruitment of potential faculty members at other communication-related events that cater to persons of color is also an excellent way to enhance the applicant pool for faculty positions. Such events include the Annual Howard University Communications Conference and the regional job fairs sponsored by the American Society of Newspaper Editors.

Develop Partnerships with Predominantly or Historically Minority Institutions. Predominantly or historically minority colleges and universities represent an excellent source of potential faculty members, especially on short-term arrangements. Through creative partnerships with these institutions, arrangements can be made for (a) faculty (and student) exchanges; (b) jointly sponsored courses and seminars; (c) dual listings of courses at majority and minority institutions taught by faculty members of color; (d) sabbatical leaves and leaves of absence for faculty of color to come to majority institutions (and vice versa); and (e) study leaves for faculty of color from minority institutions for graduate or postdoctoral study. In such arrangements, however, it is imperative for two principles to be followed: the partnership should enhance the educational environment at both institutions; and majority institutions must not raid the faculty (or student body) of minority institutions.

CONDUCTING THE INTERVIEW

If cultural diversification of a faculty is likened to a baseball game, then enrichment of the pool is merely the process of reaching first base. Reaching second base involves holding a successful interview with candidates of color. A successful interview is one that permits candidates of color to present their strengths and weaknesses in a fair and comprehensive manner. In addition, candidates need to be given a comprehensive and accurate view of the unit, the institution and the community. The interview should also present sufficient information to make the recruiting institution as attractive as possible to the candidate.

To achieve these goals, the following strategies might be employed:

Emphasize Career Advancement Possibilities to the Candidate. Persons of color, like all candidates, do not want to be locked into dead-end jobs. Inform the candidate of career opportunities in the unit and within the institution. Cite the track records of other faculty members of color.

Discuss Campus/Community History and the Current Social Situation. Interviewees should be thoroughly and candidly informed of the social environment of the campus and of the surrounding community with respect to racial and ethnic issues. Where possible, provide candidates with data derived from organizations that maintain records and statistics on this topic, such as the Office of Human Relations and the Civil Rights Commission. Discuss the history and background of negative aspects of how the campus and the community have handled racial and ethnic issues. Candidates of color will probably appreciate candid discussion of important negative information during the interview.

Arrange Meetings for Interviewees with Student, Faculty and Community Leaders of Color. Potential faculty of color frequently want to get a perspective on the unit, institution and community from persons from cultures like their own. This desire is especially important when interviewees are considering an appointment in a unit or institution in which members of their culture are not currently on the faculty, or are present only in small numbers. Such meetings may provide interviewees with highly desired information and play an important role in encouraging them to accept employment, if offered.

PREPARING FOR A CULTURALLY DIVERSE FACULTY

Many institutions or units make the mistake of believing that once the interview process is completed and persons of color are selected for their faculties, the biggest part of their work is finished. In reality, nothing is further from the truth. Institutions and units must prepare themselves to receive and maintain culturally diverse faculties, in addition to merely attracting them for employment. Without such preparation, institutions and units are not likely to achieve their diversity goals.

The most important dimension of getting a unit prepared for increased cultural diversity is developing a philosophy or attitude within the unit that faculty diversity is an asset. If necessary, the unit might assert that diversity is in its own self-interest because diversity increases the unit's potential for student recruitment and external grants and increases its national reputation. Indeed, the unit should develop the view that increased faculty diversity might help to attract some White faculty who prefer to work in a culturally diverse environment.

The following strategies might be employed to prepare the unit for increased faculty diversity:

Increase Faculty/Staff Development. The sponsorship of unit-wide faculty/staff (and possibly student) development programs in cultural awareness and sensitivity, preferably under the direction of an outside expert, is often effective in preparing units for cultural diversity. A major component of the faculty/staff development program should be in the area of intercultural communication, in which emphasis is placed on how to use verbal and non-verbal communication which is least likely to be misunderstood, misinterpreted or found to be socially offensive across cultural lines. Some attention might also be given to how to talk about race and ethnicity in a comfortable and nonintimidating manner.[4]

Cross-cultural simulations like BAFA BAFA[5] and role-playing activities are often effective in such sessions, as are nonintimidating videotapes such as the *Valuing Diversity*[6] series. The Society for Intercultural Education, Training and Research (SIETAR) in Washington, DC, can provide information on contemporary training strategies for enhancing intercultural competence. It is imperative for the entire faculty/staff to participate in these activities; participants should not be limited to those who are already committed to diversity or who are reasonably well informed on the subject.

Recruit a Culturally Diverse Student Body. Recruitment, retention, graduation and placement of a culturally diverse student body enhance faculty diversity. The presence of a culturally diverse student body sends the message that cultural diversity is taken seriously by the institution or unit. Equally important, a culturally diverse student body allows faculty of color an opportunity to share their talents with students from their culture, if they so desire.

Celebrate Diversity Throughout the Unit's Environment. Diversity should be demonstrated in a natural, unforced manner throughout the unit's physical environment. Pictures on walls, artifacts on shelves, newspapers in the reading room, books in the library and clippings on bulletin boards all reflect the values of a unit and what it considers to be important. If these elements of the environment reflect diversity, faculty diversity is enhanced. Moreover, they set a tone within the unit, showing that diversity is valued and celebrated.

Infuse Cultural Diversity Topics Throughout the Curriculum. In many ways, the curriculum reflects the academic and intellectual perspectives and values of the faculty. Moreover, the curriculum sets a tone for both faculty and students. Therefore, one very effective strategy for preparing a unit for faculty diversity is to have the faculty conduct a thorough review of each course in their curricular offerings, as well as of the philosophy of the curriculum itself. While in-depth courses that focus directly on diversity issues and topics are desirable, such courses should be complemented by an infusion of diversity topics throughout all courses within the curriculum.

ENHANCING RETENTION, PROMOTION AND TENURE

And now for the ultimate issue in faculty diversity—the home run if you will—retention and promotion! Obviously, enriching the candidate pool, successful interviews, and unit and institutional preparation mean little if faculty of color are not retained, promoted or tenured. Success in these areas is critical for long-term, institutionalized cultural diversification of faculties. The track record in promotion and tenure of faculty of color is perhaps the poorest of all aspects of cultural diversity on journalism and mass communication faculties. One only has to examine the small numbers of faculty of color on predominantly White campuses who hold tenure and the rank of professor. Of course, the numbers in this area are small partly because many faculty members of color have not been on faculties long enough to achieve the rank of professor or tenure. At the same time, anecdotal reports—and perceptions of faculty of color—suggest that considerable work needs to be done in the areas of retention, promotion and tenure.

The following actions are likely to heighten a unit's chances for retaining, promoting and tenuring faculty of color:

Provide Competitive Salary and Perks. Retention of all faculty members is greatly enhanced if they are paid competitive salaries and provided with other perquisites that enhance their academic and professional careers. The unit and the institution must be prepared to address the fact that because of high demand and low supply, faculty of color can often obtain higher salaries and more perks than other faculty at comparable ranks. This situation might produce significant human relations problems within the unit which must be addressed frontally and candidly by the leader. The best response to such complaints from other faculty is to state that there is a long-standing tradition within academia for salaries to be based, at least partly, on market demand. The current demand for faculty of color is high and the supply is small.

Provide Seed Funds for Research. It is a good idea to provide seed funds for research and faculty development for *all* new faculty. Such actions are particularly useful for faculty of color, especially those who wish to pursue research programs that are traditionally underfunded, and those so heavily extended in service activities that they have little time to seek external funding for scholarly or creative interests. Funds for faculty development, particularly for travel to professional meetings or attendance at professional or continuing education seminars, help candidates acquire credentials essential for promotion and tenure.

Provide Leadership and Career Opportunities. Faculty of color are more easily retained if they feel that they can advance their careers to the fullest in accordance with their abilities and interests. In other words, they are more likely to be retained if there is no real or perceived "glass ceiling" within the unit or institution. This is particularly true if the individual has leadership abilities and interests. These individuals need to be allowed to make use of leadership opportunities, leadership training and leadership mentoring—and not just on minority issues. If national statistics on faculty of color in predominantly White institutions are embarrassingly low, the record for those groups in leadership positions is disastrous. The small number of persons of color who hold positions of leadership as chairs, deans, directors and division heads in journalism and mass communication attests to this assertion.

Encourage Mentoring. It is important to make certain that junior faculty of color have mentors who understand the unit and the institution and who can facilitate their quest for promotion, tenure and grants. Mentors need *not* be from the same culture as the persons they mentor!

Enhance Expertise. Faculty of color should not be expected to be experts on topics pertaining to cultural diversity, or even to have a particular interest in such topics. These faculty members should be given an opportunity to focus on academic and professional areas of primary interest and competence. Above all, they should not be limited in teaching, curricular and committee assignments to topics and issues pertaining to cultural diversity.

Facilitate Access to Other Faculty of Color. One of the biggest problems that faculty of color typically face on predominantly White campuses is a feeling of isolation. Units can help to reduce or eliminate this problem by facilitating access of faculty of color to other faculty of color throughout the academic community. Of course, it is desirable to facilitate access of *all* new faculty to other faculty throughout the university community with comparable or complementary academic or professional interests.

Avoid the Minority-in-Residence Syndrome. Faculty of color should not be relegated to the role of Minority-in-Residence, either in fact or by perception. This role occurs when faculty members of color are placed on an inordinate number of committees, given excessive assignments, or invited to a myriad of social events to assure "minority representation." This overinvolvement is not only discriminatory in relation to the time demands placed on other faculty members, but also takes faculty of color away from other valuable pursuits required for tenure, such as teaching, doing research and publishing.

Provide Credit for University, Community and Professional Service. In most academic units, priority is properly placed on teaching, research and creative activity in decisions regarding reappointment, promotion and tenure. In those instances wher ⸱ faculty of color are required or expected to participate in an inordinate amount of service to the unit, university, community or profession, it is obvious that such persons are hindered in obtaining promotion and tenure. In many cases very promising faculty of color have failed to obtain promotion or tenure for these reasons. In such cases, the institution loses and the individual most certainly loses.

The best way to address this unfortunate situation, of course, is not to place faculty of color in this position—or at least to advise them against being placed in such a position. If it does occur, however, units or institutions should seriously consider giving significantly increased weight to the service component in promotion and tenure decisions and decreased weight to the scholarly/creative component and perhaps to the teaching category also.

Respect All Publication Sources. Many faculty of color publish their works in peer-reviewed journals or with publishing houses that have a particular interest in and commitment to topics pertaining to culture and communication. Sometimes these faculty members find that mainstream journals and publishing houses have little or no interest in the topic of cultural diversity. Hence, faculty members are caught in a Catch–22 situation: they either have no publications in mainstream sources, or a publication record in sources about which traditional departments know little or for which they have little respect. Departments must be sensitive to this point and not discriminate against individuals who publish in lesser-known, though peer-reviewed, journals or with publishing houses that meet professional publication standards but that do not have big names.

CONCLUDING REMARKS

This chapter has presented some proactive suggestions that can be employed to enhance cultural diversity on the faculties of journalism and mass communication units and within colleges and universities in general. While the suggestions are largely anecdotal in nature, many have been tried in several locations with success.

Some may feel a bit weary in pursuing the cultural diversity agenda, feeling that we never seem to get to a position of finality on this topic. There always seems to be something more to do! Such persons may take heart from the fact that institutional change is difficult, particularly if it is going against trends that have been deeply ingrained over a long period of time. Faculty diversity within the nation's institutions of higher learning—and especially within journalism and mass communication—has been an emerging priority for only a little more than two decades. And the progress has been extremely slow.

Moreover, faculty and institutional circumstances, like the nation's demographics, are not static. Because they constantly change, in a certain sense we are seeking a finality that we may never find. Yet, we must remain committed to seeking that finality.

In this regard, Alfred Tennyson's poem "Ulysses" comes to mind. The poem is about positive commitment. Its speaker is a man who has returned to his homeland after a 10-year hiatus, only to find that, like him, it has changed. Ulysses recognizes humankind's essential dilemma: though no experience brings ultimate fulfillment and no reorientation is conclusive, humankind must continue to seek the finality that one knows one cannot really find:

> . . . Come, my friends
> 'Tis not too late to seek a newer world.
> Push off, and sitting well in order smite
> The sounding furrows; for my purpose holds
> To sail beyond the sunset, and the baths
> Of all the western stars, until I die.

The task of achieving diversity at our institutions requires a similar level of commitment and vision.

NOTES

1. William Henry III, "Beyond the Melting Pot," *Time*, 9 April 1990, p. 28.

2. New York *Times*, 21 April 1992, p. 1.

3. Lee B. Becker, "Annual Enrollment: Comparisons and Projections," *Journalism Educator* 46 (1991), 50–60.

4. Orlando Taylor, *The Pragmatics of Race, Ethnicity and Diversity* (Rockville, MD: American Speech-Language-Hearing Association), in press.

5. R. Garry Shirts, *BAFA BAFA: A Cross Cultural Simulation* (Delmar, CA: Simile II, 1977).

6. *Valuing Diversity* videotape (San Francisco: Copeland-Griggs Productions, 1987).

8 THE SERVICE COMPONENT IN COLLEGE JOURNALISM: PITFALLS FOR FACULTY OF COLOR

Sharon Bramlett-Solomon

During her first year as an assistant journalism professor, Kathy Smith (not her real name) was immediately immersed in college service activities. In addition to teaching two classes, she coordinated the college's summer high school journalism newspaper, served as editor of the school's quarterly alumni newsletter, and organized the school's annual journalism awards banquet.

She also served as a board member of the state journalism association, co-chaired activities for the college's twentieth anniversary celebration, and coordinated the school's Journalism Orientation Day program for some 20 minority students and parents. In addition, Smith advised students and devoted time to mentoring minority journalism students.

At the national level, she was active in the Association for Education in Journalism and Mass Communication (AEJMC), served on the AEJMC Teaching Standards Committee, and served on the executive board of AEJMC's Minorities and Communication division. She also presented numerous speeches to various community groups. All of these service activities drew heavily upon Smith's time and away from her research.

In Smith's second year, her service activities list grew even longer. Despite her efforts to "just say no" to colleagues, deans and local community groups, she was overwhelmed by service duties. After three years, Smith found herself in a situation familiar to many AHANA (African, Hispanic, Asian and Native American) faculty members. Too much of her precious tenure clock time had been devoured by service activities that dominated her time, stifled her research, and counted little toward tenure and promotion.

The road to tenure is not easy for any faculty member, but it is often more difficult for AHANA faculty, who find themselves immersed in service activities.

At the 1991 Boston convention of the AEJMC, a panel on "The Service Component and Standard 12: Pitfalls for Faculty of Color" concluded that service overload is a serious impediment for AHANA faculty members. Panelist Mike Kautsch, dean of the William Allen White School of Journalism at the University of Kansas, said that service work is especially troublesome for AHANA faculty because they often are bombarded with it.

"Faculty members of color sometimes feel their lives are full of 'honey-do'—'Honey do this; honey do that,' " said Kautsch. "Their peers, deans and administrators ask them to perform an array of service activities. . . . Sometimes the minority affairs service expectations come in addition to the service expected of all faculty members. This could be a pitfall, for the faculty member who meets all of these expectations does so at the risk of his or her teaching and research, and ultimately, his or her career in higher education," Kautsch warned.

This chapter addresses the problem of service overload often experienced by Blacks, Hispanics and other faculty of color, and offers suggestions for avoiding service pitfalls that thwart successful efforts to achieve tenure. The topic is important, first, because many tenure track AHANA faculty members have experienced the trap of service overload. Second, many AHANA faculty members as well as some journalism administrators are frustrated by the service dilemma but are unsure how to handle the problem.

SERVICE AND THE TENURE PROCESS

It is essential that AHANA journalism faculty seeking tenure remember foremost that service never counts as much as teaching and research in the tenure process. Good teaching and publishing in refereed publications are vital for tenure track journalism faculty members in most programs.

This conclusion is supported by a 1991 tenure and promotion study by Leigh and Anderson, which revealed that most successful tenure candidates have superior teaching and research records. The study found that candidates who did not receive tenure generally had insufficient publications.[1]

In other words, no matter how much service one does, without good teaching and research, tenure is unlikely. Thus, junior faculty must consider what is necessary in the long run to achieve tenure and must determine where service fits into that process.

Because service counts least in the tenure process, AHANA faculty should concentrate on teaching and publications before service. However, because some service is necessary, the best way to use service in the tenure process is *to make service enhance teaching and publishing*.

Dean Kautsch suggested that faculty of color seek creative links between service, teaching and research. "Service should enhance the other functions,"

Kautsch said. "For example, the placement of student interns might be linked to research on the value of internships . . . or teaching about diversity could be joined with a survey of its effect."

PRIORITY VERSUS NONPRIORITY SERVICE

One reason the service component spells trouble for AHANA faculty is that they often attach greater importance to service than do their tenure committees. Therefore, a good place to start in balancing the service requirement is to determine what is and is not "priority service."

The importance of faculty service is articulated in the mission and goals statements of most schools. Universities and colleges expect tenure track faculty members to perform institutional, community and/or national service. For most journalism faculty, at least some service is a fact of life. Therefore, any faculty member or administrator trying to prioritize service and its relationship to teaching and research should start with an examination of the unit's mission and goals statement.

Kautsch advised at the 1991 AEJMC convention that deans and faculty members review the unit's mission and goals statement together: "The unit chief and faculty member should review it together and develop an understanding of how the mission should influence the professional life of the faculty member. They also should mutually understand the value of service and how that value will be measured."

For example, at the Walter Cronkite School of Journalism and Telecommunication at Arizona State University, service is given an articulated weight of 20 percent, compared to 30 percent for research and 50 percent for teaching. The Cronkite School's mission and goals statement emphasizes that faculty service should be recognized and rewarded as an important professional responsibility. Most highly valued is service that enhances the school's link to community organizations and to the professional print and broadcast media.

Thus, prioritizing service is also important because it helps to determine service that tenure committees find most important. However, faculty should remember that tenure and promotion committees examine service in terms of both quantity and quality. Often it is not *how much* service a faculty member does but the *kind* of service. Just because someone has a longer list of service work than someone else does not mean that the former's service work is more valued. Quality outweighs quantity.

Douglas Anderson, director of the School of Journalism and Telecommunication at Arizona State, finds the quality of service to be an important consideration.

A long list of service may look impressive, but may not be considered the most significant service to the unit or college. The quality or value of the service must be considered and assessed. Service promotes good citizenship and should be legitimately appreciated. For example, we recognize service by giving an outstanding service award to faculty each year for it. I can't imagine someone who does no service being respected by colleagues. Everyone must do some service, so we look at service quality.[2]

In prioritizing service duties, AHANA faculty should keep in mind that academic and professional service generally is more important to tenure committees than local community service such as giving speeches, serving on panels or setting up exhibits. Academic and professional service increases the school's academic visibility and promotes networking among faculty from the various journalism schools across the country. Such activities include serving on journal editorial boards, serving as paper reviewer, chairing school or university committees, or serving in executive positions in professional organizations such as AEJMC, the Broadcast Education Association, the Radio and Television News Directors Association, the American Newspaper Publishers Association or the International Communication Association.

THE SERVICE COMPONENT AND STANDARD 12

ACEJMC's Standard 12 calls for increased minority and female representation and cultural diversity in the journalism curriculum. It states: "Units must make effective efforts to recruit, advise and retain minority students and minority and women faculty members for their intended career paths. They also must include in their courses information about the major contributions made by minorities and women to the disciplines covered in the unit."

In order to comply with Standard 12, college journalism administrators often depend on AHANA faculty service to reach their goals. However, AHANA faculty members must be able to show clearly on their vitae and promotion and tenure applications how their service work fulfills Standard 12. AHANA faculty must make it clear to tenure committees and colleagues that their service work is important to the university or college and is a legitimate criterion for tenure and promotion.

Just as some faculty offer creative activities (writing magazine articles or producing broadcast programs) for credit toward tenure, service important to the university's multicultural mission also could—and should—merit tenure credit. If this service does not receive measurable tenure credit, then AHANA faculty who are unfairly bombarded with service duties should receive special compensations for their work.

AHANA faculty should receive either reduced course loads, extra pay or measurable credit toward tenure when the service they perform meets three conditions:

1. The service helps the school meet its multicultural mission and goals;
2. The AHANA faculty member's service clearly exceeds the service performed by the majority faculty; and
3. Such service duties place the AHANA faculty member at a tenure disadvantage.

In other words, journalism deans and administrators should do the right thing and recognize and reward the contributions of AHANA faculty members when the service they perform benefits the school's multicultural mission and goals and when such service is not expected of the majority faculty. If deans and administrators do not reward AHANA faculty with either reduced course loads, extra pay or measurable tenure credit, then AHANA faculty members should give service work minimum emphasis and should refuse to perform service activities that detract from research time and publishing efforts.

NOTES

1. Frederic Leigh and Douglas Anderson, "Tenure and Promotion in Schools of Journalism and Mass Communication: A Box Score," paper presented at the Southwest Education Council for Journalism and Mass Communication Conference, Corpus Christi, TX, 6–7 October 1991.

2. The Cronkite School each year presents three faculty awards (called the Leg-of-the-Stool Awards) for outstanding achievement in teaching, research and service.

BIBLIOGRAPHY

Carolyn Martindale

American Newspaper Publishers Association. *Recruiting and Retaining Newspaper Minority Employees: How to Do It*. 1986. Available from ANPA Foundation, the Newspaper Center, Box 17407, Dulles Airport, Washington, DC 20041.

American Society of Newspaper Editors. *Help Is Available*. Available from ASNE, P.O. Box 17004, Washington, DC 20041.

———. *Minorities and Newspapers: A Report by the Committee on Minorities, ASNE*. Washington, DC: ASNE, 1982.

Astin, A. W. *Preventing Students from Dropping Out*. San Francisco: Jossey-Bass, 1975.

Beal, P., and L. Noel. *What Works in Student Retention*. Boulder, CO: National Center for Higher Education Management Systems and the American College Testing Program, 1980.

Brown, S. V. *Increasing Minority Faculty: An Elusive Goal*. Princeton, NJ: Educational Testing Service, 1988.

Clayton, R. "Advising Minority Students." In D. S. Crockett, ed., *Academic Advising: A Resource Document*. Iowa City: American College Testing Program, 1978.

Dodge, S. "A Center Helps Minority Students Solve Academic, Social Problems." *Chronicle of Higher Education*, 29 November 1989, p. A38.

Green, M. F., ed. *Minorities on Campus: A Handbook for Enhancing Diversity*. Washington, DC: American Council on Education, 1989.

Greenman, John. *Recruiting and Retention of Minority Students: A "How to" Guide for Journalism Schools*. A report of the ASNE Minorities Committee, 1988. Available from ASNE (see above).

Gutiérrez, Félix. "Racial Inclusiveness: Journalism Education's Second Chance." Paper presented at the Institute for Journalism Education's conference on "Racial Diversity—The Media: A Blueprint for Action," Washington, DC, 9–11 March 1987.

Hall, Diane, Barbara Hines and Robert M. Ruggles. "Recruiting and Retaining Black
    Students for Journalism and Mass Communication Education." Special issue
    of *Insights*, July 1989. Limited quantities available from Association of Schools
    of Journalism and Mass Communication, University of South Carolina, 1621
    College St., Columbia, SC 29208–0251.
Kavanaugh, Molly. "Lessons in Journalism." *Scripps Howard News*, October/Novem-
    ber 1990, pp. 19–21.
Lewis, B., C. Dorsey-Gaines and W. DeGarcia. "Personal Contact Strategies for
    Minority Recruitment." *Journal of College Admissions*, Winter 1989, pp. 10–13.
Manning, Jane, and Anne Steward. "Marketing for Minorities: Have We Done Our
    Homework?" *Journal of Marketing for Higher Education* 1 (1988).
Martindale, Carolyn. "Recruiting Minority Students with Limited Resources." *Jour-
    nalism Educator* 45 (Spring 1990), 71–77.
Odell, M., and J. Mock, eds. *A Crucial Agenda: Making Colleges and Universities Work
    Better for Minority Students*. Boulder, CO: Western Interstate Commission for
    Higher Education, 1989.
Paddon, Anna R., and Lona Cobb. "Overlooked Faculty Resource in Historically
    Black Colleges." *Journalism Educator* 45 (Spring 1990), 64–70.
"Pluralism and Diversity: A Special Collection of Articles." Special issue of *Insights*
    (journal of the Association of Schools of Journalism and Mass Communication),
    Winter 1990–91. Limited quantities available from ASJMC (see above).
Romero, Manny. "Strategies for Recruiting and Retaining Minority Students." Paper
    presented at National Convention of Association for Education in Journalism
    and Mass Communication, Minneapolis, 9–12 August 1990.

III PLURALIZING THE CURRICULUM

9 TEACHING THE VALUE OF MULTICULTURAL SKILLS

Carolyn Martindale

Most journalism educators teach their students in essentially the same ways they themselves were taught. They teach the same news values and the same basic news-gathering techniques. They explain the who, what, when, where, why and how that should be answered in the lead. They teach the history of the media as the history of the mainstream White press and broadcasting outlets. The mass communication pioneers they discuss are outstanding White, usually male, journalists. They presume the same media audience of middle class, predominantly White, persons of European ancestry.

But American society today is vastly different from the one in which today's mass communication faculty were educated, and is changing rapidly. Consider these facts, presented in 1992 by the Center for Demographic Policy in Washington, DC:

- By the year 2010, the number of minority youngsters below age 17 in the United States will increase by 4.4 million, while the number of White children will decrease by 3.8 million.
- Two-thirds of the world's immigrants come to the United States.
- For these reasons, in 30 years one out of every three Americans will be a member of a racial or ethnic minority.[1]

These rapidly accelerating changes have already begun to alter the face of American society. According to the Center for Demographic Policy, today 31 percent of the children in the United States are minorities; by the year 2010 minority children are expected to comprise 37 percent of the youth population of the country.[2] Within another decade what used to be the White majority will become smaller than the combined minority populations in several of the nation's fastest-growing states: California, Texas, New York and Florida.[3]

Thus the society in which today's journalism and mass communication students will work and about which they will report will be vastly different in the future. These students need to be informed about groups other than their own so that they can report about these groups intelligently. They need to learn how to expand their news-gathering techniques so that they can go beyond official and customary sources and write about the concerns of persons not in the mainstream of power. They need to become aware of past stereotypes about minority groups so that they can avoid inadvertently perpetuating such stereotypes. And they need to be prepared to work and to succeed in a multicultural workplace.

The importance of such journalistic training has begun to be reflected in the concerns of some of today's media managers. Several years ago executives of the Gannett newspaper chain, which owns *USA Today*, informed reporters that they were to bring a multicultural perspective into every story in which it was possible to do so. Within the past two years more and more articles with titles like "Reaching Minority Readers" and "Are We as Sensitive as We Should Be?" have begun appearing in news industry trade journals, and a committee of representatives from national editors' and publishers' organizations recently published a report called *Cornerstone for Growth: How Minorities Are Vital to the Future of Newspapers*. A small but growing number of news organizations have begun employing diversity consultants and providing cultural sensitivity training for their employees.

More and more often, journalism and mass communication graduates are being asked at job fairs whether they have had training or student publications experience in covering diverse groups and working in a multicultural workplace. Advertisements for reporters in trade publications also are beginning to reflect this requirement. One copy editor stated recently: "Multicultural awareness greatly enhances one's ability to establish rapport, interpret verbal and non-verbal signals, gain access to and report the story as the people involved experience it. Those without multicultural awareness," he added, "are imprisoned in their own perceptions and can report nothing else."[4]

But multicultural education is not easy for today's journalism and mass communication faculty to provide, because they themselves were not trained that way; they have no model to follow. They were not educated about other cultures or how to report with cultural sensitivity, and they have no idea how to train their students that way. They don't know how to teach what Pam Creedon and Kevin Stoner of Ohio State have termed "the D for Diversity" as well as the time-honored five Ws and the H.[5]

Across the nation a few school systems and universities have made a commitment to learning how to provide multicultural education, but few journalism educators are in the fortunate position of being able to take advantage of such trail-blazing efforts. Those faculty members who recognize the need to educate their students to cover other cultures study and develop lecture material on their own, flock eagerly to panel discussions and training sessions on this topic at professional conventions, and read each article they can find. But not much information is available.

The purpose of Part III of this book is to provide guidance, resources and ideas for faculty who want to educate their students to cover and work in a multiethnic, multicultural society by presenting teaching ideas, suggestions for books and audiovisual resources, assignments, and many other techniques for getting started in multicultural teaching. The material provided here is not exhaustive, because the subject is too multifaceted to be covered in one book. Also, the field is new, and educators are just beginning to develop techniques and find resources for teaching it. But enough material and suggestions are provided here to keep one faculty member busy throughout his or her whole teaching career.

The following chapters have been written by a variety of educators from all areas of the country—men and women of various races and ethnic groups, of varying ages and backgrounds. Some are relatively new faculty members, not many years out of graduate school, while others are deans of their communications schools or chairs of their departments; some come from a newspaper background, while others have spent most of their careers in academe. What they have in common is a long-standing interest in informing their students about other cultures and training them how to cover other groups in a balanced and sensitive fashion. They also have developed a growing repertoire of methods for doing so, and these are the ideas they have shared in the chapters that follow.

Underlying all the subsequent teaching suggestions is a concept about what the educators are trying to do. They want to inform their students about other races and cultures so that the students can *value* differences among people, not be hostile to or suspicious of them. They want their students to understand that the insights and experiences and talents of people different from themselves can enrich their work experience and their stories, not threaten them.

Their aim is not to train their students to provide compensatory coverage that emphasizes only the positive or the problematic about other racial or ethnic groups. Instead, they want to encourage future journalists to produce balanced coverage that shows the bad but illuminates the good as well. Equally important, their aim is to help students see that most of their coverage, from the most mundane stories to the most important, should reflect the multiplicity of races and cultures that comprise American society.

APPROACHES TO TEACHING

A few words of caution seem necessary here. As Cohen, Lombard and Pierson explain so clearly in a 1992 *Journalism Educator* article, many White students today feel very threatened over issues they see as related to multicultural and gender diversity.[6] Professors attempting to bring information about various groups into their courses will occasionally encounter resistance from some students, ranging from mild irritation ("How come we have to spend all this time learning about other groups? What does it have to do with us?") to resentment over attention paid to various racial and ethnic groups ("Why do we have to have a Black History Month, or a Black Students' Union? Blacks would be offended if we had a *White* Students' Union!") to real anger over a perceived threat to their sense of self and their future ("I'm tired of all this affirmative action stuff! The group that's really discriminated against these days is White males!").

Several approaches, all equally valid, can be used in situations such as these. First of all, before objections even arise, students should be made aware of the absolute necessity of acquiring multicultural knowledge and communication skills if they are going to succeed as professionals in today's—and tomorrow's—world. As noted above, such abilities are, or are rapidly becoming, prerequisites to professional success. The emphasis in the syllabus and throughout the course should be on acquiring information about other cultures and developing skills in cross-cultural communication that will enable students to succeed in their chosen field. Debra Miller offers suggestions for achieving this approach in a public relations course that could be applied to any communication course.[7]

Second, it is important that a critical thinking approach be used in the classroom. Statements of opinion or supposed fact, both by students and by other speakers and writers, should be submitted to examination by critical thinking techniques. The underlying questions should always be, Is this statement true? How can we investigate to see whether or not it is true? Throughout class discussions the focus should be on facts, not opinions; on identifying unvoiced assumptions and beliefs; on gathering evidence and analyzing arguments. Numerous books and articles on critical thinking are available to help faculty in this endeavor. If students are encouraged to see their own and their classmates'—and their professor's—beliefs as ideas to be investigated in a search for truth, they may learn to feel less threatened. During the course they may even come to feel relieved at acquiring some knowledge and developing skills for dealing with these explosive issues.[8]

Third, the professor needs to be scrupulously careful not to force his or her views on the students. In manner, body language and words the teacher must encourage students to feel that the classroom is a safe place to express their views and that they will be listened to with respect. It is important that students in the class retain their right of free speech, and that the class be a forum for the free exchange of ideas. At the same time, students with particularly vehement views—on either end of the political spectrum—should not be allowed to harass or intimidate students with different ideas. The professor can prevent this by setting ground rules for classroom behavior.

Just as the faculty member can require that students raise their hands before speaking, he or she can require civility in the expression of ideas, and can ban personal attacks.[9]

Throughout the course, the students should be moving from unexamined perceptions to ideas based on fact, from feeling threatened to becoming empowered, from being familiar with only their own culture to knowing something about others' cultures as well. Ideally, they will someday carry this knowledge with them into their professional work and will help impart this understanding to their readers and viewers.

NOTES

1. Dr. Harold L. Hodgkinson, *A Demographic Look at Tomorrow* (Washington, DC: Center for Demographic Policy, 1992), p. 5; and keynote address by Dr. Hodgkinson at the Third Annual National Conference on Racial and Ethnic Relations in American Higher Education, Santa Fe, 4 June 1990.

2. Phone conversation with Janice Hamilton Outtz, associate director, Center for Demographic Policy, 23 November 1992.

3. Henry G. Cisneros, former mayor of San Antonio and president and CEO of Cisneros Asset Management Co., San Antonio, keynote address at the Fourth Annual National Conference on Racial and Ethnic Relations in American Higher Education, San Antonio, 1 June 1991.

4. Edward Pease, "Still the Invisible People: Job Satisfaction of Minority Journalists at U.S. Daily Newspapers," doctoral dissertation, Ohio University, June 1991.

5. Kevin Stoner, preconvention workshop on "Incorporating Diversity into the Curriculum," Association for Education in Journalism and Mass Communication convention, Boston, 6 August 1991. Tape available from ACTS, 14153 Clayton Rd., Ballwin, MO 63011.

6. Jeremy Cohen, Matthew Lombard and Rosalind M. Pierson, "Developing a Multicultural Mass Communication Course," *Journalism Educator* 47 (Summer 1992), 4.

7. Debra A. Miller, "Multicultural Communications: Sensitizing Public Relations Students to Multicultural Society," paper presented at the Association for Education in Journalism and Mass Communication convention, Montreal, August 1992.

8. Jeannette Ludwig, SUNY-Buffalo, "CT vs. PC: Enhancing Teaching about Multiculturalism Through Critical Thinking," speech at the Fifth Annual National Conference on Racial and Ethnic Relations in American Higher Education, San Francisco, 9 June 1992.

9. Charles R. Calleros, Arizona State, "Defending the Multicultural Curriculum from Charges of Political Correctness," speech at the Fifth Annual Racial and Ethnic Conference, San Francisco, 7 June 1992.

10 INFUSING MULTICULTURAL INFORMATION INTO THE CURRICULUM

Carolyn Martindale

Some programs of journalism and mass communication already offer whole courses, usually electives, devoted to topics like The Mass Media and People of Color. Such courses are excellent because they enable faculty to explore the history of various minority groups in the United States, their presses, their contribution to American society, and the way mass circulation media have portrayed them and their concerns. The courses often include examination of the media portrayal of women and women's issues and information about outstanding women journalists and women's contributions to mass communication history. Such courses help prepare journalism students to provide more sensitive and accurate coverage, because the students gain some knowledge of the background of different groups, some appreciation of their contributions, and some understanding of their problems and concerns.

Equally beneficial, however, is the practice of infusing multicultural information into the whole range of courses in the journalism or mass communication program. This method involves bringing a multicultural perspective to every course and including modules of information about all racial and ethnic groups, their contributions, their journalists and their treatment by the mainstream media.

The infusing approach has several distinct advantages. One is that, using this approach, the information reaches a larger number of students. Also, the importance of multicultural knowledge and sensitivity is emphasized through repetition. All students come to understand that being sensitive to and informed about various cultural and racial groups are standard parts of a journalist's job, not extra skills. They begin to realize that the D for diversity is as important to their stories as the five Ws and the H, and that sensitivity to potential racial, ethnic and gender bias is as crucial as sensitivity to potential libel. As one reporter observed recently: "Sensitivity has *everything* to do with how well a good journalist can cover a story. Sensitivity to racial issues should be part of a good journalist's tools."[1]

In addition, when multicultural information is to be integrated across the journalism curriculum, *all* journalism faculty members are required to expand their knowledge of other cultural groups. That means that all faculty members as well as students come to understand the importance of a multicultural perspective.

Also, minority journalism students will be better able to identify with the material studied if that material includes information about, and role models from, their group. This should help alleviate the feeling reported by many minority journalism students that they are being prepared to enter "somebody else's profession," as Félix Gutiérrez, vice president of the Freedom Forum (formerly the Gannett Foundation), puts it.[2] In addition, the material will educate students of color as well as White students about the contributions made by journalists from their own racial or cultural background.

The first section of this chapter offers ideas for infusing multicultural information into various kinds of writing courses. It also discusses educating students about a journalist's responsibility to bring a multicultural approach to reporting and how this can be achieved. The discussion suggests showing audiovisual materials that illustrate coverage inadequacies, exposing students to other cultures in their writing assignments, and using as examples the writings of minority journalists.

The second portion of the chapter deals with teaching nonwriting courses. For teachers of journalism history, suggestions include audiovisual materials, books and guest speakers who can provide information on the history of minority media, coverage of people of color by mainstream White media, and the history of various minority groups in the United States. Topics and resources are also provided for use in courses on mass media and society, ethics, law, newspaper management, and photography and advertising. In addition, ideas for student research projects and seminars are provided.

The final portion of the chapter presents suggestions relevant to the teaching of all journalism and mass communication courses. The chapter ends with several sample exercises to help students explore stereotypes, examine the role media have played in relations between the races, and learn more about the contributions of various racial and ethnic groups to journalism and to the building of the nation.

A bibliography that will enable educators to find helpful resources is presented at the end of Part III. It includes information on how to obtain materials on the various topics discussed in this chapter. It also suggests audiovisual resources, materials on sensitizing faculty, general histories of various ethnic and racial groups, and many other materials. Numerous other resources can be found in the bibliographies at the end of the individual chapters in Part III.

NEWS AND FEATURE WRITING

The process of sensitizing students to other races and cultures should start with the first news-writing course the students take. Aspiring journalists should be taught that they have a responsibility to reflect in their stories all parts of society, not just the White middle and upper classes. This means that, on stories about matters that affect the general public, reporters should be sure to seek the viewpoint of, and information from, various cultural and racial groups.

For example, journalists doing a story on inflation should attempt to discover the views of Black wage earners as well as White, of Hispanic professionals and Asian American citizens. A story about racial interactions in city schools should include information from Black as well as White school board members, teachers and students.

In a particularly striking example, George Curry of the Chicago *Tribune*, who was assigned to do a piece on opinions about welfare, included among his sources an affluent African American woman from the suburbs and a White welfare mother from the inner city.[3]

Also, students should be taught to be alert to opportunities to cover the everyday activities of people of color as well as Whites. A cleanup project in a Black neighborhood, a new restaurant in a Hispanic community, Native American fishermen's efforts to protect salmon, the views of Asian Americans on the recent outbreak of Japan-bashing—all are examples of ordinary concerns that should be covered. Reporters need to reflect in their work the many different communities and perspectives that comprise American society.

Students should be taught to go beyond official sources, especially in controversial situations, and seek out the voices of the disenfranchised. They should be encouraged to be creative in finding knowledgeable sources. For instance, George Curry suggests going to the Black Muslims, who have an effective drug rehabilitation program, for information on drug treatment.[4]

It has been suggested by professional journalists that reporters in the 21st century are going to need to be most adept at covering communities unfamiliar to them. This challenge can be approached as a sourcing problem, suggests Carlos Sanchez of the Washington *Post*. Reporters can approach covering stories in a Hispanic or Asian American community, for example, just as they would approach coverage if they had been assigned to their news organization's Moscow bureau: They must establish contacts, begin to understand the community's culture and values, and learn whom they can trust, who the community leaders are, and to whom they can go for alternative viewpoints.[5]

Faculty should teach students to expand their definition of news beyond coverage of isolated "newsworthy" events to include undramatic but long-standing situations that profoundly affect the lives of their audience. In their coverage of controversies, especially those involving minority groups, they should be taught the importance of digging below the surface rhetoric and violence to uncover the root causes of the controversies.[6] They need to be introduced to the inadequacies of past media coverage of various racial and ethnic groups and the stereotypes this coverage has perpetuated so that they can avoid similar mistakes in their own reporting.

Further discussion of ways coverage of minorities can be improved can be found in my 1986 book on White press coverage of Black Americans. (This book and others that examine how the news media have covered minority groups in this country are cited in the bibliography at the end of Part III.) A sample assignment for helping students examine racial stereotypes also is presented at the end of the chapter.

Several audiovisual materials are available to help students become more aware of the journalistic skills needed to avoid prejudicial or superficial media coverage of minorities. These include *Race Against Prime Time*, an excellent documentary analyzing media coverage of the 1980 Miami race riots; *Black Pols/White Press*, which uses former Chicago mayor Harold Washington's experiences to illustrate the adversarial relations that often arise between Black politicians and the media; and *Drugs in Black and White*, an exploration of the media's role in promoting the idea that the nation's drug problem is primarily a Black problem.

An excellent method of promoting multicultural awareness has been devised by Mercedes de Uriarte at the University of Texas at Austin. She has introduced students in her feature-writing class to life in an Austin *barrio* (Latino neighborhood) to seek story ideas and information.

After lectures on the U.S. Latino culture and the historical development of the local Latino community, the class met with Latino community leaders, including administrators of a school, a refugee shelter, an art gallery, a park and recreation center, as well as church and local government officials and a range of Latino activists. The students also visited key sites in the *barrio*. They were then asked to do four different types of feature stories on Latino themes.[7]

This approach can be adapted by faculty members who require each student in a writing class to submit at least one story about a minority person or concern on campus. If desired, these stories can be saved and the class can put together a special page or section to be published in the student newspaper. The class members also can find the photos and graphics for the page, do the layout and write the headlines, or these jobs can be given to students in a make-up and design class.

In a related activity, students can compile a directory of persons who can serve as sources of information about campus minority groups and issues. This directory can be used in subsequent journalism classes and even shared with the editors and managers of the campus media, to help them further pluralize their coverage.

Sharon Bramlett-Solomon of Arizona State offers additional suggestions for incorporating cultural sensitivity training into reporting courses. She also has assigned students stories that required them to become familiar with a culture different from their own. Students have written about the lives of residents of a nursing home and of nuns attending the university, the atmospheres of a Mexican and a soul food restaurant, and the work of a Mexican and a Black newspaper publisher.[8]

Kevin Stoner of Ohio State assigns each of his reporting students to 1 of 30 diversity beats, which cover not only various minority student organizations but also gay and lesbian organizations and groups for disabled students. During the course of the term students must write six stories from their diversity beat: a personality profile, an issue story, a breaking news story, a speech story, a meeting story and a budget story on how the group or department is funded.[9]

In another kind of diversity exercise, Stoner has his students do an opinion story which requires them to meet and talk to persons from different age groups with whom they might not ordinarily communicate. He requires the students to get a viewpoint on an issue from a person under 10 years old, a teenager, a person the student's own age, someone in their fifties, and someone in their seventies. The person interviewed cannot be a family member or neighbor of the students. Stoner says that students frequently return to class amazed at the new and unexpected ideas they have discovered.[10] Like the above-mentioned exercises, this assignment broadens the student journalists' perceptions and understanding in addition to teaching them how to communicate with persons different from those they ordinarily encounter.

Students venturing to cover cultures and racial groups different from the one familiar to them may need some special preparation in dealing with sources. Just as students are trained to deal with reluctant and suspicious sources, and even how to interview hostile sources, they should be prepared to deal with occasional racial animosity. Being called racist or hearing their newspaper accused of racism is especially difficult for students to endure, and they need to be trained how to cope with such accusations and still obtain the information they need. Such problems may never arise, but students should be given some ideas about the best ways to deal with them if they do. A faculty member from the psychology department can be helpful in this undertaking.

Using examples of outstanding news and feature stories written by minority journalists provides another approach to infusing multicultural information in writing courses. Newspaper chains like Scripps Howard often include such prize-winning stories in their trade magazines or in special collections of articles. Organizations of minority journalists, like the national associations of Black and Hispanic journalists, also are possible sources of stories, as are the newspapers of various racial and ethnic groups. (See Chapter 17 and Chapter 18.)

Several outstanding works by African American journalists include Acel Moore's Pulitzer-winning series on prisons and mental hospitals, published in the Philadelphia *Inquirer*; Milton Coleman and Leon Dash's coverage of 1978 city elections for the Washington *Post*; and Earl Caldwell's stories on the Black Power movement and Tom Johnson's on the experiences of Black soldiers in Vietnam, both published in the New York *Times* in the 1960s.

One of the best ways of obtaining such stories is to require students to find them and bring them to class. This exercise not only lessens the burden on the faculty member but also helps the students become more cognizant of the contributions of journalists of color.

Also important is the practice of exposing students to the publications of racial and cultural groups different from their own. The journalism department or the faculty member should assemble a collection of, or subscribe to, African American newspapers and English-language papers directed to Hispanics, Asian Americans and Native Americans. The students also should examine publications for older Americans, gays, lesbians, the homeless and other groups so that they will begin to encounter alternative viewpoints. Assignment ideas and subscription information can be found in Chapters 17 and 18.

Finally, most writing courses include some training in copy-editing, and this instruction should include information about avoiding racial and ethnic bias, sexist language and assumptions, ageism, and other forms of biased writing. See the bibliography at the end of Part III for publications helpful in this area.

REVIEWING AND OPINION-WRITING

As with news and feature stories, excellent opinion columns and editorials written by journalists of color past and present can be included in the readings required for opinion-writing classes. Works by contemporary African American columnists like Jesse Jackson and William Raspberry can be found in daily newspapers, while exploration of Black, Hispanic and other minority newspapers and magazines can yield additional examples. Finally, biographies of outstanding minority editors of the past, like Frederick Douglass and Ida Wells-Barnett, can provide examples of stirring editorials.

In courses that teach reviewing of film and other art forms, faculty members can insure that at least one of the movies or plays the students review deals with a minority culture. Examples of the many excellent films available include *Malcolm X*, *Glory*, *The Milagro Beanfield War* (Latinos), *Black Robe* (Native Americans), and *Alamo Bay* (Asian Americans).

Students in reviewing courses also should be exposed to the art, music, dance, food, literature and other cultural manifestations of various racial and ethnic groups. A guest speaker who can trace a particular group's art would be an invaluable contribution to the course.

In addition, the bibliography at the end of Part III lists a variety of resources available for exploring past stereotypes of various minority groups in the entertainment media. An examination of these images can add another valuable component to the course.

JOURNALISM HISTORY

Contrary to the belief of many journalism teachers, newspaper publishing in North America did not begin with Benjamin Harriss' *Publick Occurrences* in 1690. It began nearly 150 years earlier, with the publication of a Spanish-language newspaper in Mexico City in 1541.[11]

Faculty who teach courses on the history of American journalism should be sure to include information on the history of the Black, Hispanic and other minority media and on outstanding journalists of color of the past and present. Useful for teaching these topics are slide collections on the histories of the African American press, the Hispanic press and the Native American press available from Vis-Com.

Presented at the end of the chapter is an exercise useful for the first day of a journalism history course, to help students recognize the sketchiness of their knowledge of other cultures' contributions to American history. Other exercises to inform students about various groups are included.

Teachers of communication history should be sure to inform their students about the slowly increasing employment of journalists of color in the mass media. Career opportunities for minority journalism students could be touched upon here.

The history course also should include information on the prejudicial ways the mass media have covered people of color in the past. Consult the bibliography at the end of Part III for books that explore mass media treatment of Blacks, Hispanics, Native Americans and people of color in general. Sample exercises on exploring stereotypes are provided at the end of this chapter.

Much information of this kind can be introduced by guest speakers. History faculty members can discuss the history of various minority groups in the United States, explaining the contributions these groups have made as well as the discrimination they have faced. Almost any faculty member of color will have a perception of the way the media have portrayed his or her group in the past and may be willing to share this with the class. Students of color and those who are members of other minority groups could be asked to give their views of the campus newspaper's coverage of the group of which they are members.

A psychology faculty member can discuss how prejudices are formed and retained, while a sociology faculty member can discuss the purpose discrimination serves in society. Reporters or editors from the local minority press can explain the role their media play in covering information the mainstream media ignore.

OTHER LECTURE COURSES

In Mass Media and Society courses, faculty members can show how the social responsibility role of the press, which requires interpreting component groups within a society to each other, applies with special pointedness to mass media coverage of racial and ethnic minorities. The role the press plays, even inadvertently, in relations between groups can be explained. Special insight into this topic can be provided by local print and broadcast journalists of color, whose accounts of personal experiences and observations concerning media coverage of people of color can be compelling.

Courses exploring media ethics should include a component on the role the media have played in the past in reinforcing prejudice and promoting persecution of people of color, as they did during the Chicago riots against Blacks early in this century and during the 1943 "Zoot Suit Riots" against Mexican Americans in Los Angeles. Also pertinent here would be information about how the media sometimes stifle social change, as they did after the 1954 Supreme Court school desegregation decision by focusing on bombastic segregationists vowing "massive resistance" and ignoring the voices that suggested desegregation could be accomplished peacefully.[12] Exercises for exploring stereotypes are offered at the end of this chapter.

Teachers of communication law courses could invite minority TV station managers to talk to the students about the effect of television deregulation on minority coverage and on the community service and fairness doctrines. The speakers also could discuss opportunities for minority ownership of broadcast media.

Courses in newspaper management can include information showing that the continued existence of newspapers depends upon appealing to readers—and advertisers—who are people of color. The course can stress the importance of sensitivity training, informing the staff about minority stereotypes and making sure these are avoided. Students also should be introduced to the necessity of countering racist and sexist attitudes in the newsroom, establishing sources within the various communities of color, periodically surveying minority readers about how well the paper is serving them, and perhaps even establishing a community review board to provide input and story ideas about the paper's coverage of people of color.

Management courses also should address the media's responsibility to recruit and retain more minority employees and to make full use of the perspective they offer. Faculty could discuss how to do this through a management-by-objective method, as the Gannett newspapers have done.

PHOTOGRAPHY AND ADVERTISING

In photojournalism, advertising and public relations courses faculty can stress the importance of including images of people from the different groups that comprise American society and doing so in a way that avoids reinforcing stereotypes. Student research projects that examine past images of people of color in news photos and ads could be useful here.

Also, the photographic work of outstanding minority photojournalists can be examined. Examples of these can be found in the publications of the Knight Ridder, Scripps Howard and other newspaper chains. The work of Gordon Parks, a Black photographer for *Life* in the fifties and sixties, could be included.

Students in advertising courses should be introduced to demographic data on the growing minority populations in the United States and these groups' substantial purchasing power. Students also should be made aware of minority businesses as potential clients.

SPECIAL TOPICS

An endless variety of ideas for student research projects or independent study courses on topics concerning minority coverage can be devised. A few examples include a comparison of how a Black and a White newspaper covered a race-related event, such as an urban riot or the candidacy of a Black politician; White press coverage of the June 26, 1975, siege at Wounded Knee or of the U.S. government's internment of Japanese Americans during World War II; changes in images of African Americans in ads in one magazine over time; and mass media portrayal of other kinds of minority groups, like the disabled, the elderly, or American Jews.

Graduate seminars and special topics courses, which allow faculty members to change the focus each time the course is taught, could be used to explore in greater detail any of the ideas mentioned in this chapter, or even to devise a Mass Media and People of Color course.

As all these suggestions indicate, the amount of information on people of color and other minorities that should be conveyed to journalism students is so abundant that a journalism program would do well to include both a separate Mass Media and People of Color course *and* modules of information about minorities in all the other courses in the curriculum.

Whatever the arrangement, faculty members willing to examine some of the materials listed in the following pages will find interesting information on a wide range of topics to infuse into their courses. Such infusion can start slowly, but it becomes an ongoing process that will certainly enrich the faculty member as well as help to better prepare students to cover this nation's increasingly pluralistic society.

GENERAL CONSIDERATIONS

The faculty of a journalism program can emphasize their commitment to multicultural education by mentioning the pluralistic aspect of their courses on their syllabi, and the chairperson of a department committed to diversity could check syllabi for this component as well as for other kinds of information that should be included. Also, faculty could ask, on the course evaluations they require of students at the end of the term, what the students have learned about another culture or cultures through the course.

Faculty also could make a strong effort to introduce persons of other racial and ethnic heritages to their students as guest speakers, as guest faculty through the American Society of Newspaper Editors' professional-in-residence program, as judges for writing contests and leaders of workshops, and as honorees at journalistic events.

In addition, faculty can try to build up their university's library holdings, audiovisual resources, subscriptions to periodicals, and other materials for informing their students and other faculty members about diverse cultural groups.

Finally, they should ask themselves, "What do I have in my office that speaks to students of another race or culture about them? How many of the journalists whose writings we will study will be of the same racial or cultural group as my students of color or—equally important—different from the majority of my students? How much does the content of my courses include and appreciate the contributions of persons from other racial and cultural groups?"

Demographic information indicates that by the year 2000 two-thirds of the workforce in the United States will be comprised of minorities and women; in 30 years two-thirds of the *supervisors* in the workforce will be people of color and women.[13] Today's educators can help their students immeasurably if they begin preparing them now to report on, as well as work in, this new world. In addition, the journalism program can then claim that it has prepared its students to communicate with diverse audiences, an increasingly important ability in our changing society.

NOTES

This chapter is an expansion of Carolyn Martindale, "Infusing Cultural Diversity into Communication Courses," *Journalism Educator* 45 (Winter 1991), 34–38.

1. Edward Pease, "Still the Invisible People: Job Satisfaction of Minority Journalists at U.S. Daily Newspapers," doctoral dissertation, Ohio University, 1991.

2. Félix Gutiérrez, panel on "Expanding Our Vision, Part II: Multiculturalizing the Journalism Curriculum," Association for Journalism and Mass Communication convention, Boston, 8 August 1991.

3. George Curry, panel on "News Media Performance in Covering Politics and

Race," Association for Education in Journalism and Mass Communication convention, Washington, DC, 13 August 1989.

4. Ibid.

5. Carlos Sanchez, speech on "Reporting Racial Controversy," Associated Collegiate Press/College Media Advisers convention, Washington, DC, 3 November 1990.

6. See Carolyn Martindale, *The White Press and Black America* (Westport, CT: Greenwood Press, 1986), pp. 32–43, 150–68. See also *New Directions for News*, a study of newspaper coverage of women's issues, Women's Studies Program and Policy Center, George Washington University, 2025 Eye St. NW, Room 212, Washington, DC 20052.

7. Mercedes Lynn de Uriarte, "Texas Course Features Barrio as Story Source," *Journalism Educator* 43 (Summer 1988), 78–79.

8. Sharon Bramlett-Solomon, "Bringing Cultural Sensitivity into Reporting Classrooms," *Journalism Educator* 44 (Summer 1989), 28.

9. Kevin Stoner, preconvention workshop on "Incorporating Diversity into the Curriculum," Association for Education in Journalism and Mass Communication Convention, Boston, 6 August 1991. Tape available from ACTS, 14153 Clayton Rd., Ballwin, MO 63011.

10. Ibid.

11. Gutiérrez, "Expanding Our Vision."

12. See Martindale, *White Press*, pp. 20–29, 53–59, 62–64, 182–183. See also Randall Hines, "Selected Press Coverage of Wounded Knee," thesis, Kent State University, Kent, OH, 1974.

13. Caryl M. Stern, workshop on "A Campus of Difference: The Anti-Defamation League's Anti-Prejudice Training Program," Third Annual National Conference on Racial and Ethnic Relations in American Higher Education, Santa Fe, NM, 2 June 1990.

EXERCISE 1: EXPLORING STEREOTYPES

To the faculty member: The purpose of this exercise is to encourage students to examine stereotypes about other racial and ethnic groups, to become aware of them and to try to ascertain whether or not they are founded on fact. It is hoped that it will serve to make students more aware of the power that stereotypes exert over people's thinking.

Part One

As part of a copy-editing exercise, give students a copy of a newspaper or magazine photo of a Black man and a White man dressed in business suits, walking together. Explain that the students are to write a caption for the photo. Provide them with names for the men and explain that they are on their way to court where one man is to be arraigned for armed robbery; the other man is his lawyer. Give the time and place of the arraignment and ask students to write a caption for the photo.

You will probably find that many of the class members will assume that the Black man is the person to be arraigned and will write their captions accordingly. Whether that happens, or whether one of the class members spots the trick and asks you which person is the accused and which is the lawyer, you will be able to lead the class into a discussion of the stereotype of Black men as violent and as lawbreakers, and an exploration of the power of unconsciously held stereotypes to lead people to erroneous assumptions.

(This situation actually happened to a journalist for a Gannett newspaper, who wrote a caption identifying the White man as the lawyer when he was really the accused; the Black man was the lawyer. Someone on the copy desk caught the mistake before it got into print, and the shaken reporter, who had previously prided himself on his freedom from bias, said that he had never before realized that his thinking could be so influenced by stereotypes.)

Part Two

Show the class the film *Drugs in Black and White* and discuss how the logistics of television have led the media inadvertently to perpetuate the impression that the drug problem in America is primarily one of inner city Blacks. The class also could discuss how this kind of coverage could be avoided or balanced.

Part Three

Present the class with the following facts, and discuss which stereotypes they contradict.

1. Eighty percent of the crimes in this country involve a perpetrator and a victim of the same race. In other words, the chances are 8 out of 10 that a person who attacks or robs us will be someone who looks like us.[1]
2. The typical Aid to Dependent Children mother is a 27-year-old White woman with two children.[2]
3. Eighty percent of the cocaine use in the United States is by Whites, mostly middle class Whites who live in the suburbs.[3]

Have the class members identify other stereotypes about various racial and ethnic groups. As an exercise in obtaining information from various sources, have each class member take one stereotype and research whether or not the stereotype is founded on fact. The aim is to research the validity of the stereotype.

EXERCISE 2: THE MEDIA AND RACE RELATIONS

To the faculty member: This exercise is designed to help students realize that the mass circulation news media have played an influential role in

White perceptions of other racial and ethnic groups. Their influence has been exerted not just in subtle ways, by omissions and distortions and perpetuation of stereotypes, but in blatant appeals to racism. It will benefit students to realize that both the covert prejudice sometimes found today and the bold racism of past newspaper performance occur because newspapers are staffed by persons who share the dominant culture's attitudes about race. For example, if the prevailing sentiment in the late 19th century West was that "the only good Indian is a dead Indian," it is not really surprising to find editorials in South Dakota newspapers applauding the U.S. Army's massacre of Native American women and children at Wounded Knee in 1893. Students can discuss ways this problem can be corrected.

Part One

Put on reserve at the university library books that include capsule histories of this nation's various racial and ethnic groups, such as the books by Banks and Sowell listed in the bibliography at the end of the chapter. Assign several students to study each racial and ethnic group, with the instruction to bring back to the class information about how the press coverage of that group led to an action detrimental to the group, such as violence against them, legislation targeting them, deportation or imprisonment. Explore the relationship between press coverage and oppression of the group.

Useful examples of biased newspaper coverage of various racial groups and discussion of the media's role in race relations can be found in the following works:

Coward, John. "The Newspaper Indian: Native Americans and the Press in the Nineteenth Century." Doctoral dissertation, University of Texas at Austin, 1989.
Hines, Randall. "Selected Press Coverage of Wounded Knee." Master's thesis, Kent State University, 1974.
Martindale, Carolyn. *The White Press and Black America*. Westport, CT: Greenwood Press, 1986. See pp. 14–31, 53–71, 125–150.

Part Two

Require students to scan actual issues of the newspapers that ran prejudicial coverage, if these are available, in order to find examples of the biased coverage. The assertions or impressions about the group conveyed by this coverage could be compared to the reality about the group, which could be discovered in histories of the group and similar sources. (The idea here is, once again, to measure the stereotype against reality as much as possible.)

Part Three

Using information gained in the previous segments of this exercise, discuss what possible motives the editors of the newspapers studied might have had for running such inflammatory and inaccurate coverage and editorials. This could lead to a discussion, perhaps augmented by a presentation by a psychology professor, about the roles prejudice plays in a society and the functions and the economic classes that it serves. A useful resource for such a discussion is Teun Van Dyke's *Communicating Racism* (Newbury Park, CA: Sage, 1987).

Part Four

Require students to read the articles listed below, which present examples of more recent—and more covert—bias in coverage. Compare the current examples of racism to those of the past in terms of cause, nature and effects.

Cox, Clinton. "Meanwhile in Bedford Stuyvesant . . . " *MORE*, August 1976, pp. 18–21.

Johnson, Kirk A. "Black and White in Boston." *Columbia Journalism Review* 26 (May/June 1987), 50–52.

Moore, Linda Wright. "Can the Press Do the Right Thing? How Your News Looks to Us." *Columbia Journalism Review* 29 (July/August 1990), 21–24.

Noland, Thomas. "Old News from the New South." *Columbia Journalism Review* 18 (May/June 1979), 41.

Williams, Edwin N. "Dimout in Jackson." *Columbia Journalism Review* 9 (Summer 1970), 56–58.

EXERCISE 3: VALUING CONTRIBUTIONS

To the faculty member: The aim of this exercise is to enable students to see how much they have learned about contributions to American history and culture by groups other than Whites of European ancestry. The first part of the exercise is based on a quiz used by the Anti-Defamation League. A list of books useful for researching answers to these questions is also provided.

Part One

Ask the students to answer the following questions as best they can, giving them a few minutes for each question. Explain that this is an ungraded exercise to test their knowledge and that they should not consult among themselves to pool their knowledge.

First explain to the students that they can define what is meant by "great" in the following exercise, and the persons they name can be living or dead.

The exercise: name five famous persons who are White American males;

White American females; Black American males; Black American females; Jewish American males; Jewish American females; Hispanic males; Hispanic females; Asian American males; Asian American females; Native American males; Native American females; gay Americans; lesbian Americans.

After the students have completed the exercise, discuss their answers in class, providing them with five or more names in each of the more difficult categories so that they can see that there are famous persons in each category, even if they can't think of them. As an alternative, have the students do research to find the answers for themselves for some of the harder categories.

Part Two

Have the students answer the following questions as best they can. Afterwards, pool the students' knowledge and then provide the answers to each question. Discuss how the answers contradict an assumption or fill a void in the students' knowledge, and discuss why they were ignorant in those areas.

1. When and where was the first permanent European settlement in this nation established?
2. What Native American tribes inhabited your state before the arrival of White settlers?
3. How many African Americans fought in the Revolutionary War? The Civil War?
4. On what major project were Chinese men imported to this country to work? When?
5. What group was granted the right to vote in Wyoming Territory in 1869 and was protected by the territorial legislature when Congress said that it would grant Wyoming statehood only if this group's voting rights were revoked?

The answers to the questions above are: 1. St. Augustine, in 1565, by the Spanish (followed by San Gabriel, in what is now New Mexico, in 1598; the Jamestown and Roanoke colonies, neither of which survived, were established in 1587 and 1607, respectively). 2. The answer to this question will vary with each state, of course, and must be researched. For Ohio, the author's state, the tribes were the Miami and Delaware tribes of the Algonkian confederacy, and the Eries and Senecas of the Iroquois confederacy. 3. A total of 5,000 African Americans fought in the Revolutionary War, and 180,000 fought in the Civil War. 4. The Transcontinental Railroad, which was built to connect the East Coast with the developing West, in the years just after the Civil War. 5. Women. The territorial legislature granted Wyoming women the right to vote 50 years before the national women's suffrage amendment was passed, and refused to revoke women's voting rights when Congress made that a condition of receiving statehood. Congress backed down and allowed Wyoming (and its women voters) into the Union anyway.

Part Three

Have the students answer the following questions. When they have finished, discuss the answers and the reasons behind the answers, so that they will have a better understanding of each of the cultural groups. They may have to do research to get to the "why" of each answer.

1. What group places great importance on the extended family, family ties and loyalty?
2. What group places great importance on education and is ferocious in argument?
3. What group tends toward a confrontational and sometimes heated style in discussion and problem-solving?
4. What group highly values reserve and privacy, and used to train its members that it is impolite to look strangers in the eye?
5. What group's young people make strong leaders because of the group's training example?

The answers to the above questions are: 1. Hispanics. 2. Jewish Americans. 3. African Americans. 4. Asian Americans. 5. Native Americans.

Part Four

Assign students to interview local journalists who are women and people of color about their experiences in the media. Have the students write up biographical sketches that cover not only the persons' journalistic experiences, but what influence they feel their gender or race has had on their career, and what contribution they feel they have made. Compare their responses to see whether any common patterns can be found. The sketches can be offered to local or student media for publication, to archives that collect local history, or to the university library.

NOTES

1. Kathleen Hall Jamieson, speech on "Race and Crime in Televised Politics" at conference on "Race, Politics and the Press: Recommendations for the Future," Harvard University, 4 May 1990.
2. Ron Wade of the Minneapolis *Star Tribune*, panel on "Media Professionals Respond to the 'Quiet Riots' of the ALANA Community: 22 Years after Kerner," Association for Education in Journalism and Mass Communication convention, 9 August 1990, Minneapolis.
3. Ibid.

BIBLIOGRAPHY

Banks, James A. *Teaching Strategies for Ethnic Studies*. 2nd ed. Boston: Allyn and Bacon, 1979. This includes brief histories on Native Americans, European Americans,

Jewish Americans, African Americans, Mexican Americans, Asian Americans, Puerto Rican Americans, Cuban Americans and Native Hawaiians.

Dennis, Henry C. *The American Indian: 1492–1976*. 2nd ed. Dobbs Ferry, NY: Oceana Publications, 1977.

Franklin, John Hope, and Afred A. Moss, Jr. *From Slavery to Freedom: A History of Negro Americans*. 6th ed. New York: McGraw-Hill, 1988.

Hymowitz, Carol, and Michaele Weisman. *A History of Women in America*. New York: Bantam, 1978.

Sowell, Thomas. *Ethnic America: A History*. New York: Basic Books, 1981. Offers chapters on the Irish, Italians, Germans, Jews, African Americans, Chinese, Japanese, Mexicans and Puerto Ricans.

Takaki, Ronald. *Strangers from a Different Shore*. Boston: Little, Brown, 1990. This tells why, when and where Asian Americans came to the United States.

Thernstrom, Stephan. *Harvard Encyclopedia of American Ethnic Groups*. Cambridge, MA: Harvard University Press, 1981.

11 THE AFRICAN AMERICAN HERITAGE IN JOURNALISM

Clint C. Wilson II

Journalism history professors and countless numbers of their students are familiar with the "Penny Press" and its role as precursor of modern mass communication. Benjamin Day's New York *Sun*, established in 1833, is usually singled out for particular attention because it had the distinction of being the first successful Penny Press newspaper. The significance of the *Sun* was that it brought news to the common man, an achievement noted in the paper's famous motto: "It Shines for ALL."

In the late 1960s this writer—at the time one of fewer than half a dozen African American journalism majors in a large urban university—was fascinated by the notion of a newspaper that proclaimed social inclusiveness as an objective in 1833. The *Sun*'s claim was especially intriguing because I was an aspiring journalist in a city where at that time no person of color held an editorial position on any of its daily newspapers. None of my textbooks had much to say about Black people in journalism, although the communications law text noted that it was libelous in many states to misidentify a White person as Black.

The fascination with "It Shines for ALL" remained with me, much as the phrase "All men are created equal" has reverberated in the thoughts of African Americans for more than two centuries. But perhaps the most valuable lesson to be learned from the New York *Sun* was never imparted to that journalism class nearly 25 years ago: The *Sun*'s interpretation of "all" did not include African American citizens. In 1847 Willis Hodges, a Black man who had been denied the opportunity to express his opinions in the pages of the *Sun*, started his own newspaper, the *Ram's Horn*. The details of Willis Hodges' story (covered later in this chapter) make for fascinating classroom lecture material, but Willis Hodges and his paper were nowhere to be found in journalism history classes in most universities during the 1960s. Unfortunately, the same is true today.

Many other examples illuminate the contributions of African Americans to the history of journalism in the United States. The inclusion of African American perspectives in all facets of the journalism curriculum makes for more enlightened students of all cultural backgrounds and ultimately better professional newspersons. Just as many parents brace themselves for the day when their child asks the inevitable question, "Where did I come from?," so must journalism educators be ready for queries by students whose professional heroes include Robert Maynard, Carl Rowan, Charlayne Hunter-Gault and Bernard Shaw. It is as useful to know the heritage of those and other outstanding Black journalists as that of Jack Anderson, Dan Rather and Helen Thomas. It is the purpose of this chapter to provide a brief outline of the heritage of today's African American journalists and to suggest ways in which the Black perspective may be incorporated into the fabric of classroom instruction.

THE AFRICAN ROOTS

While many survey and introductory courses in mass media and journalism history briefly trace the development of human communication from antiquity, few dwell specifically on the contributions of people on the African continent. The thriving and sophisticated ancient African cultures relied heavily on complex communications systems for social maintenance and advancement. The techniques of making pictographs (hieroglyphics), using clay tablets for preserving public records, and using drums to transmit information between villages were all communication methods uitilized in Africa before the arrival of Western Europeans.

Also important was the oral communication tradition maintained by the African griots, individuals charged with transmitting historical information and cultural values to succeeding generations. Griots used the technique of story telling to fulfill this vital social function. Also, in the subSaharan cultures, communication took on meaning beyond the utilitarian. It also served as an art form expressed in music, painting and dance, often with religious overtones.

After the slave trade began, slave traders and owners went to great lengths to prevent effective organization of their African chattels and to mitigate the potential for rebellion by the slaves. The enslaved Africans not only faced the communications obstacle of being separated from family and tribal groups, but also encountered in their new world the barrier of antiliteracy laws that forbade teaching the slaves how to read and write.

Such efforts, however, were only temporarily effective in disrupting the elements of African communication systems that had been developed for centuries. Ironically, it was the extreme degradation of the "peculiar institution" of slavery which helped the disparate African people in America to bond and forge a sense of common identity. Ultimately the bonding effect was evident not only among slaves but among free Blacks in America as well.

Historian John Hope Franklin has suggested that the survival of certain African cultural traits in America was facilitated because Whites excluded slaves and free Blacks from participation in the mainstream culture. Unlike other ethnic groups, which gradually achieved access to the dominant culture and means of power within a century of their arrival in the United States, Blacks were excluded from the mainstream American culture for well over 300 years, consequently developing a sense of common culture and identity.

Crucial to the survival of the sense of Black community in America—both slave and free—was the strong religious and oral communication tradition shared by the various African cultures and the intertwining of spirituality and communicative expression. Just as the griot held a revered place in the tribal cultures of Africa, so did the Black clergy assume the mantle of both religious and communications leadership in America. These two threads became the basis for Black protest against the evils of slavery in the South and racial discrimination in the North. They were threads with roots in ancient Africa.

THE RELIGIOUS FACTOR

The development of organized communicative expression by Blacks in America from the colonial period to the establishment of the Black press took place against the backdrop of virtual exclusion of Blacks from the White press. Clearly, Black expression had to develop as an alternative to the mainstream channels of communication. Religious belief in a force beyond temporal life, manifested in the Black church, was vital to the emergence of the African American press.

Two incidents serve as examples of religion's role in organized Black political expression and as precursors to the Black press. One took place among free Blacks in the North, the other among slaves in the South.

One Sunday morning in 1787 a group of Black Philadelphians came to worship at St. George's Methodist Episcopal Church in a new edifice they had helped build along with White members of the congregation. When the Black parishioners were directed to seating only in the balcony, they were led out of the building by minister Richard Allen in the first recorded instance of organized nonviolent protest against discrimination in the United States. Allen and a colleague, the Rev. Absalom Jones, became the religious and political leaders of the Black community in Philadelphia and spearheaded a number of organized activities aimed at eliminating racial discrimination in the North and slavery in the South. Among those activities was the drafting of petitions to argue their positions.

In 1822 former slave Denmark Vesey set in motion his plan to mount a slave rebellion in South Carolina. Among his chief lieutenants was Gullah Jack, an African-born sorcerer whose reputation as a mystic and spiritualist earned him great credibility and respect among the slaves. Vesey himself used religion as a means of inspiring the slaves to revolt, often quoting the Bible during his orations. Although the planned revolt ultimately failed because informers betrayed him, Vesey had rallied as many as 9,000 slaves to his call. The idea that religious faith coupled with forceful action could overcome the institution of slavery had proved effective in mobilizing thousands of people.

BIRTH OF THE BLACK PRESS

It comes as no surprise, therefore, that there was a religious influence in the beginnings of the Black press in America. In 1827, only five years after Denmark Vesey's ill-fated slave uprising attempt, the first issue of a Black newspaper appeared in the United States. That publication, *Freedom's Journal*, was a New York–based weekly under the guidance of a Presbyterian minister, Samuel Cornish, and John B. Russwurm, who was one of the first African Americans to earn a college degree in the United States. Using the motto "Righteousness Exalteth a Nation," the editors set forth the objective of Blacks pleading their own cause in the struggle for emancipation of slaves and equality of citizenship for free Blacks.

With the idea of a newspaper firmly established as a practical vehicle for expression of Black thought and aspirations, other religious leaders joined the publishing ranks. Before the onset of the Civil War they included the Rev. Samuel Ringgold Ward (Boston *Impartial Citizen*), the Rev. Charles B. Ray (New York *Colored American*) and the Rev. Thomas Woodson (Cincinnati *Colored Citizen*). These and other Black publishers reached a readership comprised of free Blacks and ex-slaves primarily in northern states, a group that was increasing in size and economic stature.

Newspaper publishing in the early history of the Black press was not confined to clergymen. While contemporary journalism history courses almost always cover the prolific journalistic career of Frederick Douglass, they ignore the contributions of various other Black journalists and editors of his era who had no call to the ministry.

This brings us again to Willis Hodges and how he came to interface with that icon of journalism history, the New York *Sun*, the newspaper that ushered in the age of mass communication in America. In 1847 New York was in the midst of debate concerning whether voting rights should be extended to Blacks. The *Sun*, founded on the motto "It Shines for ALL," had taken a negative editorial stance on the issue. Hodges, in the mistaken belief that the *Sun*'s letters-to-the-editor policy encompassed Black readers, submitted a letter expressing the Black community's general support of voting rights.

Instead of publishing the letter as written by Hodges, the paper took the liberty of altering it and inserting it in the advertising section. Hodges was then sent an invoice for $15, accompanied by a note explaining that the editorial pages of the *Sun* were not open to Black men. Moreover, the note suggested that if Hodges wanted to express his opinions publicly he would have to publish his own newspaper.

Within a relatively short time Hodges raised capital for his venture, *The Ram's Horn*, by taking whitewashing jobs. His persistence demonstrated the urgent need for a people to communicate publicly concerning major social is sues.

OTHER HISTORICAL HIGHLIGHTS

Willis Hodges is only one of numerous Black contributors to press history in America and is part of the legacy of contemporary Black journalists. Following are several other historical highlights that can help journalism educators better diversify their curriculum by adding an African American perspective.

• T. Thomas Fortune was once called the dean of Black journalism in America. He began his editorial career in 1879 and earned his reputation primarily as editor of the New York *Age*. Fortune was also among the first Black journalists to write for a White daily newspaper when he became a reporter for the New York *Sun* in 1887.

• The Philadelphia *Tribune* in 1992 was the oldest continuously published Black newspaper in the United States. It was founded in 1884 by Christopher J. Perry, whose publishing acumen enabled the *Tribune* to acquire its own office facility and printing plant.

• Henry O. Flipper was not only the first Black American to graduate from the U.S. Military Academy at West Point, New York, but also became the first of his race to edit a White newspaper when he became editor of the Nogales, Arizona, *Sunday Herald* in 1889.

• Ida B. Wells-Barnett was perhaps the most renowned Black woman journalist. A courageous editor of the Memphis *Free Speech* who campaigned vigorously against lynchings of Blacks during the height of Jim Crowism, Wells-Barnett was herself the target of a lynch mob in 1892. Fortunately she escaped and continued her brilliant career, which included contributions to the New York *Age*.

• The 1896 U.S. Supreme Court ruling in *Plessy v. Ferguson* gave legal sanction to what was already the practice of the mainstream press: "separate but equal" segregationist news coverage. This set the stage for the emergence of several major Black newspapers led by prominent publishers during the next two decades.

• Henry J. Lewis was probably the first Black political cartoonist. In 1889 he began working for the Indianapolis *Freeman*, which had been founded the previous year as the first Black illustrated newspaper. Earlier he had enjoyed success as a contributor to the widely respected *Harper's Weekly*.

- Claude Barnett founded the Associated Negro Press in 1919. The ANP became the predominant news-gathering cooperative for the Black press and continued operations until 1964.

- In 1962 Mal Goode became the first Black television network news reporter when he joined ABC-TV. Goode found himself covering the year's biggest story, the Cuban missile crisis, as ABC's United Nations correspondent. His earlier career included 14 years on the staff of the Pittsburgh *Courier*, the nation's preeminent Black newspaper during his tenure there in the 1940s and 1950s.

- The Kerner Report, issued by a federal commission established by President Lyndon Johnson in 1967, found that a major cause of urban rioting in various U.S. cities was inadequate and biased news reporting about African Americans and issues affecting them and society. The report's call for increased hiring of Black journalists fueled raiding of Black newspaper talent by the White press.

BENEFITS OF AN INCLUSIVE CURRICULUM

What other benefits are to be derived from including African American press history in the contemporary journalism curriculum? Willis Hodges' story adds a perspective to the Penny Press as the beginning of mass communication in America. It dramatically illustrates a policy of exclusion of African Americans from mainstream news media and clearly explains the need for a Black press. This is an issue that is rarely addressed in contemporary courses. But Hodges' story is merely one of numerous examples of how the Black perspective would serve to enrich and illuminate the study of journalism in the United States.

Equally important are the creative ways in which Black people adapted their African communications heritage to the unique social circumstances they faced in America. That fact alone makes the journalism and communications heritage of Black Americans a worthy subject for curricular inclusion in a variety of undergraduate and graduate courses. It is an element certain to enhance the understanding of future practitioners of all ethnic backgrounds as they prepare for life in a multicultural professional world. In this way educators can be assured that their curriculum will indeed "shine for ALL."

BIBLIOGRAPHY

Dann, Martin E., ed. *The Black Press: 1827–1890*. New York: Capricorn, 1972.
Dates, Jannette, and William Barlow, eds. *Split Image: African Americans in the Mass Media*. Washington, DC: Howard University Press, 1990.
Detweiler, Frederick G. *The Negro Press in the United States*. College Park, MD: McGrath Publishing, 1968.

Hill, George. *Black Media in America: A Resource Guide*. Boston: G. K. Hall, 1984.

LaBrie, Henry G. *Perspectives of the Black Press: 1974*. Kennebunkport, ME: Mercer House, 1974.

Penn, I. Garland. *The Afro-American Press and Its Editors*. Springfield, MA: Wiley, 1891. Reprint. New York: Arno Press/New York Times, 1969.

Snorgrass, J. William, and Gloria T. Woody, eds. *Blacks and Media: A Selected, Annotated Bibliography 1962–1982*. Tallahassee: Florida A&M University Press, 1985.

Tripp, Bernell. *Origins of the Black Press: New York, 1827–1847*. Northport, AL: Vision Press, 1992.

Wilson, Clint C. *Black Journalists in Paradox: Historical Perspectives and Current Dilemmas*. Westport, CT: Greenwood Press, 1991.

Wilson, Clint C., and Félix Gutiérrez. *Minorities and Media: Diversity and the End of Mass Communication*. Beverly Hills: Sage, 1985.

Wolseley, Roland E. *The Black Press U.S.A.* Ames: Iowa State University Press, 1990.

Biographies are available on Frederick Douglass, Ida Wells-Barnett, editor P. D. Young, Civil War correspondent Thomas Morris Chester and many other journalists of color.

Sources for further information about the treatment and portrayal of African Americans in various media, including television and advertising, can be found in the bibliographies at the end of Chapter 20 and at the end of Part III and in the notes at the end of Chapter 19. For subscription information on selected African American newspapers, see Chapter 17.

12 THE LATINO PRESS IN AMERICAN JOURNALISM HISTORY

Carlos E. Cortés

The history of American journalism, like the history of the United States, has traditionally been viewed and taught from an east-to-west perspective.[1] The printing press accompanied the westward movement of Anglo-Americans. Western Union built its telegraph wires west across the country. Commercial radio expanded west from eastern network offices and flagship stations. The coaxial cable connected the East to the West.

But while this East-to-West process was occurring, another dimension of the American experience, including American journalism history, was unfolding along a south-to-north axis. As Anglos moved west, Latin Americans moved north. First they came as pioneers, conquerors and settlers of the northern reaches of Spain's Viceroyalty of New Spain. Following Mexican independence in 1821, settlers continued to come north to establish themselves in that territory that ultimately would become the U.S. Southwest. Ev en after the U.S. annexation of the northern half of Mexico during the mid-19th century, the northward flow of Latinos continued, with Puerto Ricans, Cubans and other Latinos ultimately joining Mexicans in that process.

Part of that Latino experience involved journalism. The Mexican press tradition stretches back to 1693, when the periodical *Mercurio Volante* was established in Mexico City (the first printing press was brought there from Spain in 1535).[2] As Mexicans and other Latinos migrated north, they brought with them this press tradition. The incorporation of this south-to-north process can provide an enriching dimension to the study and teaching of American journalism history.

THE DILEMMAS OF IDENTITY AND TERMINOLOGY

Identity and terminology both illuminate and complicate the study of the Latino press. The terms *Latino* and *Hispanic* have developed as linguistic umbrellas to embrace Americans of different Latin American (and sometimes Iberian—Spanish and Portuguese) ancestries. Some U.S. Latinos/Hispanics feel comfortable with either word. Some prefer Hispanic, for various reasons—because it has become an official government category, because it implies that the Spanish language is a unifying element, or because it incorporates people of direct Spanish as well as Spanish American ancestry. Some prefer Latino because it includes all persons of Latin American origin, including Portuguese-speaking Brazilians, and many even reject Hispanic, feeling that the latter suggests the marginalizing of the powerful Indian and African elements of the Latino heritage. Some avoid both umbrella terms as artificial and prefer to stick only to their national-origin heritage identities or to be viewed simply as Americans.

While Latinos share certain common characteristics and experiences, they also reflect significant internal diversity. Much of this intra-Latino diversity results from the fact that U.S. Latinos enjoy various national-origin heritages. Take, for example, the circumstances of their entry into the United States.

Mexican Americans (Chicanos) as a group came into existence through the U.S. annexation of northern Mexico: the 1845 U.S. annexation of what is today Texas; the 1848 annexation of most of present-day New Mexico, Arizona, California and other Western states through the Treaty of Guadalupe Hidalgo at the close of the 1846–1848 U.S.-Mexican War; and the 1854 Gadsden Purchase of what is today southern Arizona and New Mexico. Mexicans living in these annexed lands did not immigrate into the United States; the United States came to them. Their descendants, therefore, are not the descendants of immigrants.

Likewise, Puerto Ricans found their political status modified without participating in the immigration experience. In this case, the 1898 Treaty of Paris following the Cuban-Spanish-American War transformed Puerto Rico from a part of the Spanish empire into a part of the United States. As a result, Puerto Ricans do not immigrate into the United States, because by law they travel freely between Puerto Rico and the rest of the United States. However, the majority of U.S. Latinos, including most Mexican Americans, are immigrants, refugees or the descendants of immigrants or refugees. According to the 1990 U.S. Census, there were 22,354,059 Hispanics in the United States, although many Latinos have criticized these figures as a significant undercount.[3]

Moreover, greatly as a result of their varying heritages, each individual Latino group has had special experiences and concerns. Mexican Americans have had a special concern with the United States–Mexican border and with U.S. immigration policy, because most Latino immigrants come from Mexico. Puerto Ricans have had a special concern about the legal relationship between Puerto Rico and the United States, including the ongoing debate over Puerto Rico's official language (or languages) and the island's future political status (as a commonwealth, state or independent nation). Cuban Americans have had a special concern with the political situation in Cuba. Many El Salvadoran immigrants and refugees have undergone forced relocation and have had a special concern with the ongoing turmoil in their homeland. Many highly trained Argentine and Uruguayan professionals have been part of the critical "brain drain" from Latin America to the United States.

THE LATINO PRESS IN THE UNITED STATES: A HISTORICAL OVERVIEW

The history of the Latino press in the United States reflects both general commonalities and specific national-origin diversity. Spanish-language newspapers like *La Gaceta de Texas* and *El Mexicano* began in Texas during the 1810–1821 Mexican struggle for independence. After 1821 several newspapers operated in New Mexico, such as *El Crepúsculo de la Libertad*, while California Mexicans published books but no newspapers.[4]

Following the U.S. conquest and annexation of northern Mexico, Spanish-language journalism expanded. Herminio Rios and Guadalupe Castillo have identified 136 Mexican American newspapers that functioned during the 19th century and 236 more that emerged prior to 1940. New Mexico, with the largest 19th century Chicano population, also had the largest number of pre–1900 Mexican American newspapers, 52.[5] It was followed by Texas with 38, California with 34, Arizona with 11 and Colorado with 1.[6] New Mexico's Spanish-language periodicals united in 1892 as La Prensa Asociada Hispano-Americana, the first U.S. Latino press association.

El Clamor Público of Los Angeles provides an example of the contributions and complexities of the 19th century Latino press. The third postwar and first Spanish-language newspaper in Los Angeles, *Clamor* was established in 1855 by 22-year-old Francisco Ramírez. A former Los Angeles *Star* compositor, he had become infuriated by the chauvinistically Anglo tone of that newspaper's stories.

Ramírez used the one-page weekly (later biweekly) *Clamor* for a variety of purposes. He protested against slavery, religious bigotry and Anglo discrimination against Mexican Americans, including such acts as lynchings. At the same time, he lauded the ideals espoused in the U.S. Constitution and Declaration of Independence. He also encouraged Mexican Americans to learn English, become knowledgeable about U.S. culture, send their children to school, devote greater attention to the education of women, and become more involved in the American political process. However, lack of funds ultimately undermined Ramírez' efforts, and the newspaper closed in 1859.[7]

The fate of *El Clamor Público* exemplifies the ongoing economic struggle of the undercapitalized Latino press. Lack of money has forced the Latino press to become heavily dependent upon outside resources, such as government and private Anglo advertisers. This financial dependence on non-Latinos, who have had the ability to sever the monetary arteries, has tended historically to moderate editorial policy, mute the critical voice of the press and restrict the social activism of many Latino newspapers. The problem of undercapitalization continues to the present, as reflected in the frequent demise of contemporary Latino newspapers and magazines.

In survival terms, the greatest success among Mexican American newspapers belongs to Los Angeles' Spanish-language daily, *La Opinión*, established by Mexican immigrant publisher Ignacio Lozano. After escaping from the turmoil of the 1910–1920 Mexican Revolution, Lozano launched his first U.S. newspaper, *La Prensa*, in San Antonio in 1913. When *La Prensa*'s circulation expanded to the West Coast, Lozano decided to found his second newspaper, *La Opinión*, in Los Angeles in 1926.

By appealing to Mexican and increasing numbers of Central American immigrant readers with news on such topics as Latin America, Latinos in the United States, and U.S. immigration policy, *La Opinión* has operated continuously ever since. *La Prensa*, which was sold by Ignacio Lozano, Jr., in 1959, no longer exists. The Times-Mirror Corporation recently purchased a 50 percent interest in *La Opinión*, providing further recognition of the growing importance of the nation's Spanish-reading public.[8]

While the Mexican American press developed principally in the Southwest during the 19th century before expanding into other sections of the country during the 20th century, a parallel quest to establish a Latino journalistic presence took place in the East, led by Puerto Ricans and Cubans. As early as 1865, the Republican Society of Cuba and Puerto Rico launched *La Voz de América* in New York City, with satellites in Philadelphia and New Orleans. *La Voz* was followed by other publications from New York City to Ybor City, Florida. Many were united ideologically by one major goal: the quest for Cuban and Puerto Rican independence, first from Spain and later (in the case of Puerto Rico) from the United States.

However, the East Coast Latino press has experienced its major growth since World War II. *El Diario de Nueva York*, owned by a Dominican and having a Puerto Rican as its first editor, was established in 1948, while in 1958 a Puerto Rican was named editor of *La Prensa*, which had been founded in 1913 by Spanish immigrants. The two newspapers merged in 1962 as *El Diario de Nueva York/La Prensa*, with Anglo ownership but Puerto Rican editorship. In 1981 the Gannett media empire purchased *El Diario/La Prensa*, but it continued the practice of appointing Puerto Ricans as editors.[9]

Newspapers comprised the predominant form of Latino media throughout the 19th century and the first half of the 20th century. However, the rise of Latino activism, beginning in the 1960s, has sparked the expansion of other elements of the Latino and the Spanish-language media in addition to news-papers. (It is important to recognize the Latino media and the Spanish-language media as distinct but overlapping media categories, because non-Latinos own many of the Spanish-language media, while many of the Latino media use English as their primary language.) According to one estimate, from 1980 to 1983 an average of 16 Hispanic newspapers and magazines were launched each month. However, only 20 percent of the newspapers and 5 percent of the magazines lasted more than two years.[10]

While Latino periodicals have been increasingly successful, some of the earlier, ephemeral attempts to establish Latino national magazines deserve recognition. The first extended Latino effort to gain a national magazine foothold was *La Luz*, established in Denver by Daniel Valdez in 1971 and published until 1981. While *La Luz* covered the U.S Latino community and even Latin America in general, it devoted most of its attention to Mexican American life. More ambitious was the slicker *Nuestro*, published first in New York and later in Washington, DC. Launched with great fanfare in 1974, it survived until 1987 despite an inconsistent editorial focus and continuous economic problems. *Agenda*, a bimonthly publication of the National Council of La Raza in Washington, operated from 1970 to 1981. Less popular in orientation than *La Luz* and *Nuestro*, *Agenda* engaged in a more serious dis-cussion of major Latino concerns and often published thematic issues on such topics as immigration, politics, civil rights and the media.

FUNCTIONS OF THE LATINO PRESS

From mid–19th century newspapers to late–20th century magazines, the Latino press has carried out a variety of functions. It has provided news about Latino individuals and communities locally and nationally, about Latin America, and about the United States and the world in general. It has served as a source of ethnic identity, a voice of social commentary and an outlet for cultural expression. It has informed readers about current events, Latino community activities, employment opportunities, local services and impor-tant social issues, while also providing an outlet for poetry, essays, letters, art and other forms of Latino expression.

The Latino press has sought to inculcate values. For example, in analyzing the 19th century Mexican American press, historian Richard Griswold del Castillo uncovered numerous examples of articles aimed at teaching youth, particularly young women, how to act, and lecturing parents, particularly mothers, on parental responsibilities. Likewise, newspaper writers com-monly used the press to champion such values as the sanctity of marriage.[11]

In a seminal 1977 article, Félix Gutiérrez hypothesized that Chicano news-papers (his generalization can also be applied to other Latino newspapers and magazines and possibly even to some of the broadcast media) have served as instruments of both social control and social activism.[12] As instruments of social control, they have spread official government information about how Americans are supposed to act and have socialized Latinos into the "American way of thinking." As instruments of social activism, they have protested against discrimination, pointed out the lack of public services for Latinos, raised Latino social consciousness and exhorted Latinos to take action.

The social activism function of the Latino press expanded during the civil rights heyday of the 1960s and early 1970s. During that period, Latino media tended to be more militant or at least more reform-oriented than their media predecessors. While that press militancy has declined somewhat since the mid–1970s, elements of social activism still appear even in the more moderate, commercially oriented newspapers and magazines that now dominate the Latino press spectrum.

Finally, language has been one of the critical historical and contemporary issues facing the Latino press. Language-usage statistics are very imprecise and unreliable. According to some estimates, approximately 50 percent of U.S. Latino readers are biliterate (to varying degrees) in English and Spanish, while the other half read only English or Spanish.

As a result, the Latino press has developed in different linguistic packages involving Spanish and English, a reflection of the diversity of the Latino reading community and the fact that non-Latinos comprise part of the readership. Many Latino publications are issued completely in Spanish or English; some carry all articles in both Spanish and English; others print some articles in Spanish and some in English; and a few carry full articles in one language and brief synopses of articles in the other language. Publications that use only Spanish or English necessarily lose one monoliterate part of the Latino audience.

Even those publications that employ Spanish differ in approach. Some use only traditional Spanish, while others include U.S. Latino variations of Spanish. Some incorporate interlingual writing that integrates Spanish and English words, often within the same sentence or line of poetry.

THE FUTURE OF LATINO JOURNALISM

Particularly since the mid–1980s, the U.S. Latino press has established an increasingly firm and resonant presence, while national Latino media organizations have provided important networks for media and journalists. In December 1982, the National Association of Hispanic Publications was formed during the First National Chicano Media Conference in San Diego. The association has established a series of goals, including the promotion of Hispanic publications as an important form of communications and as an effective outlet for advertising.[13] This was followed by the formation of the National Association of Hispanic Journalists at the Second National Hispanic Media Conference in Washington in April 1984.[14]

According to Eddie Escobedo, vice president of the National Association of Hispanic Publications and publisher of Las Vegas' *El Mundo*, the Latino press had grown to more than 350 newspapers and magazines by 1990.[15] These range from daily and weekly newspapers to such varied publications as the English-language monthly national magazine *Hispanic*, the Spanish-language monthly magazine *Temas* (which has been operating since 1950), the English-language Sunday newspaper supplement *Vista* and various special interest magazines like *Hispanic Business*. Moreover, the Hispanic Media Association's national feature service, Hispanic Link, has provided columns about Latino issues for both Latino and mainstream publications.

Latino newspapers and magazines still face significant obstacles, particularly undercapitalization, the struggle for advertising and the need to make choices as to the language or languages of publication. However, they have increasingly provided an important service both to the nation's rapidly growing Latino community and to non-Hispanics interested in the Latino experience. In doing so, the Latino press has etched a rich, if underrecognized, chapter in American journalism history.

NOTES

1. While *American* is used in the United States to describe people or things of the United States, it should be recognized and explained to students that many Latin Americans have been rightfully indignant about the U.S. appropriation of this term, correctly pointing out that Latin Americans, too, are Americans (the Western Hemisphere includes the continents of North and South America).

2. Nonreaders of Spanish may find the following translations useful in understanding the names of the publications mentioned in this chapter: *volante* means flying; *crepúsculo* means twilight; *prensa* is press; *voz* is voice; *nuestro* means our or ours; *luz* is light; *mundo* is world; *temas* means themes or subjects; *grito* is cry; *Atzlán* roughly refers to a homeland to the northwest, as viewed from central Mexico; *caminos* are roads. While *raza* may be translated literally as race, a more appropriate translation of *la raza* would be the people.

3. U.S. Bureau of the Census, Current Population Reports, Series P–20, No. 455, *The Hispanic Population in the United States: March 1991* (Washington, DC: U.S. Government Printing Office, 1991), p. 2.

4. For a historical analysis of the Mexican American press, see Carlos E. Cortés, "The Mexican-American Press," in Sally M. Miller, ed., *The Ethnic Press in the United States: A Historical Analysis and Handbook* (Westport, CT: Greenwood Press, 1987), pp. 247–260.

5. For a discussion of the Latino press in 19th century New Mexico, see Annabelle M. Oczon, "Bilingual and Spanish-Language Newspapers in Territorial New Mexico," *New Mexico Historical Review* 54 (January 1979), 45–52, and Henry R. Wagner, "New Mexico Spanish Press," *New Mexico Historical Review* 12 (January 1937), 1–40.

6. Herminio Rios and Guadalupe Castillo, "Toward a True Chicano Bibliography: Mexican-American Newspapers: 1848–1942," *El Grito: A Journal of Contemporary Mexican-American Thought* 3 (Summer 1970), 17–24, and Herminio Rios,

"Toward a True Chicano Bibliography—Part II," *El Grito: A Journal of Contemporary Mexican-American Thought* 5 (Summer 1972), 40–47.

7. See Leonard Pitt, *"El Clamor Público*: Sentiments of Treason," chapter 6 in *The Decline of the Californios: A Social History of Spanish-Speaking Californians, 1848–1890* (Berkeley: University of California Press, 1966), pp. 181–194.

8. Among the studies of *La Opinión* are Francine Medeiros, *"La Opinión,* a Mexican Exile Newspaper: A Content Analysis of Its First Years, 1926–1929," *Aztlán, International Journal of Chicano Studies Research* 11 (Spring 1980), 65–87; and Ricardo Chavira, "A Case Study: Reporting of Mexican Emigration and Deportation," *Journalism History* 4 (Summer 1977), 59–64.

9. Joseph P. Fitzpatrick, "The Puerto Rican Press," in Miller, *Ethnic Press*, pp. 304–310.

10. Kirk Whisler, "The Growth of Hispanic Print Media," *Caminos* 5 (January 1984), 13. One preliminary but incomplete listing of Hispanic (not just Spanish-language) publications can be found in Joshua A. Fishman, ed., *Language Resources in the United States*, Vol. 1, *Non-English-Language* (Rosslyn, VA: National Clearinghouse for Bilingual Education, 1981), pp. 26–30.

11. Richard Griswold del Castillo, *La Familia: Chicano Families in the Urban Southwest, 1848 to the Present* (Notre Dame, IN: University of Notre Dame Press, 1984), pp. 81–83, 85.

12. Félix Gutiérrez, "Spanish-Language Media in America: Background, Resources, History," *Journalism History* 4 (Summer 1977), 38–41, 65–66.

13. *Caminos' 1983 National Hispanic Conventioneer*, p. 49. Special convention issue.

14. Juan González, "On the Road to Equality: Latino Journalists Organize," *Nuestro* 8 (June-July 1984), 35.

15. "National Association of Hispanic Publications Fifth Annual Convention a Success," *National Hispanic Reporter* (March 1991), p. 9.

BIBLIOGRAPHY

Cortés, Carlos E. "The Mexican-American Press." In Sally M. Miller, ed., *The Ethnic Press in the United States: A Historical Analysis and Handbook* (Westport, CT: Greenwood Press, 1987), pp. 247–260.

Fitzpatrick, Joseph P. "The Puerto Rican Press." In Sally M. Miller, ed., *The Ethnic Press in the United States: A Historical Analysis and Handbook* (Westport, CT: Greenwood Press, 1987), pp. 304–310.

Greenberg, Bradley S., Michael Burgoon, Judee K. Burgoon and Felipe Korzenny. *Mexican Americans and the Mass Media.* Norwood, NJ: ABLEX Publishing, 1983.

Gutiérrez, Félix. "Reporting for La Raza: The History of Latino Journalism in America." *Agenda* 8 (July-August 1978), 29–35.

Oczon, Annabelle M. "Bilingual and Spanish-Language Newspapers in Territorial New Mexico." *New Mexico Historical Review* 54 (January 1979), 45–52.

Pitt, Leonard. *"El Clamor Público*: Sentiments of Treason." Chapter 6 in *The Decline of the Californios: A Social History of Spanish-Speaking Californians, 1848–1890* (Berkeley: University of California Press, 1966), pp. 181–194.

"Spanish-Language Media Issue." *Journalism History* 4 (Summer 1977).

Veciana-Súarez, Ana. *Hispanic Media, USA.* 1987. The Media Institute, 3017 M St. NW, Washington, DC 20007.

Wagner, Henry R. "New Mexico Spanish Press." *New Mexico Historical Review* 12 (January 1937), 1–40.

Additional resources on Latinos can be found in the bibliographies at the end of Part III and at the end of Chapter 18 and in the notes at the end of Chapter 19.

13 ASIAN AMERICANS IN THE JOURNALISM CURRICULUM

Alexis S. Tan

Asian Americans are the fastest-growing minority population in the United States. Recent immigration and an increase in birth rates have accounted for this growth. In the last decade, all Asian and Pacific Islander groups in the United States increased in population by 107 percent, compared to a 53 percent increase for all Hispanics. The make-up of the Asian American population has also changed in recent years. The fastest-growing subgroups are Vietnamese (a 134.8 percent increase from 1980 to 1990), Indians (125.6 percent) and Koreans (125.3 percent.)[1]

Asian Americans, therefore, are a major component in the increasing diversity of the American population. This growth in numbers, as well as differences in the cultures of Asians and other American groups, is a compelling reason for the inclusion of Asian Americans in the journalism curriculum. Here are some suggestions on how this can be accomplished.

REPORTING COURSES

A diversified American society requires more frequent and more accurate coverage of its many cultural groups. To cover the Asian American population competently and accurately, a reporter should first have a basic understanding of Asian American culture. It would be ideal to require journalism students to take a course in Asian American cultures. When this is not possible, material about Asian cultures related to reporting (e.g., interviewing and information-collecting) can be incorporated into the reporting class. For example, the following differences between traditional Asian and Western cultures can be covered:

1. Existential worldviews, or the relation of humans to the universe, their place in nature and society, the relations of humans to one another;
2. Terminal and instrumental values, or desirable goals in life, and traits needed to obtain those goals;
3. Temporality, or the concept of time;
4. Space and proxemics;
5. Religions.

An underststanding of Asian cultures will help the journalist report on Asian Americans more accurately, completely and fairly. A good reference for this material would be any of the intercultural communication textbooks currently in print. One that is particularly useful is *Intercultural Communication*, edited by Samovar and Porter.[2]

In addition to examining cultural differences, a reporting class could also cover differences in communication styles between Asians and other Americans. An understanding of these differences will enable the reporter to establish rapport with people in Asian American communities. Sources of information will open up, and respondents will be more willing to be interviewed and share information.

Several studies at Washington State University have identified major differences in the communication styles of Asians and Anglo-Saxon Americans.[3] Communication styles were defined as how people verbally exchange information in face-to-face situations.

Differences perceived in communication styles showed up when Asian respondents were asked to characterize their own styles and then to characterize the communication styles of Americans. Chinese and Japanese respondents, for example, agreed that American communicators were sociable, not shy, direct, relaxed, expressive, happy, energetic, strong, friendly and confident. They perceived themselves to be inhibited, unexpressive, indirect, sensitive, considerate, tense, quiet and humble.

These differences can be traced to differences in culture and use of language.[4] First, let's look at cultural differences. In our studies, Asian respondents agreed very strongly with the following cultural values related to communication, while Anglo-Saxon Americans disagreed:

"In dealing with other people, 'saving face' or avoiding being 'shamed' is very important to me."

"Disagreement between members of a group should not be discussed in the open to preserve a good 'atmosphere' for the group."

These values are explained by the influence of Confucianism in the thinking and lifestyles of most Asians.[5] Confucianism places high value on hierarchical order in relationships, including human relationships. An individual's worth is measured largely by his or her ability to maintain good relationships with others and by the ability to consider the interest of the group over personal interest. Conflict is avoided, and emphasis is placed on pleasing others.

Language also explains communication differences between Asians and Anglo-Saxon Americans. Asian communication styles (use of language) have been described by linguistic scholars as "high context" rather than "low context." In high context communication, most of the information is "either in the physical context or internalized in the person, while very little is in the coded, explicit transmitted part of the message."[6] Thus, the high context communicator, like most Asians, tends to be ambiguous and indirect, leaving the receiver to figure out what is really meant or what is in the speaker's mind. On the other hand, low context communicators, like most Anglo-Saxon Americans, prefer clear and direct communication.

A journalist obviously will have serious difficulties in obtaining information from the Asian American community if he or she does not understand these differences. A reporting class could make students aware of the important differences in communication styles between Anglo Americans and most Asian Americans by discussing some of the most basic differences. Inter-cultural communication readers are useful sources of information, as are guest speakers from the Asian American community.

Another focus of reporting classes should be how to cover and portray Asian Pacifics accurately and fairly in the news. An excellent source for this material is *Asian American Handbook*, a 1991 expansion and revision of *Asian Pacific Americans: A Handbook on How to Cover and Portray Our Nation's Fastest Growing Minority Group*, published by the National Conference of Christians and Jews, the Asian American Journalists Association and the Association of Asian Pacific American Artists.[7] This handbook provides tips on how to avoid stereotyping, racial slurs, double standards and unfair portrayals of Asian Americans. It also discusses how reporters can cover important news events about Asian Americans, and not only those that are conflict-related. A section is included on finding and developing news sources and overcoming language barriers.

A reporter's education will be more complete if he or she understands the different groups to be covered. The material discussed in this section can easily be included in a reporting class.

COMMUNICATION THEORY AND MASS MEDIA COURSES

For courses covering general material on communication, the mass media or journalism, students can be taught about stereotypes in the media and how these stereotypes affect audiences. Journalism students should be able to recognize stereotypes and know how to avoid using them. The ability of journalists to cover the news accurately and fairly will be enhanced by an understanding of stereotypes.

Considerable research has been done in communication and social psychology on media stereotypes. Here are some topics that could be covered in communication and mass media courses:

1. What is a stereotype? A stereotype is a generalized impression of an object or person, in which characteristics are ascribed to an individual simply because the individual is a member of a group. Rarely are stereotypes based on firsthand or factual information. The media, in both their news and entertainment aspects, are major sources of information on which stereotypes are based. A useful exercise would be to ask students to write anonymously about stereotypes they hold about Asian Americans and other ethnic groups. The first step in eliminating stereotypes is to recognize that we have them.[8]

2. Why are stereotypes held? Stereotypes are an easy way of perceiving others. Stereotypes help us deal with unfamiliar objects, persons and situations. Journalists should understand why they hold stereotypes. This understanding will help them avoid stereotypes in reporting the news. Considerable information about stereotypes and their functions for the individual is available in the social psychology research literature.[9]

3. Stereotypes of Asian Americans in the media. Stereotypes of Asian Americans are frequently used in media entertainment and news. These stereotypes are manifested in many ways. Here are some examples pointed out in the *Asian American Handbook*:

a. Media invisibility. Asian Americans are not represented in proportion to their populations in television entertainment programs and in the national newspapers.

b. Imbalanced coverage. Most news stories about Asian Americans focus on criminal and conflict-driven activity such as gang wars and illegal immigration. The Asian American community should be covered as a regular beat rather than used as a source for violence-related stories.

c. Use of racial slurs and conflict terminology to refer to Asian Americans. "Jap" and "Chinaman" still are used in the media. "Invasion," "trade wars" and "immigration waves" are often used to describe events relating to Asians and Asian Americans. Negative and prejudicial language should be avoided by journalists in referring to Asian Americans.

In television entertainment, Asian Americans have often been portrayed negatively—women are shown as geishas and dragon ladies, men as "evil, sinister, diabolical, myopic, buck-tooth subhuman villains, or as passive and emasculated detectives."[10] Journalists should recognize that realistic portrayals of Asian Americans should include the whole range of human experiences, from good to bad.

4. Effects of stereotyping. Journalism students should be aware of the effects of stereotypes on the stereotyped group and on the general public. Studies in communication and general psychology suggest that the media are a major source of

information used by people to form perceptions of reality. Therefore, inaccurate and negative portrayals of and information about Asian Americans in the media will lead to negative and inaccurate perceptions of Asian Americans in real life. These perceptions will reinforce negative stereotypes. Effects on the stereotyped group include lower self-esteem, low achievement in school and other dysfunctional behaviors.[11]

5. How to eliminate stereotyping. Journalists should learn how to get rid of stereotypes they now hold. The following Zen parable is a useful lesson:

Nan-in, a Japanese master during the Meiji era, received a university professor who came to inquire about Zen. Nan-in served tea. He poured his visitor's cup full, and kept on pouring. The professor watched the overflow until he could no longer restrain himself. "It is overfull. No more will go in."

"Like this cup," Nan-in said, "you are full of your opinions and speculations. How can I teach you Zen unless you first empty your cup?"[12]

Strategies for eliminating stereotypes are discussed in several intercultural communication textbooks.[13]

HISTORY COURSES

Journalism students should understand the historical events leading to the immigration of Asian Americans to the United States. By understanding this history, which can be included in journalism courses, the students will get a better understanding of Asian Americans in the United States today.

An excellent resource for this material is Ronald Takaki's *Strangers from a Different Shore*.[14] Takaki discusses the history of all Asian Americans, including the Chinese, Japanese, Filipinos, Asian Indians, Koreans and more recent immigrants. He forcefully and clearly documents the racism and discrimination that these groups faced as they struggled for acceptance as United States citizens. Most students who read this book will develop a clearer understanding of Asian American communities today. For the journalist attempting to cover these communities accurately and fairly, this understanding is essential.

NOTES

1. U.S. Census Bureau, 1991.
2. Larry Samovar and Richard Porter, eds., *Intercultural Communication* (Belmont, CA: Wadsworth Publishing, 1991).
3. Jim Du, "Impact of the Mass Media and Interpersonal Contacts on the Chinese Student Sojourners' Communicator Styles and Cultural Affinity," Master's thesis, Washington State University, Pullman, WA, 1991. See also Yuki Fujioka, "Impact of American Mass Media in Japan: U.S. Media Effects on Interpersonal Commu-

nication Patterns and Cultural Identity," Master's thesis, Washington State University, Pullman, WA, 1990.

4. Samovar and Porter, *Intercultural Communication*.

5. Ibid.

6. Ibid., p. 48.

7. *Asian American Handbook*, a 1991 revision of *Asian Pacific Americans: A Handbook on How to Cover and Portray Our Nation's Fastest Growing Minority Group*. (Copies available for $18 from the National Conference of Christians and Jews, 360 N. Michigan Ave., Chicago, IL 60601.)

8. Gordon Allport, *The Nature of Prejudice* (Reading, MA: Addison-Wesley, 1954); John F. Dovidio and Samuel L. Gaertner, eds., *Prejudice, Discrimination and Racism* (New York: Academic Press, 1986); C. McCauley, C. L. Stitt and M. Segal, "Stereotyping: From Prejudice to Prediction," *Psychological Bulletin* 87 (1980), 195–208; D. M. Taylor and R. N. Lalonde, "Ethnic Stereotypes: A Psychological Analysis," in L. Driedger, ed., *Ethnic Canada: Identities and Inequalities* (Toronto: Copp Clark, 1987), pp. 347–373.

9. Dovidio and Gaertner, *Prejudice*.

10. *Asian American Handbook*, section 7, p. 4.

11. Driedger, *Ethnic Canada*. See also A. Tan and G. Tan, "TV Use and Self Esteem of Blacks," *Journal of Communication* 29 (1979), 129–135.

12. Joe Hyams, *Zen in the Martial Arts* (New York: Bantam Books, 1979), p. 10.

13. Samovar and Porter, *Intercultural Communication*.

14. Ronald Takaki, *Strangers from a Different Shore* (Boston: Little, Brown, 1989).

BIBLIOGRAPHY

Asian Women United of California, eds. *Making Waves: An Anthology of Writings by and about Asian American Women*. Boston: Beacon Press, 1989.

Beekman, Alan. "Japanese Language Press of Hawaii, What Now?" *Pacific Citizen*, 23–30 December 1983, p. B–1.

Chinese America: History and Perspectives, 1987. San Francisco: Chinese Historical Society of America, 1987.

Crouchette, Lorraine Jacobs. *Filipinos in California*. El Cerrito, CA: Downey Place Publishing, 1982.

Daniels, Roger. *Asian America: Chinese and Japanese in the United States since 1850*. Pullman: University of Washington Press, 1988.

Fawcett, James T., and Benjamin V. Carino, eds. *Pacific Bridges: The New Immigration from Asia and the Pacific Islands*. New York: 1987.

Flores-Meiser, Enya P. "The Filipino-American Press." In Sally M. Miller, ed., *The Ethnic Press in the United States*. Westport, CT: Greenwood Press, 1987.

Glick, Clarence E. *Sojourners and Settlers: Chinese Migrants in Hawaii*. Honolulu: University Press of Hawaii, 1980.

Hart, Donn V. "The Filipino Press in the United States: A Neglected Resource." *Journalism Quarterly* 54 (Spring 1977), 135–139.

Irons, Peter. *Justice at War: The Story of the Japanese American Internment Cases*. New York: Oxford University Press, 1983.

Kitano, Harry H.L. "The Japanese-American Press." In Sally M. Miller, ed., *The Ethnic Press in the United States*. Westport, CT: Greenwood Press, 1987.

————. *Japanese Americans*. Englewood Cliffs, NJ: Prentice-Hall, 1976.

Knoll, Tricia. *Becoming Americans: Asian Sojourners, Immigrants, and Refugees in the Western United States*. Portland, OR: Coast to Coast, 1982.

Lai, H. M. "The Chinese-American Press." In Sally M. Miller, ed., *The Ethnic Press in the United States*. Westport, CT: Greenwood Press, 1987.

Lo, Karl. "Kim Shan Jit San Luk, the First Chinese Paper Published in America." *Chinese Historical Society of America Bulletin* 6 (December 1971).

Lo, Karl, and Him Mark Lai. *Chinese Newspapers Published in North America, 1854–1975*. Washington, DC: Center for Chinese Research Materials, 1977.

Melendy, H. Brett. *Asians in America: Filipinos, Koreans, and East Indians*. Boston: Twayne, 1977.

Morrison, Joan, and Charlotte Fox Zabusky, eds. *American Mosaic: The Immigrant Experience in the Words of Those Who Lived It*. New York: Dutton, 1980.

National Conference of Christians and Jews. *Asian American Handbook*, a 1991 expansion and update of *Asian Pacific Americans: A Handbook on How to Cover and Portray Our Nation's Fastest Growing Minority Group*. $18 from the National Conference of Christians and Jews, 360 N. Michigan Ave., Chicago, IL 60601.

Reimers, David. *Still the Golden Door: The Third World Comes to America*. New York: Columbia University Press, 1987.

Takaki, Ronald. *Iron Cages: Race and Culture in 19th Century America*. New York: Oxford University Press, 1990.

————. *Strangers from a Different Shore: A History of Asian Americans*. Boston: Little, Brown, 1989.

Wain, Barry. *The Refused: The Agony of the Indochina Refugees*. New York: Simon & Schuster, 1981.

Additional resources on Asian Americans can be found in the bibliographies at the end of Chapter 18 and at the end of Part III and in the notes at the end of Chapter 19.

14 NATIVE AMERICANS IN JOURNALISM AND MASS COMMUNICATION EDUCATION

John M. Coward

Who is the most famous American Indian in U.S. history? This is hardly a trivial question, because the answer reveals something about the place of Native Americans in American culture. If the answer is Geronimo, for instance, then the idea of the Indian is linked to fierceness and savagery, two qualities associated with the great Apache leader. If the answer is Sitting Bull or Crazy Horse, the idea of the Indian is much the same; they too were known for courage and battlefield prowess.

But if the answer is Pocahontas or Sequoyah or Chief Joseph or Sacagawea, the "Bird Woman" who served as guide for the Lewis and Clark expedition, then the idea of the Indian takes a different turn. These natives were best known for their grace, eloquence and wisdom, qualities presumably arising from their innate intelligence and their special relationship to the natural world.

Either way—as savage warriors or as wise children of nature—Native Americans have been defined in the public mind in terms of extremes. Moreover, these extremes have been perpetuated and amplified by the mass media, so that a wide variety of indigenous cultures, traditions and lifeways have been collapsed into a handful of memorable clichés: the demonic Sioux warrior, the idealized Indian princess, the proud chief grieving over the ruin of his homeland, to name a few. By such means Native Americans—when they have been noticed by the dominant society at all—have been reduced to cardboard characters on the margins of history, to images as narrow as they are shallow. What is missing from popular conceptions of Native Americans is a broad middle range of native images, a cultural space where the stereotypical Indian can be broadly explained and understood as someone from a complex and significant set of indigenous cultures that have existed in the Western Hemisphere for centuries—and that exist today.

Journalism and mass communication teachers have a special responsibility to address this topic because the native image has long been tied to the popular media. In fact, the first (and only) issue of the first newspaper published in the British colonies, Benjamin Harriss' *Publick Occurrences, Both Foreign and Domestick*, discovered stereotypical Indians near Boston. Harriss praised the "Christianized Indians in some parts of Plimouth" but, a paragraph later, speculated that some "barbarous Indians" were the prime suspects in the disappearance of two children.[1]

Harriss' story foreshadowed the rise of the Indian captivity narrative, an extremely popular genre in early American publishing which emphasized the savagery of Indians.[2] James Fenimore Cooper and Henry Wadsworth Longfellow, by contrast, popularized the nobility of the natives, Indians who were brave, stoic and gentle in spirit. Later in the 19th century, the savage Indian dominated the cultural landscape, as hordes of sinister, painted warriors rode through the pages of dime novels and illustrations of *Harper's Weekly* and *Frank Leslie's Illustrated Monthly*. In the modern era, the Indian, sometimes a friendly sidekick but more often a terrifying enemy, has been a staple of Hollywood Westerns in movies and on television.

The purpose of this chapter is to suggest some ways that journalism and mass communication teachers can move beyond such stereotypes and open their classrooms to a more sensitive and thoughtful discussion of Native Americans and their place in a cultural landscape dominated by mass communication. Another aim is to help students discover the long and complex history of the Native American press. This chapter offers a number of ideas for accomplishing these goals and provides a selected bibliography designed to suggest a variety of additional approaches to these important topics.

THE IDEA OF THE INDIAN

Misconceptions about Native Americans can be traced as far back as Christopher Columbus. In 1492 Columbus used a single term, *los Indios*, to identify a wide variety of native societies and cultures. This term, as historian Robert Berkhofer has noted, de-emphasized "the social and cultural diversity of Native Americans then—and now—for the convenience of simplified understanding." Unfortunately for Native Americans, this simplification persists today. "Native Americans were and are real," Berkhofer writes, "but the Indian was a white invention and still remains largely a white image, if not a stereotype."[3]

An example of the continuing power of Indian stereotypes can be demonstrated by referring to a single hour of American history. "To almost every American, to almost everyone who knows anything about America, a reference to Custer's Last Stand is meaningful," writes Western historian Don Russell. Custer's defeat at the hands of the Sioux and Cheyenne in 1876 was a battle that quickly escalated into a national myth. "No single event in United States history, or perhaps in world history, has been the subject of more bad art and erroneous story than Custer's Last Stand at the Battle of the Little Big Horn," Russell notes.[4] His study of Little Big Horn images, completed in 1968 and "by no means exhaustive," he says, turned up 848 paintings and illustrations. This mythologizing suggests how the popular image of all Native Americans came to be a Plains Indian warrior on horseback, circling a dying, golden-haired hero named George Armstrong Custer.

Even the acclaimed Kevin Costner movie *Dances with Wolves* was, despite its sympathetic treatment of the Sioux, yet another story about a White man and his encounter with a "vanishing" race of Plains Indians. In other words, Native Americans are most often portrayed in terms of their encounters with Whites, as if they have no history of their own and no stories to tell. Native peoples have been assigned to a specific place in the American mind, a place that is romantic, often brutal, but always safely in the past.

Yet Native Americans have not vanished. Recent census figures show a population of nearly two million American Indians, Eskimos and Aleuts.[5] But this population is widely dispersed in the West, far from the centers of political and media power. In Alaska, natives make up 15 percent of the population, but only five other states have a native population of more than 5 percent. Even Oklahoma, once known as "Indian Territory" and designated as the government's official Indian homeland, has a native population today of only 8 percent. Moreover, Native Americans as a group have little economic power. As a result, Native Americans are easily overlooked in contemporary America, and what little attention they do receive is largely restricted to media stereotypes and clichés—all the more reason to incorporate them in classroom discussions of the mass media.

INCORPORATING NATIVE AMERICANS IN MEDIA COURSES

If Native Americans should be part of the ongoing dialogue about contemporary mass communication, a check of some standard textbooks shows that this is not the case now. For example, Don Pember's *Mass Media in America*, a good introductory text currently in its sixth edition, includes a discussion of minorities and mass media, including minority hiring practices. Native Americans are not mentioned. The only hint of Native Americans in Pember's book is two still photos from *Dances with Wolves* in the chapter on movies.[6] Edward J. Whetmore's *American Electric*, an introduction to the electronic media, which are the source of many myths about Indians, does not discuss Native Americans, despite an exploration of stereotyping and a sensitivity to other minorities.[7] Journalism history texts do a little better, most noting the beginning of the native press in the early 19th century. Still, the discussion in these texts is limited to a few paragraphs and an illustration or two.[8] As a minority within the minority community itself, Native Americans are sometimes overlooked even by scholars who write about the problems of minorities.[9]

Perhaps the first step in incorporating Native Americans into journalism and mass communication courses is an explicit recognition in the classroom that major media institutions serve a pluralistic society made up of a variety of groups and cultures. Each of these cultures is affected by media processes and products, and each has to struggle against the media's power to distort, exaggerate or oversimplify news and information about their cultures. Recognizing the diversity of the American audience and the lack of access to media power is a modest step, but an emphasis on this point opens the way to a broad examination of the way media institutions constitute culture, process information, reproduce power relationships and create or perpetuate stereotypes. As a small but nonetheless significant part of American society, Native Americans are often shut out of this meaning-making process. Their example offers a powerful case study of the problems of all minorities in the media-saturated society.

STUDY OF BIASED LANGUAGE AND SYMBOLS

Once native peoples are recognized as part of the American mosaic, specific lectures and assignments can highlight the complex relationship between Native Americans and specific media practices and images. In news-writing and editing classes, for example, assignments about Native Americans and their concerns can introduce students to real-world problems involving biased language and racial group sensitivity. Similar assignments are also appropriate for mass communication and society classes and for discussion of media ethics.

The controversy over the "tomahawk chop" during the 1991 baseball season, for instance, can be used to illustrate the media's power over symbols as well as the sensitivity of native peoples. Was the "chop" racially biased or simply a harmless gesture? Would it be harmless if it offended another minority or religious group, one with more political and media clout? On a higher level, what responsibility do the media have to present fair and accurate representations of any minority group? Who decides what is fair and how far the media should go to accommodate minority views? These are important questions and are likely to generate vigorous classroom discussions. With a little planning, professors can develop similar cases involving other Native American issues.

EXAMINATION OF NATIVE JOURNALISTS

In introductory mass communication or journalism history classes, students can write short biographical sketches of native editors, taking advantage of a number of recent guides to the native press (see the bibliography at end of this chapter). This assignment pushes students beyond the usual list of "Great Men in Journalism" and emphasizes the role of native journalists in the development of the American media.

Students should do more there than read *about* native journalists. Indeed, they should be asked to describe and analyze some writing *by* native journalists. This allows students to make their own assessments of native writers and to connect their ideas and opinions to larger themes in American history. In short, a combination of both primary and secondary sources will help students place native journalists within the social, cultural and economic times in which they lived. The sources also will open the way toward an enlarged understanding of the role of native journalists in defining their own cultures and articulating the place of those cultures in relation to the dominant culture.

STUDY OF NEWS PROCESSES

A more dynamic assignment, and one that may engage students more fully in the study of media processes, combines the study of the news-making process and the coverage of native news. Such an assignment might ask students to locate and analyze two news stories in the mass circulation media about the same Indian news event and to compare these stories against the best historical record of this event. The idea is for students to evaluate the effects of the news-making process on news stories involving Indians. Instead of merely copying facts from reference books, students are forced to develop their own analysis of news stories and to draw conclusions about the effects of the journalistic method on these stories.

The impact and immediacy of this assignment—the fact that, in this context, 19th century Indian news stories seem fresh and important—makes historical research more interesting. Students will discover various ways that the news-making process worked for and against American Indians, as well as a host of factual errors, newspaper romanticism, exaggerations and other more subtle patterns of journalistic framing. In short, this assignment is effective because it gives students a way to draw their own conclusions about journalistic processes in a way they find interesting and significant.

COMPARISONS BETWEEN NATIVE AND MAINSTREAM JOURNALISM

An active native press has existed in this country almost continuously since the founding of the *Cherokee Phoenix* in 1828. So there is a great opportunity for comparisons between these two press systems. How has the native press differed from the mainstream press on the major political or social issues of the day? For example, how did they differ on issues related to the Indian wars or, more recently, the Vietnam War? How did their coverage differ on the confrontation between federal agents and Native Americans at Wounded Knee, South Dakota, in 1973 and again on June 26, 1975? How did they compare in their portrayal of the Canadian government's siege of Mohawks protecting an ancestral burying ground at Oka, Quebec, in the summer of 1990? The answers to such questions will shed light on the functions of the native press as well as the strengths and weaknesses of mainstream news coverage of native views.

Research about the native press and its history requires some planning, however, since native journals are not widely available and must be obtained through interlibrary loan. Fortunately, a number of excellent reference books on the native press are available, including Greenwood Press' wonderful three-volume study *American Indian and Alaska Native Newspapers and Periodicals* by Daniel F. Littlefield, Jr., and James W. Parins (see bibliography). This work provides a short history of each native periodical as well as a description of the paper's content, a list of its editors, and the location of the paper.

Contemporary native papers can be studied, too, especially if they are readily available in department reading rooms. A leading independent native paper is *Indian Country Today*, formerly the *Lakota Times*, published in Rapid City, South Dakota, by Tim Giago. Giago's award-winning weekly offers nationwide coverage of Native American issues and is an excellent example of native journalism which deserves attention in journalism classrooms. Another important native newspaper is the *Navajo Times*, the official newspaper of the nation's largest tribe. Published in Window Rock, Arizona, this weekly provides a good overview of news and opinion from the Southwest. Subscription information on both newspapers can be found in the bibliography at the end of this chapter.

ANALYSIS OF INDIAN IMAGES IN THE ILLUSTRATED PRESS

Indians were popular subjects for illustrations in *Frank Leslie's Illustrated Newspaper*, *Harper's Weekly* and other 19th century publications. But little scholarship has been done on these illustrations. Since many students today enjoy working with visual images, research projects might be developed to include illustrations of Indians in such materials as dime novels, popular prints, advertising, postcards or children's stories. A collection of such images can also supplement lectures about media stereotyping and stimulate class discussions.

COMPARISON BETWEEN PUBLIC AND PRIVATE IMAGES OF THE INDIAN

This idea comes from Glenda Riley, whose book *Women and Indians on the Frontier* shows that the media portrayal of Indians often differs markedly from the portrayal found in women's private letters and diaries. Riley also shows that women's views of the natives were often more sympathetic than those of men, thereby introducing gender as a factor in the perception of Native Americans.

Following Riley's lead, students with access to frontier diaries—or perhaps diaries from their own families—could contrast those Indian images with images from the frontier or Eastern press.

ANALYSIS OF THE ROLE OF NATIVE WOMEN IN THE NEWS

Stereotypes often control the public's perceptions of native people. Thus the image of the Indian woman is often reduced to an Indian princess: Pocahontas. But surely Indian women made news over the years in many ways. By focusing on the lives of individual native women or events in which they participated, students could identify the mainstream press treatment of these women and the consequences of such news coverage.

For example, one researcher has detailed how the Boston and New York press lionized an Omaha Indian woman named Bright Eyes, who was in the East on behalf of the Ponca tribe. At the same time, the newspapers remained cool toward a Ponca chief named Standing Bear, noting that Bright Eyes was attractive and spoke good English, while describing Standing Bear as "an athletic savage."[10] Such differences reveal how the press filtered its image of the natives through a preconceived set of ideas, a practice that perpetuated White stereotypes of natives.

THE INDIAN IMAGE IN POP CULTURE

Popular culture offers a rich source of material for investigating the image of Native Americans. In mass communication and society or similar courses, for instance, professors can highlight the Hollywood treatment of Indians and the narrow range of native images that make it to the silver screen. Class discussions can be stimulated by screening Western movies and television shows or listening to old radio programs. Student research papers can also be designed around the image of Native Americans in other forms of pop culture. Postcards and tourist brochures featuring Indians can provide telling details about the idea of the Indian in American life.

The 20th century is the age of mass advertising, another powerful force in the image of Native Americans. In advertising classes or in discussions of media ethics, the use and misuse of the native image can be a stimulating topic.

REASONS FOR INCLUSION

American journalism and mass communication can be taught—quite competently, perhaps—without any serious discussion of Native Americans and their cultures. But to do so is to leave out crucial aspect of American history and to slight the journalistic achievements of native peoples.

Native Americans have long been outsiders in American life, literally and figuratively pushed to the margins of our history. And though they were devastated by disease, defeated on the battlefield and overwhelmed by European technologies and ideas, the people have not disappeared, and their cultures have not vanished. Indeed, both are thriving. And this persistence is perhaps the most compelling reason to include Native Americans in the study of journalism and mass communication.

NOTES

1. The paper was published September 25, 1690. Authorities prevented Harriss from further publication, and he eventually returned to England. Quoted from Calder M. Pickett, *Voices of the Past: Key Documents in the History of American Journalism* (Columbus: Grid, 1977), p. 20.

2. See, for example, Richard VanDerBeets, ed., *Held Captive by Indians: Selected Narratives, 1642–1836* (Knoxville: University of Tennessee Press, 1973).

3. Robert F. Berkhofer, Jr., *The White Man's Indian* (New York: Vintage Books, 1979), p. 3.

4. Don Russell, *Custer's Last* (Fort Worth: Amon Carter Museum of Western Art, 1968), p. 3.

5. *Statistical Abstract of the United States, 1991* (Washington, DC: U.S. Bureau of the Census, 1991), p. xiii.

6. Don R. Pember, *Mass Media in America*, 6th ed. (New York: Macmillan, 1992), p. 260. The caption to the *Dances with Wolves* photos concerns movie audiences, not Native Americans.

7. Edward J. Whetmore, *American Electric* (New York: McGraw-Hill, 1992).

8. See, for example, Michael and Edwin Emery's *The Press in America*, 6th ed. (Englewood Cliffs, NJ: Prentice-Hall, 1988), pp. 95–96, or Jean Folkerts and Dwight Teeter, *Voices of a Nation* (New York: Macmillan, 1989), pp. 167–169.

9. Native Americans are not included in the nine ethnic groups discussed by Thomas Sowell in his *Ethnic America* (New York: Basic Books, 1981).

10. John M. Coward, "The Newspaper Indian: Native Americans and the Press in the Nineteenth Century," doctoral dissertation, University of Texas at Austin, 1989, pp. 223–227.

BIBLIOGRAPHY

Native American Newspapers

Indian Country Today, formerly the *Lakota Times*. P.O. Box 2180, Rapid City, SD 57709. $38 for one-year subscription, $29 for six months, $17 for three months. Telephone 605–341–0011.

Navajo Times. P.O. Box 310, Window Rock, AZ 86515–0310. $25 for one year, $20 for nine months. Telephone 602–871–6641.

Bibliographies and Research Guides

Green, Rayna. *Native American Women: A Contextual Bibliography*. Bloomington: Indiana University Press, 1983.
Prucha, Frances Paul. *A Bibliographic Guide to the History of Indian-White Relations in the United States*. Chicago: University of Chicago Press, 1977.
———. *Indian-White Relations in the United States: A Bibliography of Works Published 1975–1980*. Lincoln: University of Nebraska Press, 1982.
Woll, Allen, and Randall M. Miller, eds. *Ethnic and Racial Images in American Film and Television: Historical Essays and Bibliography*. New York: Garland, 1987.

European and Early American Views of Native Americans

Axtell, James. *The Invasion Within: The Contest of Cultures in Colonial North America*. New York: Oxford University Press, 1985.
Berkhofer, Robert F., Jr. *The White Man's Indian: Images of the American Indian from Columbus to the Present*. New York: Vintage Books, 1979.
Crosby, Alfred W., Jr. *The Columbian Exchange: Biological and Cultural Consequences of 1492*. Westport, CT: Greenwood Press, 1972.
Pearce, Roy Harvey. *Savagism and Civilization: A Study of the Indian and the American Mind*. Rev. ed. Berkeley: University of California Press, 1988.

Native American-White Relations since 1800

Dippie, Brian. *The Vanishing American: White Attitudes and U.S. Indian Policy*. Middletown, CT: Wesleyan University Press, 1982.
Horsman, Reginald. *Race and Manifest Destiny*. Cambridge, MA: Harvard University Press, 1981.
Prucha, Frances Paul. *American Indian Policy in the Formative Years: The Indian Trade and Intercourse Acts, 1790–1834*. Lincoln: University of Nebraska Press, 1962.
———. *The Great Father: The United States Government and the American Indians*. 2 vols. Lincoln: University of Nebraska Press, 1984.
Riley, Glenda. *Women and Indians on the Frontier, 1825–1915*. Albuquerque: University of New Mexico Press, 1984.
Slotkin, Richard. *The Fatal Environment*. New York: Atheneum, 1985.

Indian Wars in the 19th Century West

Brown, Dee. *Bury My Heart at Wounded Knee: An Indian History of the American West*. New York: Bantam Books, 1972.
Rosenberg, Bruce A. *Custer and the Epic of Defeat*. University Park: Pennsylvania State University Press, 1974.
Smith, Sherry L. *The View from Officers' Row: Army Perceptions of Western Indians*. Tucson: University of Arizona Press, 1990.
Svaldi, David. *Sand Creek and the Rhetoric of Extermination: A Case Study in Indian-White Relations*. New York: University Press of America, 1989.

Utley, Robert M. *The Indian Frontier of the American West, 1846–1890.* Albuquerque: University of New Mexico Press, 1984.

Native American Journalism

Danky, James, ed. *Native American Periodicals and Newspapers, 1828–1982.* Westport, CT: Greenwood Press, 1984.

Littlefield, Daniel F., Jr., and James W. Parins. *American Indian and Alaska Native Newspapers and Periodicals, 1826–1924.* Westport, CT: Greenwood Press, 1984.

———, eds. *American Indian and Alaska Native Newspapers and Periodicals, 1925–1970.* Westport, CT: Greenwood Press, 1986.

———, eds. *American Indian and Alaska Native Newspapers and Periodicals, 1971–1985.* Westport, CT: Greenwood Press, 1986.

Luebke, Barbara. "Elias Boudinott, Indian Editor: Editorial Columns from the *Cherokee Phoenix*." *Journalism History* 6 (Summer 1979), 48–53.

Murphy, James E., and Sharon M. Murphy. *Let My People Know: American Indian Journalism, 1828–1978.* Norman: University of Oklahoma Press, 1981.

Murphy, Sharon. "Neglected Pioneers: 19th Century Native American Newspapers." *Journalism History* 4 (Autumn 1977), 79–82.

Native Americans and the Press

Blankenburg, William. "The Role of the Press in an Indian Massacre, 1871." *Journalism Quarterly* 45 (Spring 1968), 61–70.

Coward, John M. "The Newspaper Indian: Native Americans and the Press in the Nineteenth Century." Doctoral dissertation, University of Texas at Austin, 1989.

Hines, Randall. "Selected Press Coverage of Wounded Knee." Master's thesis, Kent State University, 1974.

Knight, Oliver. *Following the Indian Wars: The Story of Newspaper Correspondents among the Indian Campaigners.* Norman: University of Oklahoma Press, 1960.

Nichols, Roger L. "Printer's Ink and Red Skins: Western Newspapermen and the Indians." *Kansas Quarterly* 3 (Fall 1971), 82–88.

Watson, Elmo Scott. "The Indian Wars and the Press, 1866–1867." *Journalism Quarterly* 17 (December 1940), 301–312.

———. "The Last Indian War, 1890–91: A Study of Newspaper Jingoism." *Journalism Quarterly* 20 (September 1943), 205–224.

Native Americans in Popular Culture

Bataille, Gretchen M., and Charles Silet, eds. *The Pretend Indians: Images of Native Americans in the Movies.* Ames: Iowa State University Press, 1980.

Friar, Ralph, and Natasha Friar. *The Only Good Indian: The Hollywood Gospel.* New York: Drama Book Specialists, 1972.

Marsden, Michael, and Jack Nachbar. "American Indians in the Movies." In *Handbook of American Indians*, Vol. 4. Washington, DC: Smithsonian Institution, 1985.

O'Connor, John. *The Hollywood Indian: Stereotypes of Native Americans in Film*. 1980. New Jersey State Museum, 205 W. State St., Trenton, NJ 08625.

Tuska, Jon. *The American West in Film: Critical Approaches to the Western*. Westport, CT: Greenwood Press, 1985.

Native American Women

Green, Rayna. "The Pocahontas Perplex: The Image of Indian Women in American Culture." *Massachusetts Review* 16 (1975), 698–714.

Welch, Deborah. "American Indian Women: Reaching Beyond the Myth." In Colin G. Calloway, ed., *New Directions in American History*. Norman: University of Oklahoma Press, 1988.

Additional resources on Native Americans can be found in the bibliography at the end of Part III, in the notes at the end of Chapter 19, and in the bibliography for Chapter 18.

15 INCLUDING INFORMATION ABOUT WOMEN

Marion Marzolf

Women now make up 61 percent of the enrollment in journalism schools and communication departments, but they usually don't hear much about women journalists in their courses. They don't often learn about women's contributions to journalism history, or how the media cover women and women's issues, or how women employed in communications are faring today. Many of the journalistic standards and traditions being passed along to the next generation of reporters were shaped in the early 20th century by White male publishers, editors and reporters. In fact, journalism is just beginning to assess the sensibilities women bring to the reporting and editing process, where they now represent 40 percent of the staff.

Attempts to incorporate more diverse views in the news process began in the early 1970s as a result of pressure from the women's movement and faculty. Educators and professionals set goals for attracting and incorporating more women into the classroom and the newsroom. There has been much positive talk about the democratic value of including differing sensibilities in the reporting and editing process, but the challenge remains: how do we start taking off our cultural and gender blinders and seeing anew?

At least four approaches to incorporating gender diversity into the curriculum are being used in some schools: offering a stand-alone course about women and media; incorporating material on women throughout the curriculum; sensitizing faculty, students and staff; and hiring and promoting women to positions of responsibility and leadership.

The stand-alone course offers the advantage of dealing in depth with the subjects of women in journalism, mass media professions for women, media coverage of women, and treatment of issues concerning women. But attempting to incorporate examples using women into all aspects of the curriculum is perhaps the more popular approach. This task includes asking women professionals to serve as guest lecturers, editors-in-residence and seminar panelists for career days, and promoting opportunities for jobs and graduate study for women and men on an equal basis.

The value of sensitivity training workshops for faculty, staff and students has been accepted in university communications programs, but is regarded by some as unnecessary after the past two decades of experience in gender-related awareness. The Clarence Thomas hearings suggest, however, that there is still room for improvement in communications between men and women, as does new linguistic research like that of Deborah Tannen, reported in her book *You Just Don't Understand*. Access to education and jobs appears to be open for women, although hiring and promotion patterns suggest that barriers to upward mobility still exist.

OBSTACLES TO CHANGE

When efforts to develop courses on women and media began in American universities in the early 1970s, proponents were warned that the courses would not be considered legitimate or substantive. They also were told that research on topics concerning women was not appropriate or weighty enough to be considered seriously in tenure and promotion decisions, and that feminist recommendations and demands for change not only threatened the status quo but were also ideological, biased and suspect. It was implied—and sometimes baldly stated—that chances for tenure, promotion and the respect of one's peers could be jeopardized by pursuing the path of feminist scholarship and teaching. But eventually changes did occur in the university as well as in the workplace.

The lesson to be learned from these beginnings is that social changes of the sort sought by feminists do challenge power, and they involve educational goals and politics as well as human relationships and attitudes. But change must start at the basic level with individuals, in this case faculty members.

Whether diversity or affirmative action goals are mandated by law or by the institution, whether they are set by example from the top down or from the bottom up, people's minds have to open, and individuals at all levels in the institution have to be willing to challenge their habitual ways of seeing and behaving. A department can dictate that all course materials will reflect diversity, but each teacher has to deal with how this goal fits into a particular field, course and teaching style.

Today multicultural seminars, workshops and videotapes are available and can be used to raise these issues in a learning environment where female and male faculty and students can interact. Some schools provide funding, released time or research assistance to faculty who are developing new diversity courses or incorporating new material on gender and race into their courses. Academic and professional associations like the Association for Education in Journalism and Mass Communication (AEJMC), the International Communication Association, Women in Communications, Inc., and the Society for Professional Journalists sponsor seminars and workshops on these topics, as do some corporate training programs.

Acceptance of the need to practice and teach diversity is taking various forms at the faculty and college level, from a multicultural course requirement for all students and incorporation of diversity as an accreditation standard to the addition of a female or minority faculty member who is expected to take care of the matter single-handedly.

At the institutional level, however, backlash can occur in the form of arguments over a core curriculum, preserving a traditional canon, and charges of "political correctness" inhibiting free expression. These are familiar defenses by the dominant culture protecting their turf against those with new ideas and different views who insist on sharing the stage and power. Faculty members engaged in "opening up" the curriculum to diverse voices need to be prepared for these obstacles.

Getting a new course through the curriculum committees is the next stage. Women who have successfully introduced courses in women in media history, gender and communication, and the like have found it helpful to provide examples of courses at peer institutions as part of the course proposal. The AEJMC Women's Commission has provided several compilations of course syllabi and continues to update the selection. Sample assignments and discussions of methods and theories contained in these syllabi are useful. (See the bibliography at the end of this chapter.) At schools with women's studies departments or programs, communications faculty have succeeded in crosslisting courses on media and gender, which not only adds strength to the course proposal but populates the classes with students from different disciplines and thereby greatly enriches the experience. A computer database or message network that would enable participants to share course information and experiences would be a helpful addition to the available resources.

TECHNIQUES

Once such a course is in the curriculum, teachers need to be aware that there will be attempts to denigrate it as a "cake" course, a "gripe" course or an "indoctrination" course. Each teacher will, of course, handle these objections in an individual way. Some have found it helpful to make sure that exams and assignments are rigorous, to provide new ways of applying traditional theories and methods, and to introduce competing feminist approaches. Letting colleagues know about the course content, sharing student work of high quality and inviting speakers who add credibility and personal experience or research to the course are also helpful techniques. Finally, it is vital to get other faculty members educated so that the teacher doesn't have to carry the entire burden for this social responsibility alone.

The stand-alone course is valuable as a means of introducing the subject of women as media professionals, as news content and as audience in ways that make use of mass media and feminist theory. Students gain both knowledge and understanding of the discipline by using mass media theories about effects, audience or images, or by using historical analysis, on the subject of women. Students also learn to make specific topical or case applications. This type of course is extremely valuable as a means of stimulating student research in the field and providing ideas and case studies that further the field and whet student interest for research and academic careers.

Some of these stand-alone courses now emphasize the theoretical, using feminist and mass communication theories to examine gender and media. Others deal more with the professional status of women in the media or with history. In all cases, the students are learning methods and theories and applying them to issues and actions involving women.

These courses tend to attract only female students, and it is rare to have a male faculty member teach them, but some do. Doubtless more males will be attracted to these courses as feminist theory continues to challenge traditional approaches in the social sciences and in the humanities. Courses that take a wider perspective, incorporating race and gender and media, are still few but can be expected to increase as global multiculturalism becomes a reality in the 21st century, as many predict.

Experience in a recent University of Michigan course entitled Media and Women, with an enrollment comprised entirely of female students, showed that a mixed group of grads, undergrads, African Americans, Asian Americans and Anglo-Saxon Americans were easily able to create mixed study groups for projects based on students' special interests, not along racial lines. The atmosphere of this seminar was nonthreatening; everyone worked and spoke freely in discussions. Because the students had read and thought deeply about the issues of women in media professions, their forthright questioning impressed the media professionals who spoke to the class. Classes such as these not only prepare women students for the realities of the media workplace, but help them challenge and think through the social, ethical and professional values of contemporary mass media work.

A course about gender issues and the media is an appropriate place to begin moving toward feminist teaching methods, for those attracted to this pedagogical style. Feminist pedagogy seeks to change the traditional classroom model of teacher as authority and students as passive recipients of knowledge to a more dynamic and interactive one. In the ideal of the feminist classroom, the teacher seeks to empower students and help them assume leadership roles in the class. The students, instead of competing with each other, are encouraged to cooperate and accept some responsibility for other students' learning as well as their own. Such a teaching style, which encourages students to express feelings, and values those feelings as important sources of information, can be especially useful in these types of courses, which are sometimes criticized as a form of indoctrination or enforced political correctness. Several articles discussing feminist teaching modes can be found in the bibliography to this chapter.

In addition to offering courses on women and media, some programs have tried to infuse information about women in all courses. This effort can often take the form of a patchwork or an add-on to the standard core of material. Sometimes that is the only way a teacher can begin to deal with the new material. But the more the teacher thinks about creative ways of being inclusive rather than exclusive, the more natural it becomes to use female and male examples in language, story assignments and guests. Recognition of bias and prejudice leads to new discoveries of sexism and racism in textbooks and in media content, and these discoveries can be used in generating classroom discussion or developing assignments or grading criteria.

SUGGESTIONS

It is likely that the first time a teacher begins infusing information about women into a communication course, it will feel artificial and forced. Several examples of approaches that have worked in a variety of classes are offered below, in the hope that they will be helpful to faculty interested in bringing gender-related information into their courses.

In Information Gathering, an introductory-level class, teachers can provide students with many library and database research assignments that teach the structure of information and search strategies while simultaneously broadening students' acquaintance with little-known minority and female persons. Biographical research can focus on finding information on people of color, both celebrities and less well known authorities, instead of famous White males. The search strategies are learned, but at the same time students are introduced to people who had been largely invisible because of their gender or race.

In the same course, research topics drawing on the social sciences of sociology, psychology or political science, for example, can highlight gender and race issues in the research question. Students can research such topics as gender and work, sex discrimination, women in politics, gender and language, sexual harassment and rape. By designing assignments to highlight gender subject matter, the teacher can introduce information on these topics into the class discussion and assignments, while retaining discussion of the search strategy process for the social sciences as the basic framework for the class work.

Courses in reporting can include a discussion of the credibility of sources of news stories and develop strategies to find alternative sources to supplement the overused core of spokespersons tapped by the media. Students can develop a source list for their campus that provides alternative experts: women and ethnic minorities who are subject experts and community leaders. Some teachers have created beats for reporting classes based on minority activities and on issues that affect the lives of women. Some libraries provide peer counseling and resources about women, race and ethnic groups, including names of local organizations and printed and video materials.

Language usage and stereotyping may be discussed in many Mass Media and Society courses. Feminists have provided ample material, including articles and guidebooks, for the use of nonsexist language. Reporting and editing classes are logical places for attention to these details and for examination of stylebooks and local news conventions.

The news that is left out of the paper, the invisible voices and issues, the silences—all have been the subject of critical analysis and study in media history, analysis, criticism and media effects courses. A competition sponsored by AEJMC in 1990–91 and repeated the following year provided the initiative for classes across the nation to develop student papers and projects on speech that is silenced, for whatever reason. Many of the silenced voices that were given a hearing through the project were female voices. The idea can be used for class projects on any kind of speech that is silenced, whether or not a competition exists. Also, such projects might be shared with other students and faculty to encourage them to talk over the meaning of the silences and what can be done about them.

Media law courses are ideal for bringing up the issue of speech that is hindered by law, self-censorship or public pressure. Examples include expressions of racial prejudice, treatment of dissent, censorship, hate speech, naming of rape victims, suppression of information on birth control and prohibition of reporters' participation in protest marches or demonstrations.

One reporting teacher developed an interviewing strategy that revealed differences in students' thinking when dealing with male and female interviewees. It was the teacher's custom to bring in a colleague for the first interview, go over the papers with the students, and then give the students a chance to improve by interviewing another faculty colleague. One year this teacher happened to invite as interviewees a male professor and a female professor of about the same age and experience. Both were single parents and untenured faculty members. In going over the student interviews and interview questions, the teacher was struck by the stereotyping they exhibited. The male teacher was described in terms of courses he taught, personal interests and goals. The child in his household was not mentioned. The female teacher was turned into a supermom, struggling to do it all. Since this illuminating coincidence, the teacher has used this set of interviews frequently to teach interviewing and awareness of gender bias and stereotyping.

Much has been written about the differing styles of male and female managers. Assignments and mock problem cases for media management courses could incorporate and discuss these differences and their appropriateness to the newsroom. The supportive, consultative style most associated with women could be discussed as well on the level of reporter-editor and team projects. How do creative people working under deadline tension work best? Is the authoritarian style more useful in some situations? Students can read the research, and then interview local newsroom managers and bring back their findings for class discussion.

The subjects taught in communications history courses obviously can be expanded not only by introducing famous women in journalism but also by discussing the roles played by women in daily and other forms of journalism and the special problems and obstacles they faced. Students can locate local women journalists, study their work and conduct interviews with them. These materials are usually welcome additions to state and local archives, or to archives for women in media such as the one at the University of Missouri. Assignments that require students to examine media content and coverage in the past can include subjects dealing with women or issues critical to women's lives. Treatment of women in advertising and other forms of media content has been a much-researched topic in the last two decades, and students can mine this research for questions to pose of historical material as well.

Almost any content area in journalism and media studies can be used to introduce diversity perspectives, as specific subjects within the course, as examples, in research assignments, through guest speakers or in video presentations. The possibilities are many. The goal is not to substitute one rigid canon for another, but to open up and expand the popular media forum that is largely responsible for enlightening the democratic society and serving as its eyes, ears and voice.

BIBLIOGRAPHY

Useful Resources

Women and Mass Communications: An International Annotated Bibliography. Compiled by John A. Lent. Westport, CT: Greenwood Press, 1991.
Women and Media Course Outlines. Compiled by Marion Marzolf for AEJMC Women's Commission, 1990, 1991. University of Michigan, Department of Communication, 2092 Frieze Building, Ann Arbor, MI 48109–1285. $10 by mail.

Writing Examples

Beasley, Maurine, and Sheila Silver. *Women in Media: A Documentary Sourcebook*. Washington, DC: Women's Institute for Freedom of the Press, 1977. Examples of women's reporting.
Ivins, Molly. *Molly Ivins Can't Say That, Can She?* New York: Random House, 1991.

Ricchiardi, Sherry, and Virginia Young. *Women on Deadline: A Collection of America's Best*. Ames: Iowa State University Press, 1991.

Rivers, Caryl. *More Joy than Rage: Crossing Generations with the New Feminism*. Hanover, NH: University Press of New England, 1991. Collected columns.

History

Belford, Barbara. *Brilliant Bylines: A Bibliographical Anthology of Notable Newspaperwomen in America*. New York: Columbia University Press, 1986.

Bennion, Sherilyn Cox. *Equal to the Occasion: Women Editors of the Nineteenth-Century West*. Reno: University of Nevada Press, 1991.

Edwards, Julia. *Women of the World: The Great Foreign Correspondents*. Boston: Houghton Mifflin, 1988.

Elwood-Akers, Virginia. *Women War Correspondents in the Vietnam War, 1961–1975*. Metuchen, NJ: Scarecrow Press, 1988.

Hudak, Leona. *Early American Women Printers and Publishers, 1639–1820*. Metuchen, NJ: Scarecrow Press, 1978.

Marzolf, Marion. *Up from the Footnote: A History of Women Journalists*. New York: Hastings House, 1977.

Mills, Kay. *A Place in the News: From the Women's Pages to the Front Page*. New York: Dodd, Mead, 1988.

Penn, I. Garland. *The Afro-American Press and Its Editors, 1867–1930*. New York: Arno/New York Times, 1969.

Robertson, Nan. *The Girls in the Balcony: Women, Men, and the New York Times*. New York: Random House, 1992.

Sanders, Marlene, and Marcia Rock. *Waiting for Prime Time: The Women of Television News*. Urbana: University of Illinois Press, 1988.

Schlipp, Madelon Golden, and Sharon Murphy. *Great Women of the Press*. Carbondale: Southern Illinois University Press, 1983.

Wagner, Lilya. *Women War Correspondents in World War II*. Westport, CT: Greenwood Press, 1989.

Wilson, Clint C. II. *Black Journalists in Paradox: Historical Perspectives and Current Dilemmas*. Westport, CT: Greenwood Press, 1991.

Excellent biographies and autobiographies are available on Nellie Bly, Ida Tarbell, Ida Wells-Barnett, Marguerite Higgins, Dickey Chapelle, Dorothy Day of the *Catholic Worker*, Freda Kirchway of the *Nation*, Georgie Anne Geyer, Martha Gellhorn, Margaret Bourke-White and many other women journalists.

Numerous articles on colonial women printers and other early women journalists can be found in *Journalism History*, *Journalism Quarterly* and *Media History Digest*.

The ERIC database includes unpublished papers on women journalists presented at AEJMC conventions and other scholarly gatherings.

News Values and Content

Benedict, Helen. *Virgin or Vamp: How the Press Covers Sex Crimes*. New York: Oxford University Press, 1992.

Creedon, Pamela J., ed. *Women in Mass Communication: Challenging Gender Values.* Newbury Park, CA: Sage, 1989.

Epstein, Laurily Kier. *Women and the News.* New York: Hastings House, 1978.

New Directions for News, a 1983 study of major newspapers' coverage of six issues concerning women. Published by the Women's Studies Program and Policy Center, George Washington University, 2025 Eye St. NW, Room 212, Washington, DC 20052.

Tuchman, Gaye, ed. *Hearth and Home: Images of Women in the Mass Media.* New York: Oxford University Press, 1978.

Audiovisuals

The American Experience: Ida B. Wells portrays the experiences of this crusading African American woman editor and writer of the 19th century. Available from PBS Video, 1320 Braddock Place, Alexandria, VA 22314–1698. Telephone 1–800–424–7963.

Dorothea Lange is a 13-minute overview of the works of this outstanding photographer of the Depression. Available from Films for the Humanities and Sciences, P.O. Box 2053, Princeton, NJ 08543–2053.

Hearts and Hands is a prize-winning one-hour film that vividly chronicles the changing role of women in American society through a social history of quilting. Available from Hearts and Hands Media Arts, 372 Frederick St., San Francisco, CA 94117.

Killing Us Softly and its update, *Still Killing Us Softly,* are powerful videos on portrayals of women in advertising. Available from Cambridge Documentary Films Inc., P.O. Box 385, Cambridge, MA 02139. Telephone 617–354–3677.

Newswomen is a half-hour discussion among leading network newswomen about the role their gender plays in their careers. Available from Films for the Humanities and Sciences, P.O. Box 2053, Princeton, NJ 08543–2053.

Women Journalists on the Persian Gulf War details the work of women reporting on the Gulf War. Available from CNN video.

Rental videos of the feature films *Double Exposure,* about the life of photojournalist Margaret Bourke-White, and *Reds,* about socialist journalist Louise Bryant, also can be used.

Other feature film videos, like *The China Syndrome, Absence of Malice, Eyewitness, Switching Channels* and *Broadcast News,* can stimulate discussion of images of women journalists in popular media. Older films of interest include *Front Page Woman* (1935) with Bette Davis, *His Girl Friday* (1940) with Cary Grant and Rosalind Russell, *Meet John Doe* (1941) with Barbara Stanwyck and Gary Cooper, and *Woman of the Year* (1942) with Katharine Hepburn and Spencer Tracy.

Loren Ghiglione, *The American Journalist: Paradox of the Press* (Washington, DC: Library of Congress, 1990), includes an excellent chapter, entitled "Newswoman: Tough and Tormented," on the portrayal of women journalists in fiction, including both novels and films.

Feminist Pedagogy

Grunig, Larissa A. "Seminars: The Intersection of Pedagogy and Content in Transforming Public Relations Education." Outstanding Research Paper on Teaching, Public Relations Division, Association for Education in Journalism and Mass Communication, Minneapolis, August 1990.

Schneidewind, Nancy. "Teaching Feminist Process." *Women's Studies Quarterly* 15 (Fall/Winter 1987).

Shrewsbury, Carolyn M. "What Is Feminist Pedagogy?" *Women's Studies Quarterly* 15 (Fall/Winter 1987).

Sources for further information about the portrayal of women and minorities in media, including advertising, can be found in the bibliographies at the end of Chapter 20 and at the end of Part III and in the notes at the end of Chapter 19. Information on feminist newspapers is included in Chapter 18.

16 OTHER STEREOTYPES, OTHER SILENCES

Carolyn Martindale

Most people have been the victims of stereotypes at some point in their lives. Athletes have had to face the "dumb jock" image; members of campus fraternities and sororities have been branded with the various stigmas attached to being a Greek; Poles have been the butt of innumerable Polish jokes; even people with blonde hair have been the targets of a recent rash of "dumb blonde" jokes. Every nationality group, many age groups, every economic class, many professions and numerous other groups have been the subject of some stereotype—and nearly always the stereotype is negative.

In some ways stereotypes are useful to us. They serve as a form of mental shorthand that enables us to make sense of the overwhelming flood of information that bombards us every day. But stereotypes also are dangerous, when they lead us to leap to conclusions about people without sufficient evidence, and lead us to see what is not there.

Like everyone else, journalists are influenced by the stereotypes floating around in our society, and they carry these stereotypes with them into the newsroom. One author, speaking of stereotypes of disabled people, noted that "attitudes of men and women in the news media toward disabled people are developed by the same influences [that affect] members of the general public. The images and stereotypes of disabled people were not left at the front door of journalism school but remained to become part of the psyche of the working reporter. With the appearance of these reporters' news stories, the cycle begins again."[1]

How does one counter stereotypes? How does a faculty member or student media adviser help journalism students become aware of the stereotypes they unconsciously hold? How can students be taught to counter the effect of the stereotypes in their own journalistic work?

The first step is to help the student examine the stereotype and begin to be curious about the degree of truth it represents. The second is to help the student gain some factual knowledge about the stereotyped group, so that the student journalist will look at new information with an informed, not an ignorant, eye. It also helps if the student begins to engage in dialogue with members of the stereotyped group, to learn which issues are of concern to them and which stereotypes and labels they find most offensive, and why. Finally, the student journalist should be provided with information that will help the student acquire some respect and perhaps even appreciation of the achievements and contributions of members of that group.

For instance, just a cursory study of several articles and pamphlets about the disabled has turned up these facts:

1. Disabled people do not want to be called handicapped. Disabled means that the person has a disability; a handicap is some sort of barrier for the disabled person.[2]

2. Disabled persons resent stories portraying someone as a "supercrip" or a "sadcrip," that is, stories portraying the disabled person as heroic and undefeatable because he or she has achieved a "normal" life, or stories that evoke sympathy for the disabled person because of his or her disability.[3]

3. About 43 million Americans, or one out of every six, has some sort of disability.[4]

Various resources for sensitizing and informing journalism students about persons with disabilities are listed at the end of this chapter.

Another large group about whom prospective journalists should be educated are older Americans—one of the fastest-growing and most politically powerful segments of the U.S. population. According to Henry Cisneros, former mayor of San Antonio, for the first time in many decades the U.S. population includes more persons above the age of 60 than teenagers. Because people are living longer, he said, the population over 80 is the fastest-growing segment of society. In previous years, a man would spend an average of 3 percent of his life in retirement; by the year 2000 a man will spend an average of 30 percent of his life in retirement.[5]

Retired persons and/or older Americans have many active organizations that publish magazines, lobby for or against certain legislation, and organize elderhostels and other activities. Their guidelines for media coverage of older Americans and some of their publications are listed at the end of this chapter.

Gays and lesbians are still another group that has suffered from extremely derogatory stereotypes, many of which have seeped into news coverage of these groups, of the AIDs epidemic, and of crime news involving homosexuals. The homophobia present in American society infects even those who feel no strong biases against persons whose sexual orientation is different from their own. The bias against homosexuals is absorbed so early in this society that a commonly heard insult among juveniles and even grade-school children is calling a fellow student a "fag" or a "queer." The term, in such cases, has nothing to do with the person's supposed sexual orientation; it is a general insult, like "jerk."

Journalism educators could help students become aware of their own prejudices and those held by society, and could provide students with information that will help them view homosexuality in a more informed fashion. Sources of information are listed at the end of this chapter.

Another useful source of information is a newspaper published and distributed by the homeless in many of the nation's largest cities. While the paper does not focus on the homeless, most issues include some letters, poetry, photos, drawings and other materials by homeless persons that will help students get a clearer picture of the humanity of those persons they pass with averted eyes in our nation's large cities.

The bibliography at the end of this chapter also includes sources of information about images of Arabs and other groups who are often reduced to stereotypes and whose voices are not often heard in the media.

In addition, faculty should be aware that they themselves probably harbor some prejudices, and may unknowingly denigrate some students or make them uncomfortable by revealing their prejudices during lectures or in off-hand remarks. Faculty also need to learn how to deal effectively with students who have special needs and to remember that persons who are members of unusual groups have additional perspectives and information to bring to a class, if they are willing to share them. Articles addressing these subjects can be found in the bibliography.

A recent article on multicultural teaching by several members of the Ohio State journalism faculty suggests some general do's and don'ts to be used in covering any minority group:

DON'T:
* Lump everyone in the group together and fail to recognize the existence of differences.
* Assume unanimity of opinion among members of the group.
* Make one or two people the spokespersons for everyone in the group.
* Condescend or portray the persons as objects of pity or as though their accomplishments are atypical.
* Focus on the bizarre in coverage.
* Refer to a person's minority status when it is not relevant to the story.

   On the other hand,

DO:
* Let the persons in the group, including children, speak for themselves whenever possible.

- Focus on the person, not the situation that makes the person different.
- Use whatever term the group or the interviewee prefers for the group.
- Use as specific a term as possible for individuals, for example, a Navajo (not Native American) man, a Cuban woman, a teenager who has diabetes.
- Mainstream the group by including the viewpoint of members of the group in general stories.[6]

NOTES

1. Michael R. Smith, "Language Use Affects Coverage of People with Disabilities," *Journalism Educator* 45 (Winter 1991), 8.
2. Jeffrey Alan John, "Students with Disabilities Win Equal Education Opportunity," *Journalism Educator* 45 (Winter 1991), 13.
3. Smith, "Language Use," p. 8.
4. Clark Edwards, "Integration of Disabled Students in Classroom with New Technology," *Journalism Educator* 47 (Spring 1992), 86.
5. Henry Cisneros, address at Fourth Annual National Conference on Racial and Ethnic Relations in American Higher Education, San Antonio, June 1991.
6. Kevin R. Stoner, Felecia Jones and Pamela J. Creedon, "Addressing Cultural Issues in Journalism Classes: The 5 Ws, the H and the D, for Diversity," *Southwestern Journal of Minorities and Media* 1 (Fall/Winter 1990), 11–24. Contact the School of Mass Communications, Texas Tech University, Lubbock, TX 79409–3082.

BIBLIOGRAPHY

American Society of Newspaper Editors, Human Resources Committee. *Alternatives: Gays and Lesbians in the Newsroom.* 1990. Copies $3.95 each from ASNE Foundation, P.O. Box 17004, Washington, DC 20041.
Arab Stereotypes in America. A slide show with taped narration. American-Arab Anti-Discrimination Committee, 1731 Connecticut Ave. NW, Washington, DC 20009. Telephone 202–797–7662.
Edwards, Clark. "Integration of Disabled Students in Classroom with New Technology." *Journalism Educator* 47 (Spring 1992), 85–89.
Guidelines for Bias-Free Publishing. New York: McGraw-Hill, 1984.
Guidelines for Reporting and Writing about People with Disabilities. 3rd ed., 1990. Research and Training Center on Independent Living, University of Kansas, Lawrence, KS 66045. Telephone 913–864–4095.
Gup, T. "Identifying Homosexuals: What Are the Rules?" *Washington Journalism Review* 10 (1988), 26–34.
John, Jeffrey Alan. "Students with Disabilities Win Equal Education Opportunity." *Journalism Educator* 45 (Winter 1991), 12–16.
Johnson, Mary, and Susan Elkins, eds. *Reporting on Disability: Approaches and Issues.* Louisville, KY: Avocado Press, 1989.
Keyser, Les, and Barbara Keyser. *Hollywood and the Catholic Church: The Images of Roman Catholicism in American Movies.* Chicago: Loyola University Press, 1984.
Michalak, Laurence. *Cruel and Unusual: Negative Images of Arabs in American Popular

Culture. American-Arab Anti-Discrimination Committee, 1731 Connecticut Ave. NW, Washington, DC 20009. Telephone 202–797–7662.

Mitchell, L. R. "Beyond the SuperCrip Syndrome." *The Quill* 77 (November 1989), 18–23.

Pickens, Judy E., ed. *Without Bias: A Guidebook for Nondiscriminatory Communication*. 2nd ed. New York: John Wiley and Sons, 1982.

Profile of Older Americans, 1991. AARP Fulfillment, 601 E. St. NW, Washington, DC 20049.

Rich, C. "Don't Call Them 'Spry.' " *The Quill* 38 (February 1989), 12–13.

Rush, William L., and the League of Human Dignity. *Write with Dignity: Reporting on People with Disabilities*. 1983. Hitchcock Center, School of Journalism, 206 Avery Hall, Lincoln, NE 68588–0127.

Shaheen, Jack. "Images of Arabs on the Screen." *Extra!* Newsletter of FAIR (Fairness and Accuracy in Reporting), 1 (January/February 1988), 13.

Smith, Michael R. "Language Use Affects Coverage of People with Disabilities." *Journalism Educator* 45 (Winter 1991), 4–11.

Sommerness, Martin D. "Stereotypes and Mediated Reality: The Naming and Valuing of the Shadow of Social Control Through the Mass Media." *Southwestern Journal of Minorities and Media* 1 (Fall/Winter 1990), 32–42.

Stoner, Kevin R., Felecia Jones and Pamela J. Creedon. "Addressing Cultural Issues in Journalism Classes: The 5 Ws, the H and the D, for Diversity." *Southwestern Journal of Minorities and Media* 1 (Fall/Winter 1990), 11–24.

Struntz, Karen A., and Shari Reville. *Growing Together: An Intergenerational Sourcebook*. American Association of Retired Persons and the Elvirita Lewis Foundation, 1985. AARP, 1909 K St. NW, Washington, DC 20049.

Names of newspapers and of special groups can be found in Chapter 18.

17 USING THE BLACK PRESS AS A TEACHING TOOL

James Phillip Jeter

The Black press is an underutilized source of material for teaching. This chapter discusses the difficulties one encounters in, and the purposes that can be achieved by, incorporating material from the Black press into journalism and mass communications courses.

DIFFICULTIES

The major obstacle to using the Black press as classroom source material is many people's belief that the Black press is an anachronism. Media scholars Fink and Wolseley, to cite two examples, predict a dire future for Black newspapers.[1] Myriad reasons are given for the decline of the Black press:

Increased coverage of the Black community by general circulation newspapers;

Poor quality of the product because of undercapitalization (which has staffing and production implications);

Decline in readership; and

Development of alternative advertising vehicles for the Black community.

These phenomena notwithstanding, one must remember that the Black press continues to publish a product that is still needed and is available on a weekly basis. The credo of *Freedom's Journal*, the first Black newspaper published in the United States, in 1827, remains valid: "We wish to plead our own cause. Too long have others spoken for us."[2]

The imbalance in the power relationship between Blacks and Whites in the United States creates the need for the Black press. American history and practices of the general circulation media have created a need and a marketing niche that the Black press fills.

If one stops to think about it, the Black press has not really been eclipsed by other Black-owned media. Many Black-owned/oriented radio stations provide little local news. Many of these stations are jukeboxes, imparting little in the way of local news, perspective or opinion. Broadcast stations produce fleeting information that is literally gone with the wind. Black Entertainment Television—the only national Black television programming service—is not widely available in the many urban areas not served by cable. Few television stations are Black-owned.

Since 1827 the Black press has performed a news and information function that cannot be totally dismissed. In today's media environment, the Black press may be viewed as the weekly of this community. Virtually every Black community of size has a Black newspaper.

The function and state of the Black press may be examined via several methods, as indicated in the following sample class assignments:

1. Have students review four consecutive issues of a Black newspaper and, using Wolseley (pp. 371–386), write a 750–1,000-word critique of the publication.
2. Compare the current version of the Pittsburgh *Courier*, the Norfolk *Journal and Guide*, the New York *Amsterdam News*, the Chicago *Defender* or the Baltimore *Afro-American* with an edition of that paper published between 1942 and 1945, when Black press circulation was at its highest. (Addresses of these papers can be found at the end of this chapter.)
3. Compare the local Black paper to one of the better-written/edited Black newspapers (e.g., the Winston-Salem *Chronicle*).

An instructor's approach will likely depend on his or her personal view of the Black press. Tripp identified five schools of Black press interpretation:

Romantic—the Black press as the effort of honest, noble intellectuals fighting the good fight.

Developmental—the Black press as an instrument for race progress.

Consensus—a press critical of society's treatment of Blacks but supportive of America.

Cultural—the Black press as the arbiter of the role of Blacks in American society.

Militant—the Black press as an instrument of political protest and societal reform.[3]

PURPOSES

In terms of teaching, faculty can use the Black press for historical purposes and for discussion of current events, keeping in mind that Black papers can provide *a* (not *the*) barometer of Black opinion on an issue.

Many of today's college students have little sense of history. Instructors must remember that many students are under age 20 and might view a current phenomenon as unique when it really is a variation on an old theme. This is true for many of the media accomplishments of Blacks in the first three-fourths of the 20th century.

For example, when students start talking about the 1991 rash of Black films, they could be exposed to a biography and the work of Black filmmaker Oscar Micheaux, who made about 30 films, including the highly regarded *Body and Soul*, between 1919 and 1948. This could lead to a discussion of Micheaux as a pioneer, his business acumen and the temerity required to achieve what he did when he did.

Students could be assigned to research and write bios/obits on Black publishers and journalists like John Sengstacke, Robert Vann or Civil War correspondent Thomas Morris Chester. Special attention to issues of the Black press during February (Black History Month) can turn up a variety of teaching material that can be used throughout the year.

The Black press is a source of material that can be used to:

Break or challenge stereotypes;

Demonstrate the diversity of Black opinion;

Provide additional perspective on local issues and commentary;

Provide alternative points of view on national issues and controversial figures; and

Compare media coverage of news stories.

BREAKING OR CHALLENGING STEREOTYPES

One of the classic criticisms of the mass circulation media's portrayal of Blacks is that they depict Blacks as less a part of American society than they are and imply that their accomplishments or problems are Black and not American. The general circulation media imply that crime, substance abuse and teenage pregnancy, to cite three examples, are peculiarly Black problems. Columnists whose work appears in the Black press frequently provide a more accurate picture by presenting facts that are often neglected by the mainstream press.

Sample class assignment: Choose a column (or story) from the Black press that contains statistical data. Before giving the column to students, ask them what they think the statistics related to the issue are. After letting them read the column, lead a discussion on the discrepancies between their perception and the column data. For example, ask students what they think is the percentage of criminals or persons accused of crimes who are Black. Examine a general circulation newspaper for a week and note the crime stories accompanied by photos or descriptions of the accused. Then give the students, or ask them to find, the Department of Justice statistics on the percentage of Blacks actually incarcerated. Discuss the differences between their expectations and what they found.

SHOWING THAT BLACK OPINION IS NOT MONOLITHIC

Black newspaper coverage of the nomination of Clarence Thomas as an associate justice of the Supreme Court provided a good example of the diversity of opinion in the Black community. An examination of the Black press for the period July and August 1991 would reveal columns both for and against Thomas' nomination.

The same diversity of opinion can be found in the Black press on many major issues.

SUPPLEMENTING LOCAL ISSUES COMMENTARY

An examination of a Black newspaper over time is likely to uncover a story or editorial criticizing the general circulation media for their coverage of an event. Or the study may turn up an editorial relating to an issue of interest to the Black community.

Taking issue with general circulation media is an example of one aspect of the Black press' role—that of speaking for elements of the Black community instead of letting Whites only speak for and interpret the Black community.

PROVIDING AN ALTERNATIVE POINT OF VIEW

Black figures such as Nation of Islam leader Louis Farrakhan and boxing promoter Don King are often the focus of negative coverage and editorials by much of the general circulation media. A regular reading of the Black press will reveal an additional dimension of controversial Black figures and provide more opportunities for students to know about the person behind the image.

Black press reportage can also put events in perspective and context. While the mass circulation media gave extensive coverage to the violent incidents surrounding the opening of the 1991 Black film *Boyz 'N' the Hood*, the Black press remarked on how little coverage these media give to violence at heavy metal concerts. Also, the Black press has always provided commentary on all branches of the government.

Sample class activities: Pick an editorial and/or column on the same subject from the Black press and a general circulation newspaper. Have the students compare or, as the instructor, take note of the position taken and the facts used to support that position. Other elements of the comparison could include an assessment of the quality of the editorial or column. Which one was most coherent, logical, convincing? Why?

PROVIDING COMPARATIVE COVERAGE OF THE SAME EVENT

Race is still a divisive issue in the United States. Consequently, a comparison of coverage by Black-owned and White-owned newspapers of the same story in which race is a factor will yield interesting material for discussion. The August 1991 handling by the New York *Times* and the New York *Amsterdam News* of a rape trial involving St. John's University students illustrates the differences in local newspaper coverage of a story in which race is an element. Similar differences might be observed by comparing coverage of the recent Los Angeles riots, the Mike Tyson rape trial and Marion Barry's arrest and trial.

Sample class assignment/activity: Have students read local Black and White newspaper coverage of a story or issue. Which paper do they think did the better job and covered the important points? How did the focus differ from publication to publication?

The preceding are a few of the ways the Black press can be used in journalism and mass communication education. The same assignments could be used to examine Latino, Asian American and Native American periodicals. Names and addresses of such newspapers are provided at the end of Chapter 18.

NOTES

1. Conrad Fink, *Inside the Media* (White Plains, NY: Longman, 1990), pp. 255–262, and Roland E. Wolseley, *The Black Press, U.S.A.*, 2nd ed. (Ames: Iowa State University Press, 1990).

2. "To Our Patrons," *Freedom's Journal*, 16 March 1827, p. 1.

3. Bernell Tripp, in W. D. Sloan, *Perspectives on Mass Communication History* (Hillsdale, NJ: Lawrence E. Erlbaum, 1991), pp. 172–185.

SELECTED BLACK NEWSPAPERS

Atlanta *Daily World*. 145 Auburn Ave., NE, Atlanta, GA 30335. Established 1928.
Baltimore *Afro-American*. P.O. Box 1857, Baltimore, MD 21201. Established 1892.
Chicago *Daily Defender*. 2400 S. Michigan, Suite 308, Chicago, IL 60616. Established 1905.
City Sun. P.O. Box 560, Brooklyn, NY 11201. Established 1984.
Journal and Guide. P.O. Box 289, Norfolk, VA 23501. Established 1900.
Los Angeles *Sentinel*. 1112 East 43rd St., Los Angeles, CA 90011. Established 1933.
New Pittsburgh Courier. 315 E. Carson St., Pittsburgh, PA 15219. Established 1905.
New York *Amsterdam News*. 2340 Frederick Douglass Blvd., New York, NY 10027. Established 1909.
Winston-Salem *Chronicle*. P.O. Box 3154, Winston-Salem, NC 27102. Established 1974.

All the papers except the *Sun* and the *Chronicle* are available on microfilm.

18 USING OTHER SPECIAL NEWSPAPERS IN TEACHING

Carolyn Martindale

Many of the benefits of using the African American press in teaching journalism also can be obtained by using the English-language versions of the newspapers of other cultural groups as well, although the history and growth patterns of these media are different from those of the Black press. Besides using the assignments suggested in the previous chapter with Black newspapers, faculty also could use many of these same ideas with Latino, Asian American and Native American newspapers.

For instance, students could be asked to discover what facts and viewpoints are omitted from mainstream news coverage of U.S. attempts to prevent Mexicans from entering this country, what the Japanese American press says about the U.S. response to the business competition between the United States and Japan, and what mainstream media fail to tell readers about land rights controversies involving specific Native American groups.

The idea could be further broadened by using some of these assignment ideas with feminist newspapers, papers serving the disabled, the gay and lesbian press, and newspapers of other special groups. Students could be asked to find feminist newspapers' coverage of the 1992 Tailhook sexual harassment scandal involving Navy personnel, or gay press coverage of the U.S. armed forces' policy on homosexual persons in their ranks, or what newspapers for the disabled say about enforcement of the new Americans with Disabilities Act.

In all cases, examination of newspapers of groups different from their own can provide students with a variety of benefits, including new information, increased understanding of other groups and enlarged perspectives about important contemporary issues.

Assignments for study of such newspapers are greatly facilitated if the journalism program or school has subscriptions to some of these newspapers. In order to make obtaining such subscriptions easier, the following list of newspapers has been compiled from the *Standard Periodical Directory*, 15th ed. (New York: Oxbridge Communications, 1992), and *Gale Directory of Publications and Broadcast Media* (formerly *Ayer*), 124th ed. (Detroit: Gale Research, 1992). Their listing here is not an endorsement of the papers; instead, it provides a sampling to make journalism faculty aware of the variety and locations of such specialty papers so that they can obtain some of them for their students.

LATINO NEWSPAPERS

Cambio! Box 33904, Phoenix, AZ 85067. Telephone 602–395–9111.

El Diario-La Prensa. 143 Varick St., New York, NY 10013. Telephone 212–807–4600.

El Hispano. Chavez Publications, 928 2nd St., 300, Sacramento, CA 95814–2201. Telephone 916–442–0267.

El Mundo. Alameda Publishing Corp., 630 20th St., Box 1350, Oakland, CA 94612. Telephone 415–763–1120.

La Prensa. 301 S. Frio, Suite 102, San Antonio, TX 78207. Telephone 512–270–4590. Headquarters in 1992 of National Association of Hispanic Publications.

Milwaukee Spanish Journal. 238 W. Wisconsin Ave., Suite 306, Milwaukee, WI 53203. Telephone 414–271–5683.

Mundo Hispanico. 1929 Piedmont Circle, Atlanta, GA 30324–0808. Telephone 404–881–0441.

Vista magazine. Horizon, 999 Ponce de Leon, Suite 600, Coral Gables, FL 33134. Telephone 305–442–2462.

ASIAN AMERICAN NEWSPAPERS

Chicago Shimpo. (Japanese.) 4670 N. Manor Ave., Chicago, IL 60625. Telephone 312–478–6170.

Chinese American Progress. Chinese American Civic Council, 2249 Wentworth Ave., 2nd Floor, Chicago, IL 60616–2011. Telephone 312–225–0234.

Hawaii Hochi. (Japanese.) P.O. Box 17429, Honolulu, HI 96817–0429.

Mabuhay Republic. Philippine Service Co., 833 Market St., Room 502, San Francisco, CA 94103–1824.

Pamir Magazine. Chinese-American Culture Association, 8122 Mayfield Rd., Box 8, Chesterland, OH 44026. Telephone 216–729–9937.

Sampan Newspaper. Chinese-American Civic Association, 90 Tyler St., Boston, MA 02111. Telephone 617–426–9492.

NATIVE AMERICAN NEWSPAPERS

Akwesasne Notes. Mohawk Nation, Rooseveltown, NY 13683. Telephone 518–358–9531.

The Eagle: New England's American Indian Journal. Eagle Wing Press, P.O. Box 579MO, Naugatuck, CT 06770. Telephone 203–274–7853.

Indian Country Today, formerly the *Lakota Times.* P.O. Box 2180, Rapid City, SD 57709. Telephone 605–341–0011.

Navajo Times. P.O. Box 310, Window Rock, AZ 86515–0310. Telephone 602–871–6641.

News from Indian Country. Rt. 2, Box 2900-A, Hayward, WI 54843. Telephone 715–634–5226.

FEMINIST NEWSPAPERS

Off Our Backs: A Woman's Newsjournal. 2423 18th St. NW, Washington, DC 20009.

Sojourner: The Women's Forum. 42 Seaverns Ave., Boston, MA 02130.

NEWSPAPERS OF SPECIAL GROUPS

AARP (American Association of Retired Persons) *Bulletin.* AARP Fulfillment, 601 E St. NW, Washington, DC 20049.

The Disability Rag. Avocado Press, P.O. Box 145, Louisville, KY 40201. Telephone 502–459–5343.

Gay Community News. Bromfield St. Educational Foundation, 62 Berkeley St., Boston, MA 02116–6215. Telephone 617–426–4469.

Jewish Week. 1457 Broadway, New York, NY 10036–7395. Telephone 212–921–7822.

Street News. 714 Ninth Ave., Suite 511, New York, NY 10019. A newspaper sold by the homeless.

Windy City Times. Sentury Publications Inc., 970 W. Montana, Chicago, IL 60614. A newspaper for gay men.

19 MASS COMMUNICATION AND ETHNIC MINORITY GROUPS: AN OVERVIEW COURSE

Federico A. Subervi-Vélez

The national and international dynamics associated with ethnic minority groups are becoming increasingly evident and complex. These changes can be observed in activities ranging from revived ethnic pride and celebrations to ethnic and racial strife and conflicts.

At the same time, the United States and the world are becoming ever more interlinked in commerce and all forms of communication. At this writing, the United States, Mexico and Canada, countries of many immigrants and diverse social and ethnic groups, have just negotiated an International Free Trade Agreement that will impact heavily on both business and communication. Europe, with many of its nations composed of diverse ethnic groups and receiving new immigrants, is also striving for unified regional markets and more dynamic international relations. On the other side of the world, Pacific Rim countries are seeking new avenues of commerce and communication to expand.

Given these realities, professionals in almost every field should learn more about selected ethnic groups in their history, politics, culture, economic development and market characteristics. Studying ethnic minority groups, especially from a communication perspective, is particularly important for students whose careers will require reporting about, and working with or for, people of diverse ethnic backgrounds. Radio, television or film producers, journalists, advertising and public relations experts, teachers, professors, counselors, or just media consumers in general should learn how to better understand, communicate with and relate to various ethnic communities in our changing nation and world.

This chapter presents an overview of a course designed to help students learn some of the fundamental issues related to ethnic minority groups in the United States from a mass communication perspective. Chances are that many students may not have had any formal exposure to information about diverse ethnic groups, nor will they be aware of the communication dimensions of ethnic America. The objective of this class is to analyze "ethnicity" from the point of view of the field of communication.

To accomplish that goal, the course is divided into five broad components: (1) the United States as a multiethnic country; (2) portrayals of ethnic minority groups in U.S. mass media; (3) social and psychological effects of the portrayals of ethnic groups in the media; (4) trends and characteristics of the employment of ethnic minority groups in various communication industries; and (5) brief history and current status of the ethnic-oriented mass media in the United States.

In the pages that follow, highlights of these five components are explained. Each component is individually important and should be included every time the course is taught. However, the specific structure of the course is subject to modifications which best suit the instructor's goals and the students' needs.[1] Thus, while a number of topics and readings are recommended, and a general outline for a 16-week course is provided, a specific syllabus with reading assignments is not part of this chapter. The reader should also note that this course is not a general multicultural and gender class. It is specifically designed to help students learn about mass communication issues pertaining primarily to the four major ethnic minority groups in the United States: African, Hispanic/Latino, Asian and Native American.

THE UNITED STATES AS A MULTIETHNIC COUNTRY: BASIC FACTS AND CONCEPTS

To teach some of the basic facts and concepts within the context of communication, the class can begin with a week or two of lectures on four issues: (1) the ethnic diversity of the class; (2) the ethnic diversity of the United States; (3) basic terms and concepts; and (4) the political economy of ethnic diversity.

Ethnic Diversity of the Class

One approach to help students get to know each other and break the ice for the new semester is to use one of the first class sessions to talk informally about the students' (and the professor's) own ethnic heritage and diversity. To promote this discussion, an in-class survey is conducted in which students indicate their place of birth and the country of origin of their parents and grandparents. Respondents are also asked to write any names or ethnic labels that they themselves use and those they like (or don't like) other people to use to refer to their ethnic background. The information gathered from this survey is promptly coded and summarized (by volunteer students, a teaching assistant or the instructor) for discussion, preferably during the second lecture, when students are soon made aware of the rich ethnic heritage and diversity of their immediate class environment. During this session, students can be prompted to share anecdotes about their family histories in the United States.

The challenge of this type of class activity in a communication course is to begin asking students about the images they may have about the countries and people represented by the ethnic mosaic of the class members. The problem of stereotypes and the possible role of media in disseminating such stereotypes may easily surface during such discussions. During this discussion the issue of ethnic names and labels can be brought forth so as to (re)sensitize students to the terms that would best be used (or not used), at least in the class.

An interesting aspect of this exercise is the debates that arise regarding the terms Hispanic versus Latino versus Chicano, and the terms African American versus Afro-American versus Black. Often no strong consensus emerges for any one of these terms, as an equal number of students may prefer and dislike the same term, for example, Chicano, Hispanic, Black. The challenge that is then posed to the communication student is to observe how the various ethnic stereotypes, names and labels are used in the media to which they are exposed. Those observations can then be used for subsequent discussions of positive and/or negative media images and labels of ethnic groups in general and ethnic minority groups in particular.

Ethnic Diversity of the United States

After those first impressions, the class can turn to discussions of the ethnic diversity of the United States as a whole. An aid for illustrating the breadth of this phenomenon is the table of contents of the *Harvard Encyclopedia of American Ethnic Groups*, which lists groups ranging from Acadians to Zoroastrians.[2] For discussing the present-day diversity of the United States, one of the best sources of information is the U.S. Bureau of the Census and the updated population figures regularly published by this agency. In presenting national and state demographics about the major U.S. ethnic minority groups (African, Hispanic/Latino, Asian and Native Americans), at least four sets of figures can be used. These assist students in understanding not only the issue of diversity but also how in numerous locations the traditional ethnic "minorities" are actually numerical *majorities*.

One useful set of figures is the percent of "U.S. population, by race and Hispanic origin: 1970 to 1990."[3] This figure shows the percentage shift of the five major groupings utilized by the Census: "White," "Black," "American Indian, Eskimo or Aleut," "Asian or Pacific Islander" and "Hispanic origin (of any race)." A distinctive feature of this figure is that for the nation as a whole, Whites are the absolute majority (80.3 percent in 1990).

Yet the second figure, "Percent change in population, by race and Hispanic origin for the United States: 1960 to 1990," illuminates the fact that the rate of growth of the White population has held at 6 percent over the last 10 years, whereas during the same period the Asian population has grown over 100 percent and the Hispanic population has grown over 50 percent. Between 1980 to 1990, the Black population grew 13.2 percent.

The third set of figures illustrates the ethnic diversity of selected states having the largest number and the largest proportions of each of these four groups. Those figures also illustrate the numerical minority status of all groups in all states except Hawaii, where Asians and Pacific Islanders constitute 61 percent of the population—the numerical majority. However, the figures also demonstrate the significant proportion that Blacks constitute in the District of Columbia (66 percent), Mississippi (36 percent) and Louisiana (31 percent), and that Hispanics constitute in New Mexico (38 percent), California (25 percent) and Texas (25 percent). Similar data are discussed regarding Native Americans and Asians.

A fourth set of figures relates to selected cities (e.g., Miami, Selma, Brownsville, Oxnard, Honolulu) where Whites are a numerical minority.

These demographic realities are new, surprising and very revealing to most students. Students are usually amazed to learn that over one-fifth of the populations of both Santa Barbara and Austin are Hispanic. Such demographics are made even more relevant to the students when they are required, as an assignment, to turn in statistics summarizing the ethnic populations of three to five cities where they would like to work upon graduation. For some students, the search for the figures can be a challenge as well as their first venture into the library section holding the numerous reports of the U.S. Bureau of the Census.

To connect these demographic lessons with the field of communication, the introductory chapter of *Minorities and Media* by Wilson and Gutiérrez is recommended, as are the first two chapters of *The White Press and Black America*, Martindale's 1986 book.[4] A fundamental question raised for continued discussion throughout the semester is "How are the major ethnic groups presented and employed in the national entertainment and news media?" Also, "How are the groups reacting to their treatment in the media?"

Terms and Concepts

As with any other course, numerous terms and concepts require some standard definitions. A few that should be discussed are ethnic group, degree of ethnicity, assimilation, acculturation, pluralism, minority/majority and stereotype.

For the purposes of this class, an ethnic group is defined, according to one essay in the *Harvard Encyclopedia of American Ethnic Groups*, as "people who are generally recognized by themselves and/or by others as a distinct subset of the population with such recognition accruing on the basis of some combination of three factors or criteria."[5] The three major factors are race, region, and culture, each of which is explained in detail in the encyclopedia. For the introductory communication lecture, this term and its criteria serve as a common ground for understanding that labels for some ethnic groups (e.g., Blacks, Whites) are racially based, while labels for other groups (e.g., Puerto Ricans, Asians) are regionally based. Still other ethnic group labels stem from particular cultural criteria, such as religion and related customs for Muslims and Jews. Moreover, it is also noted that groups are classified according to combinations of these criteria (e.g., Black Muslim), some of which can be quite complex, defying single labels (e.g., a Black Spanish-speaking Puerto Rican Jew from New York). Again, the table of contents of the *Harvard Encyclopedia* can be quite valuable for this lecture.[6]

Special attention is also given to various meanings of minority and majority. The focus here is the difference between population sizes and the controls over political and economic resources (i.e., power). Wilson and Gutiérrez review these terms and other correlates such as dominant and subordinate groups. The implications of all these terms are usually readily understood by most students, especially upon discussion of the current demographics of selected locations as alluded to above.

Another major concept that requires some discussion at the beginning of the class is stereotype. While the term is commonly used to refer to a simplified (usually negative) characterization of a particular group of people, students are guided into understanding that there are various ways to define the term and interpret its implications for analyzing ethnic minority groups. A formidable communication-oriented essay on this subject that should be required reading was published in 1990 by Charles Ramírez Berg, who discussed stereotyping from sociological, psychological, psychoanalytical and ideological perspectives.[7]

The student needs to understand important yet intricate terms such as ethnic group, degree of ethnicity, assimilation/pluralism, minority/majority and stereotype. Within the communication context, these terms and related concepts have been used inconsistently, not only in everyday media content, but also in communication research.[8]

Political Economy of Ethnic Diversity

The last lesson on basic facts could be an overview of the historical reasons for the presence in the United States of each of the major groups. In broad sketches, students are reminded (or learn for the first time) about the primary political and/or economic factors that caused the immigration of the ethnic groups during various time periods.[9] Additional explanations of the history and current status of the groups can be discussed as part of the first lecture related to each group's treatment in the media. While a communication class cannot delve deeply into the history of each ethnic group, students are provided with selected references for further inquiries into past and present issues related to the ethnic dynamics of this country. And, again, students are challenged to consider how media have historically treated the groups.

PORTRAYALS OF ETHNIC MINORITY GROUPS IN
U.S. MASS MEDIA

The second major component of the course focuses on portrayals of the ethnic minorities. The first readings on the subject of ethnic images in various media can be gathered from the introductory chapters in *The Kaleidoscopic Lens* by R. Miller, *Minorities and Media* by Wilson and Gutiérrez, and *Split Image* by Dates and Barlow.[10] After the introductory readings, students can focus on how a particular group has been treated in various media across different time periods.

For example, lessons can start with the portrayals of African Americans[11] in film over the years from the turn of the century to the present.[12] Two formidable resources for the African American component of the course are *Toms, Coons, Mulattoes, Mammies and Bucks* by Bogle and "The Dark Spot on the Kaleidoscope" by Cripps.[13] One of the advantages of the Cripps essay is that it discusses political and economic factors that influenced the changing images of Blacks in film. These and other relevant readings can be supplemented with the showing of film clips that illustrate the various predominant stereotypes and how these have changed throughout the years.[14] In discussing the changing images of African Americans, mention could also be made of portrayals of Black Africa and Africans. While lectures and readings on the early images may seem distant and of little relevance to the typical student, attention and involvement in class discussion are certain to increase when contemporary films are studied.

Following the portrayals of African Americans in film, the class can turn to the images on television. Aside from the overview in *Minorities and Media*, Dates' chapters on this subject in *Split Image* provide a comprehensive and updated synthesis on the topic.[15] That reading can be supplemented with a few others (many of which are cited in the chapters by Dates) that analyze the images of African Americans in specific shows or in various shows in a particular season or across many years.[16] A recent program that should be an indispensable audiovisual aid related to Blacks in entertainment television is filmmaker Marlon Riggs' documentary *Color Adjustment*, which was broadcast as a PBS *Point of View* special program in June 1991.[17] Among the attributes of this documentary are the presentation of various clips from old television shows along with discussions of political, economic and cultural factors that influenced the portrayals and participation of African Americans in this medium.

News portrayals of African Americans are not emphasized in *Color Adjustment*, but this issue should also be given some attention under the rubric of television portrayals. Readings on news portrayals are easily found in the aforementioned sources and in occasional journal articles on this subject. Since students have had heavy exposure to television for most of their lives, it is common for them to engage in numerous discussions about their own impressions and evaluations of African American portrayals on TV.

The next aspect of African American portrayals to be studied can be the treatment in print media news. The most systematic assessment of this subject is Martindale's previously cited work, *The White Press and Black America*. While the whole book may be too long and detailed to become required reading for an introductory overview course, it provides numerous examples of the problem of portrayals of African Americans in newspapers—examples that complement the Wilson and Gutiérrez summaries in *Minorities and Media* and Shaw's most recent analysis of the subject.[18]

Depending on the students' interest and the time available for studying African American portrayals in media, the class could continue by studying advertising in print and on television. *Split Image* deals with each of these subjects as well as with African American participation in the radio and music industries.[19]

Next the class can turn to the history and problems of the portrayals of Hispanics in the various media. While no book such as *Split Image* has been published on Latinos, numerous readings on the subject are available in the compendiums this author and others have put together in the *Hispanic American Almanac* and *The Handbook of Hispanic Cultures in the United States*.[20] Those works provide summary overviews of and numerous references about Latino portrayals in print, film and television.

A similar pattern of discussions of portrayals in film, television, newspapers and advertising can be followed with respect to Asian Americans and Native Americans (and any other ethnic minority of interest or relevance to the instructor or students). Among the indispensable readings about images of these groups are "The Yellow Menace" by Oehling, Murphy and Murphy's *Let My People Know*, Bataille and Silet's "The Entertaining Anachronism," and O'Conner's *The Hollywood Indian*.[21] Also, the best resources for examples of portrayals of any ethnic minority group are current films, the season's television shows, and printed material from newspapers, magazines and other popular culture.

Throughout the lectures on portrayals of ethnic minority groups in the media, three critical elements merit emphasis. First, too few ethnic minority groups are represented in media relative to their actual participation in society, and the few that are included are primarily shown in stereotypical or negative roles. Second, different historical periods have direct and indirect effects on the production of the stereotypes and other images of minority groups within the United States. In other words, the predominantly negative images are usually not isolated or casual; instead they are a product of political, economic and/or social factors of the times. The third critical element to emphasize in discussions of this subject is the commonalities and differences of treatment of the various minority groups. There are many parallels in the typically inferior roles given to many ethnic groups. On the other hand, there are many differences, such as the relative improvement of roles for African Americans on television—a situation yet to be enjoyed by any other ethnic minority group.

SOCIAL AND PSYCHOLOGICAL EFFECT OF PORTRAYALS OF MINORITIES

The next major component of the course is the effects that such portrayals have on members of both majority and minority members of society. Some of the recommended readings for this topic are Chapter 2 of Wilson and Gutiérrez's *Minorities and Media*, and again the first two chapters of Martindale's *The White Press and Black America*. Furthermore, the introduction to Berry and Mitchell-Kernan's *Television and the Socialization of the Minority Child*, as well as a few other chapters, is among the very few readings that directly deal with the effects of television on minority children.[22]

Throughout these readings it becomes obvious that the limited and mostly negative portrayals of ethnic minority groups have detrimental consequences not only for ethnic minority adults and children, but also for members of the majority, or Anglo, society. Under selected conditions, self-esteem and self-concepts of all groups are potentially influenced by the enduring images, especially when these are repeated constantly in dramatic form. And when in real life people lack direct exposure to a variety of "others" not like themselves, media portrayals (or lack thereof) of a particular group may become the main guide for helping predetermine many of the perceptions and social relations that prevail about those others.

EMPLOYMENT OF MINORITIES IN COMMUNICATION INDUSTRIES

By the time the course reaches this topic, it may have already become obvious that one reason for the negative portrayals of minorities in mainstream media is the lack of participation and control that members of such groups have in the decision-making processes of the various communication industries. Passages and chapters of the books alluded to above (e.g., *Minorities and Media*, *Split Image*) make reference to this problem. The reason for giving individual attention to this issue as a separate component of the course is to indicate in at least one or two lectures past and current statistics on ethnic minority hiring and participation in selected industries. Students can also be taught about some of the legal battles that have been and are being fought on the civil rights and affirmative action fronts of the communication industries.

Among the classic studies on the status of minority participation in television and the film industry are the reports published by the U.S. Commission on Civil Rights in the late 1970s.[23] Also useful are the late 1980s reports by Babbie on employment practices by the Writers Guild of America[24] and the newspaper employment statistics compiled by the Newspaper Association of America.[25] A related issue for class discussion is the question of whether minority participation in media decisions positively affects the media product.

HISTORY AND CURRENT STATUS OF ETHNIC-ORIENTED MEDIA

It is invaluable to help students learn about the growing ethnic-oriented media industries in the United States. The term *ethnic-oriented* is used because some of those media are owned or controlled by White Anglo males. Such is the case, for example, with the Spanish-language television networks in the United States—Univisión and Telemundo—presently owned by Hallmark Corporation and by Reliance Corporation, respectively.[26] Also, a variety of media specifically oriented toward some ethnic groups are produced in English. Thus it is inappropriate to refer to *all* media directed at Latinos in this country as Spanish-language media.

In this component three topics should be covered. The first topic should be facts about the foundation of ethnic-oriented newspapers, including the common and distinct sociopolitical factors that led to their establishment in the 1800s. For the introductory level of analysis, Chapter 8 of *Minorities and Media* covers this topic with respect to the Black, Hispanic, Asian and Native American presses. For students more interested in the history of these publications, extra readings can be assigned from Dates and Barlow's *Split Image*, Murphy and Murphy's *Let My People Know*, S. Miller's *The Ethnic Press in the United States*, and Wolseley's *The Black Press U.S.A..*[27]

The second topic should be information about the quantity, content, audiences and ownership status of the major national and regional ethnic-oriented media. A compendium of Hispanic-oriented media can be found in the aforementioned work by this author and collaborators. *Split Image* provides partial information about African American–oriented media. No similar compendiums are now in print about modern-day Asian American– and Native American–oriented media, but various resources are available that can assist in finding out about the variety of media for these groups at the national and local levels.[28]

Four key goals of this second topic are a basic understanding about (1) the diversity of the ethnic-oriented media in many parts of the United States and in the students' own communities; (2) the general content and/or functions of such media (i.e., entertainment, information, promoting cultural connections); (3) the particular audiences of the various stations, programs and/or publications; and (4) the major owners of some of these media (i.e., whether the media are owned and operated by ethnic minorities or by Anglo businesses). In an introductory course of this type, most of these points will be covered for one or two of the major media for each group. Yet the discussion should help students understand the status of such media and their potential value for a wide range of ethnic minority groups and their communities.

Depending on the time and resources available, a special section of this course component could be dedicated to the ethnic-oriented advertising and marketing companies. *Advertising Age* and *Adweek* magazines regularly publish information on ethnic issues in these businesses, especially about the Black, Hispanic and growing Asian markets in the United States.

For a typical 16-week semester, the material presented above can be outlined as follows:

Weeks 1–2	The United States as a multiethnic country: basic facts and concepts
Weeks 3–4	Media portrayals of African Americans
Weeks 5–6	Media portrayals of Hispanics/Latinos
Weeks 7–8	Media portrayals of Asian Americans, Native Americans
Week 9	Review, midterm exam
Week 10	Social and psychological effects of the portrayals of ethnic groups in the media
Week 11	Employment of ethnic minority groups in various communication industries
Weeks 12–14	Ethnic-oriented media
Week 15	Student presentations of projects, term papers
Week 16	Review, preparation for final

In a class of this type, especially if enrollment exceeds 25 students, significant benefits can be drawn from incorporating supplemental (but required) discussion sessions led by teaching assistants. Such sessions could meet once a week and would give students more informal opportunities for in-depth discussion of the readings, lectures and regular assignments. During these sessions, students will also be able to spend more time viewing and analyzing audiovisual materials that cannot be presented in the large lectures. Given the controversial nature of some of the subject matter of this course, the opportunity for expression of different viewpoints in a small group is pedagogically quite valuable.

CONCLUSION

Today, so-called minority journalism workshops are held on various campuses across the country and are primarily geared to prepare minority students to work in mainstream media. Little or no attention has been given to preparation of minority (or even majority) students for work in ethnic-oriented media. Yet each of those ethnic media regularly needs managers, editors, journalists and advertising executives who know the characteristics of the enterprise and can assist in their growth. Specialty curricula are particularly needed for the non–English-language media, which during the last decade have had the most notable growth. For example, Spanish-language radio has been among the most profitable broadcast media in the last few years.[29]

In addition, mainstream media and communication offices of public and private agencies also need specialists in ethnic minority populations. Advertising, marketing and survey research companies, public relations departments, newspapers, magazines, and radio and television stations are constantly seeking personnel who know how to reach, work with and expand opportunities related to ethnic minority groups. Even the Democratic and Republican parties have established branches to deal with such groups on a regular basis and particularly during elections.

It is hoped that the course outlined in these pages and other recommendations presented in this book can assist students and faculty in meeting these needs and facing the growing challenges and opportunities associated with ethnic minority groups.

NOTES

The suggestions presented in these pages are based on the author's experience in the last 10 years in teaching courses similar to the one outlined here at the University of California at Santa Barbara and at the University of Texas at Austin. Special thanks go to Patricia Constantakis-Valdes, Diana Ríos, Lucila Vargas and Elizabeth Waiters, who, as teaching assistants for the course, helped in its development. Thanks also to research assistant Sarah Harding for technical support for this chapter.

1. Since a course like this should be tailored to the instructor's and students' needs and interests, the recommended readings listed here are kept to a minimum. But articles on many of the topics discussed in this chapter are increasingly available in academic and professional journals. Also, in spring 1988 the *Howard Journal of Communications* was launched to provide a much-needed showcase for academic communication works that focus on cultural perspectives. This journal and many others should be reviewed regularly for potential new material for the class.

2. Stephan Thernstrom, ed., *Harvard Encyclopedia of American Ethnic Groups* (Cambridge, MA: Harvard University Press, 1980). This encyclopedia is highly recommended because it provides a synopsis of each group's history in the United States

as well as various thematic essays on issues used in subsequent lectures, such as assimilation and pluralism.

3. The U.S. Bureau of the Census divides its figures by race and Hispanic origin, indicating that Hispanics can be of any race.

4. Clint Wilson II and Félix Gutiérrez, *Minorities and Media: Diversity and the End of Mass Communication* (Beverly Hills, CA: Sage, 1985); Carolyn Martindale, *The White Press and Black America* (Westport, CT: Greenwood Press, 1986).

5. Harold Abramson's essay "Assimilation and Pluralism," in *Harvard Encyclopedia of Ethnic Groups*, pp. 150–160.

6. It should be noted, however, that the table of contents does not list separately the approximately 200 tribes of American Indians. Most of these are mentioned in the text under the section on American Indians.

7. Charles Ramírez Berg, "Stereotyping in Films in General and of the Hispanic in Particular," *Howard Journal of Communications* 2 (Summer 1990), 286–300.

8. Federico A. Subervi-Vélez, "The Mass Media and Ethnic Assimilation and Pluralism," *Communication Research* 13 (January 1986), 71–96.

9. Such overviews are important because most students may have very little knowledge of the factors related to the presence in the United States of any ethnic minority group. Even through a brief lecture students are exposed to some significant differences between selected groups, particularly Hispanics and Asians. For example, it is made clear that millions of Mexian Americans did not immigrate from Mexico; instead, they became residents of the United States through American conquest of thousands of miles of Southwestern territories. Because of the political changes that followed, many of the inhabitants of those lands became foreigners in their own land even though their descendants were theoretically as much a part of America as anyone else born in the United States. Also mentioned in passing are the different histories of Cubans vis-à-vis Puerto Ricans in the United States. Some facts are discussed regarding the island's political and economic status and relation with the United States.

10. Randall Miller, *The Kaleidoscopic Lens: How Hollywood Views Ethnic Groups* (Englewood, NJ: Jerome Ozer, 1980); Wilson and Gutiérrez, *Minorities and Media*; Jannette L. Dates and William Barlow, eds., *Split Image: African Americans in the Mass Media* (Washington, DC: Howard University Press, 1990).

11. The author's decision to start with African Americans is primarily based on this group's numerical size relative to the other groups. But classes could start with any other group of preference for the instructor or students.

12. While print portrayals of ethnic groups certainly preceded any film portrayals, the audiovisual format is much more dynamic. Also, there is still a paucity of good overview works on the portrayals of African Americans in newspapers and other print media throughout this century.

13. Donald Bogle, *Toms, Coons, Mulattoes, Mammies, and Bucks: An Interpretive History of Blacks in American Films* (New York: Continuum, 1989); Thomas Cripps, "The Dark Spot on the Kaleidoscope: Black Images in American Film," in R. Miller, *Kaleidoscopic Lens*, pp. 15–35. Cripps' most recent chapter on this subject, in Dates and Barlow, *Split Image*, while more updated, may be quite difficult for undergraduate students to digest.

14. The first 35–40 minutes of *Black History: Lost, Stolen, or Strayed*, a CBS news special produced in 1968 with Bill Cosby as host and narrator, are excellent for

illustrating the early negative stereotypes of Blacks in film. Available from BFA Educational Media, a division of CBS, Inc., 2211 Michigan Ave., Santa Monica, CA 90404. Even though this program is quite old, it is still one of the better resources for such illustrations. A more recent audiovisual aid focusing on Black images in a variety of popular media is Marlon Riggs' *Ethnic Notions*. This documentary and other audiovisual productions dealing with African Americans can be ordered from California Newsreel, 149 Ninth St./420, San Francisco, CA 94103; telephone 415–621–6196.

15. See her chapters on television in Dates and Barlow, *Split Image*.

16. Two other recent publications on this topic are Carolyn Stroman, Bishetta Merritt and Paula Matabane, "Twenty Years after Kerner: The Portrayal of African Americans on Prime-Time Television," *Howard Journal of Communications* 2 (Winter 1989–90), 44–56; and Sally Steenland, *Unequal Picture: Black, Hispanic, Asian and Native American Characters on Television* (Washington, DC: National Commission on Working Women on Wider Opportunities for Women, 1989).

17. *Color Adjustment* can also be obtained from California Newsreel.

18. David Shaw, "Negative News and Little Else," Los Angeles *Times*, 11 December 1990. This was one of a series of nine articles Shaw wrote on this subject for the *Times* between 11 and 14 December 1990.

19. See also *Invisible People: Depiction of Minorities in Magazine Ads and Catalogs* (report by the City of New York Department of Consumer Affairs, 1991); and Robert Wilkes and Humberto Valencia, "Hispanics and Blacks in Television Commercials," *Journal of Advertising* 18 (1989), 19–25.

20. Federico A. Subervi-Vélez, "Media," in Nicolas Kanellos, ed. *The Hispanic American Almanac* (Detroit: Gale Research, 1993); and "Mass Communication and Hispanics," in Felix Padilla, ed., *Sociology* volume of the *Handbook of Hispanic Cultures in the United States*, N. Kanellos and C. Esteva-Fabregat, gen. eds. (Houston: Arte Publico Press, forthcoming).

21. Richard Oehling, "The Yellow Menace: Asian Images in American Film," in R. Miller, *Kadeidoscopic Lens*, pp. 182–206; James Murphy and Sharon Murphy, *Let My People Know: American Indian Journalism, 1828–1978* (Norman: University of Oklahoma Press, 1981), Chapter 1; Gretchen Bataille and Charles Silet, "The Entertaining Anachronism: Indians in American Film," in R. Miller, *Kaleidoscopic Lens*, pp. 36–53; John O'Conner, *The Hollywood Indian* (Trenton: New Jersey State Museum, 1980).

22. Gordon Berry and Claudia Mitchell-Kernan, eds., *Television and the Socialization of the Minority Child* (New York: Academic Press, 1982).

23. See, for example, United States Commission on Civil Rights, *Window Dressing on the Set: Women and Minorities in Television* (Washington, DC: USCCR, 1977); *Window Dressing on the Set: An Update* (Washington, DC: USCCR, 1979); *Behind the Scenes: Equal Employment Opportunity in the Motion Picture Industry* (Washington, DC: USCCR, 1978).

24. William Bielby and Denise Bielby, *Pay Equity and Employment Opportunities among Writers for Television and Feature Films* (Los Angeles: Writers Guild of America, West, 1987); and their *The 1989 Hollywood Writer's Report: Unequal Access, Unequal Pay* (Los Angeles: Writers Guild of America, West, 1989).

25. Every two years, the Industry Development and Diversity Department of the Newspaper Association of America (NAA) conducts and publishes a survey of mi-

nority employment in newspapers. The report can be requested from NAA at 11600 Sunrise Valley Drive, Reston, VA 22091; telephone 703–648–1000.

26. As of this writing, Hallmark has accepted a bid for $550 million to sell the Univisión network and station group to the partnership of U.S.-based investor Jerrold Perenchio, and the mega-corporations Televisa of Mexico and Venevision of Venezuela. The sale is currently under review by the Federal Communications Commission and the U.S. Department of Justice.

27. Sally Miller, *The Ethnic Press in the United States: A Historical Analysis and Handbook* (Westport, CT: Greenwood Press, 1987); Roland Wolseley, *The Black Press, U.S.A.*, 2nd ed. (Ames: Iowa State University Press, 1990).

28. For example, for information about the Native American media, two sources are the Native Communications Group (P.O. Box 8311, Lincoln, NE 68501; telephone 402–472–3522) and the Native American Public Broadcasting Consortium, Inc. (P.O. Box 83111, Lincoln, NE 68501; telephone 402–472–3522). Information about Asian American media can be requested from the Asian American Journalists Association, 1765 Sutter Street, Room 1000, San Francisco, CA 94115; telephone 415–346–2051. A recent publication on Asian Americans and media arts is Russell Leong, ed., *Moving the Image: Independent Asian Pacific American Media Arts* (Los Angeles: UCLA Asian American Studies Center and Visual Communications, Southern California Asian American Studies Center, 1992). Other resources for learning about any ethnic minority media include occasional articles and special issues of various trade magazines, especially *Variety* and *Broadcasting*. Some of the national resources on ethnic-oriented media are the annual editions of the *Editor and Publisher* and *Broadcasting Yearbook*, which, respectively, have sections on "foreign" language publications and on minority stations and "foreign" language formats and programs; *Gale Directory of Publications and Broadcast Media* (Detroit: Gale Research, 1992); and *Burrell's* Media Directories (Livingston, NJ), which have included special issues on Hispanic and Black media; a 1992 edition will combine information on both groups. For Hispanic media in particular, see the quarterly reports titled "Hispanic Media and Markets" of the *Standard Rate and Data Service*, which provides convenient updates on major Hispanic-oriented media nationwide; and the December issues of *Hispanic Business* magazine, which are dedicated to major developments in these media, including the Hispanic-oriented advertising and marketing businesses. The national offices of the various ethnic journalists', broadcasters' and publishers' associations also compile directories of their group members and media. For example, the Human Resource Development Department of the National Association of Broadcasters (1771 N Street NW, Washington, DC 20036–2891; telephone 202–429–5498) keeps updated directories of minority radio and television stations. The National Newspaper Publishers Association (529 14th St. NW, Suite 948, Washington, DC 20045; telephone 202–662–7324) has directories of the African American publications of its members, as does the National Association of Black Owned Broadcasters (1730 M Street NW, Suite 412, Washington, DC 20036; telephone 202–463–8970). For information about local ethnic-oriented media, one often-neglected resource is the yellow pages of the telephone directories.

29. See *Hispanic Business*, especially the December 1987 issues.

20 SELECTING BIAS-FREE TEXTBOOKS FOR JOURNALISM COURSES

Marilyn Kern-Foxworth

Textbooks used by journalism students are an integral part of their educational experience. The copy, illustrations and language used play a vital role in the educational process. "It has been estimated that 75 percent of a child's classwork and 90 percent of the homework focus on the textbook. From elementary through high school a child reads at least 32,000 textbook pages," according to one authority.[1] The average college student reads between 25,000 and 30,000 pages prior to graduation.

Textbooks serve an important function in the development of positive self-concept of multiethnic and female students. They are also important factors in determining perceptions that White students formulate about people of color and females. Students who study from biased textbooks are not given information about the contributions people of color and women have made to the development of the United States and to the mass media industry. Consequently, they are not properly equipped with the skills necessary to cover those audiences comprehensively.

This inadequacy is serious now, and will be increasingly important as the growth of these populations escalates. In 1990 women represented 51.3 percent of the American population.[2] African Americans, Latinos and other people of color currently represent one-fourth of the American population, and futurists project that this percentage will increase to one-third by the 21st century.

In 1968 Lionel C. Barrow, Jr., a pioneer in multicultural journalism education, requested that the Association for Education in Journalism and Mass Communication (AEJMC) membership "take immediate steps to achieve and to expand the recruitment, training and placement of minority groups and disadvantaged students in the field of mass communications."[3] The next year the AEJMC Ad Hoc Committee on Minority Education outlined four goals, one of which was the "incorporation in curricula of materials on the role of minority group members in America and their portrayal by the media."[4]

In 1988 the AEJMC Task Force on Minority Affairs commissioned a study to determine the extent to which African Americans, Asian Americans and other minorities had been incorporated into journalism and mass communications textbooks.[5] Of the small random sampling of AEJMC members who responded to the survey, all said that they sought to use textbooks that are color-blind.[6]

Omission from journalism textbooks has not been limited to people of color; women also have been ignored. During the past two decades, several organizations have become involved in changing this situation. A resolution adopted in 1980 by the International Communication Association's board of directors reaffirmed female students' right to an equal educational experience. It observed that "sexism in textbooks, even at the graduate level, the absence of women faculty members to serve as role models, exclusion of women students from the 'old boy network' of tips and good advice—these are minor issues individually, but their cumulative effect is one of 'being nibbled to death by ducks.' "[7]

A study of journalism textbooks conducted at the University of Michigan by Judy Hansen in 1973 concluded that such texts included few references to women.[8] A study conducted by Roberta Evans and Ellen Meyers noted several examples of sexism in journalism textbooks. They stated, "Textbooks that teach journalistic writing imply that men 'do' while women 'appear.' It is not surprising that reporters describe appearance more often for women than for men, since a textbook once taught them to write this lead: 'Pretty in skirts and pert in slacks—that's Mildred Miller, size 12, mezzo-soprano with the Metropolitan Opera Company.'"[9]

POSSIBLE ACTIONS

In order to offer students a multicultural education, the following suggestions are made in reference to textbooks:

1. Administrators and professors should very carefully monitor the textbooks that are selected for classes and avoid using books that do not adequately address the contributions of African Americans, Native Americans and other people of color and women.

2. Journalism educators should write to publishers whose books contain blatant omissions and biases and let them know of their concerns. In fact, this task could be turned into a classroom exercise by having students write letters to publishers. Such an activity would reinforce the concerns being voiced and would offer students an opportunity to understand why the selection of textbooks is so critical.

3. Journalism and mass communication professors should make every attempt to serve as reviewers for journalism and mass communication textbooks prior to publication to make sure contributions and issues pertinent to various racial and ethnic groups and women are fully integrated into the entire text.

4. Administrators should serve as leaders in insuring that courses are not racially and gender biased. This should be a concern of administrators at all times. (Many administrators take this issue seriously only when an accreditation visit is pending.)

5. Administrators should reward those professors who successfully integrate information about women and ALANA (African, Latino, Asian and Native American) group members into their courses.

GUIDELINES

Reacting to pressure from teachers, parents and civil rights groups, major textbook companies have published guidelines for editors, authors and others responsible for textbook selection. Journalism professors can use the following guidelines in searching for textbooks that are free of gender and racial stereotypes and other forms of bias.

1. Check the index. Examining the index will provide an immediate impression of how sensitive the author is to people of color and women. The following entries can be used as a starting point in searching through indices: female, women, feminine, women's movement, Equal Rights Amendment, Equal Rights Movement, gender, race, African American, Asian American, Latino, Hispanic, Native American, American Indian, minorities, Black American and people of color.

2. Observe how information about women and people of color is presented. Are these topics discussed in only a few chapters, thereby segregating these people's contributions from the mainstream of information in the book? Or is information about women and multiethnic groups presented throughout the text, thus reinforcing the integral nature of these groups within society?

3. Check the illustrations. The illustrations, charts and graphs used in a textbook can convey as much as the printed words do. Professors should carefully scrutinize the pictures used to supplement text. The book should have an equal balance of illustrations featuring women and men and Whites and people of color. Do the illustrations exemplify the diversity that exists in society? Do the illustrations show one race in dominant positions over those of other races? Are White males the only characters featured in most of the illustrations?

4. Check the storyline, if applicable. The storyline should not be stereotypical, but instead should reinforce the contributions of women and people of color.

5. Look at the lifestyles. It should not be implied that some lifestyles or activities are intrinsically "masculine" or "feminine" or just for Whites or various racial or ethnic groups. Women and men, Whites and other racial groups should be shown as participants in all phases of life. Women should not always be portrayed as mothers and housewives.

6. Weigh the relationships between people. Women and members of multiracial

groups should not always be shown as those who need leading. They should be shown in positions of leadership, in roles as supervisors and administrators, for example. Are persons portrayed in positions of authority almost invariably White? Do Asians, African Americans, Latinos and Native Americans in high-level positions appear only when the communication has an affirmative action message?

7. Note the heroes. Personalities and profiles of those used as examples in illustrations and copy should not be limited to White males, but should highlight women, African Americans, Latinos and other people of color who would be appropriate examples.

8. Consider the effects on a student's self-image. Karen DeCrow, past president of the National Organization for Women and a former textbook editor, stated that about 15 major textbook companies control about 90 of the textbook market for grades K through 12. Most of their books, says DeCrow, present the image of woman as helpmate, as mother, as observer of male activities. Since school attendance is compulsory in the United States, DeCrow observes, this means that every young American girl must read about herself as a passive citizen for 12 years—by law.[10]

9. Carefully scrutinize the language used to convey concepts. Is "he" the only pronoun used to illustrate examples? Is the language patronizing or condescending? Examples would be sentences like the following: "The qualified Black reporter was offered the position of assignment editor," or "A well-groomed Latino student, Bob Hernandez works as a part-time clerk," or "The articulate Asian American professor. . . . "

10. Look at the copyright date. Some publishers have become very sensitive to the inclusion of women and multiracial groups in their textbooks. If a book exhibits blatant omissions or stereotypical portrayals of women and multiethnic groups, the textbook may be outdated, and a newer edition or another textbook should be selected.[11]

Selecting a textbook for classroom use should not be taken lightly. One tremendous resource is *Guidelines for Bias-Free Publishing*, published by McGraw-Hill (available from Order Services, McGraw-Hill Book Co. Distribution Center, Princeton Road, Heightstown, NJ 08520).

Materials used to train future journalists must reflect the historical roles of all racial groups accurately and completely. Students entering the job market should be prepared to create and communicate information about and to all segments of society. All journalism and mass communication textbooks should be meticulously scrutinized, because textbooks are vital to the educational process and have the power to emphasize or ignore racial and gender pluralism.

For those who teach classes on women and people of color and the mass media, and for those who would like to supplement other courses with materials about these groups, the books listed in the bibliography at the end of this chapter will be helpful, especially on depictions of women in advertising and television.

NOTES

Some material in this chapter is reflected in the author's forthcoming book, *Aunt Jemima, Uncle Ben and Rastus: Blacks in Advertising Yesterday, Today and Tomorrow.*

1. Hillel Black, *The American School Book* (New York: William Morrow, 1967).
2. U.S. Department of the Census, Economics and Statistics Administration, *1990 Census of Population and Housing: Summary Population and Housing Characteristics, United States* (Washington, DC: U.S. Government Printing Office, 1992).
3. Edwin Emery and Joseph McKerns, "AEJMC: 75 Years in the Making: A History of Organizing for Journalism and Mass Communications," *Journalism Monographs* 104 (1987), 64–65.
4. Ibid., p. 65.
5. B. Luebke, unpublished report to the AEJMC Task Force on Minority Affairs, convention of the Association for Education in Journalism and Mass Communication, Portland, OR, 1988.
6. Marilyn Kern-Foxworth, "Ethnic Inclusiveness in Public Relations Textbooks and Reference Books," *Howard Journal of Communications* 2 (Spring 1990), 226–237.
7. Matilda Butler and William Paisley, *Women and the Mass Media: Sourcebook for Research and Action* (New York: Human Sciences Press, 1980), p. 248.
8. Judy Hansen, "Women in Journalism History Textbooks," paper presented at the Women in Journalism Seminar, University of Michigan, 1973.
9. Roberta Evans and Ellen Myers, "Consequences of Sexism in Journalism Texts," paper presented at the Women in Journalism Seminar, University of Michigan, 1973.
10. Marilyn Kern-Foxworth, "Public Relations Books Fail to Show Women in Context," *Journalism Educator* 44 (Autumn 1989), 31–36.
11. Council on Interracial Books for Children, *10 Quick Ways to Analyze Books for Racism and Sexism* (New York: Racism and Sexism Resource Center for Education, 1983).

BIBLIOGRAPHY

Baehr, Helen, and Gillian Dyer. *Boxed In: Women and Television.* New York: Methuen, 1988.
Barthel, Diane. *Putting on Appearances: Gender and Advertising.* Philadelphia: Temple University Press, 1989.
Betterton, Rosemary. *Looking On: Images of Femininity in the Visual Arts and Media.* Winchester, MA: Unwin Hyman, 1987.
Butler, Matilda, and William Paisley. *Women and the Mass Media: Sourcebook for Research and Action.* New York: Human Science Press, 1980.
Mattelart, Michele. *Women, Media and Crisis: Femininity and Disorder.* London: Comedia, 1986.
Osborn, Suzanne. *Gender Depictions in Television Advertisements: 1988.* Memphis: Suzanne Osborn.

Rush, Ramona, and Donna Allen. *Communications at the Crossroads: The Gender Gap Connection*. Norwood, NJ: Ablex, 1989.

Additional resources for bias-free teaching can be found in the bibliographies at the end of Chapters 11, 12, 13 and 14 and at the end of Part III.

21 LAYING OUT PLURALISM: LABORATORY PUBLICATIONS PRACTICE FOR THE FUTURE

Mercedes Lynn de Uriarte

The newspaper industry sits today on the cusp of change. It must find ways to enfranchise new voices, tap into a new audience pool and make its product attractive to those readers.

More than a decade ago press leaders, faced with flat or declining circulations, newsrooms that failed to reflect changing American demographics, and content that overlooked potential new readers, began to address these problems. In 1978 the American Society of Newspaper Editors (ASNE) called for minority parity in the newsroom by the year 2000.

Soon after this, ASNE began its annual newsroom census. The organization also sponsors several other activities—often in cooperation with the American Newspaper Publishers Association—including conferences, panels and consultation toward improving access to the profession and coverage. Additionally, several newspaper chains, including Gannett and Knight-Ridder, established executive incentives toward diversified newsrooms.

But today, journalism education lags behind industry demand. Its faculty is less integrated, its curriculum less focused on minority coverage needs and its recruitment and retention programs only minimally effective.

"Too many publishers and editors are running their news-editorial and business operations according to a model of society that is woefully outdated," noted David Lawrence, Jr., publisher of the Miami *Herald*, who served as chair of the Task Force on Minorities in the Newspaper Business. The task force produced a 1990 industry report that called for more minority journalists and better coverage. "Between now and the year 2000, 87% of all U.S. population growth will be in minority communities. To offset flat

circulation trends, newspapers must tap into these growth areas," concluded
the report.[1]

JOURNALISM EDUCATION'S ROLE

Journalism education finds itself slumped in a cultural lag, unable to supply
21st century press needs. Industry leaders now recognize the importance of
diverse voices. A growing number of editors understand that an integrated
newsroom means different staff sensibilities and, as a result, more inclusive
content.

Although professional associations have called for changes in the newsroom
for more than ten years, most journalism educators have failed to address
the implications for their field. As a result, there are both practical and
theoretical problems to tackle.

By the year 2000 editors hope to have a representative number of minority
journalists on their staffs. Based on current U.S. Census figures and projections, minorities should make up 25 percent of the profession now.[2] But in
1991 they numbered barely 8 percent.[3]

The ASNE goal cannot be met without the active participation of journalism educators. They must not only train fledgling journalists in traditional
skills, but also prepare the next newsroom generation to cover a changing
America.

Before the turn of the century, Blacks and Hispanics will "constitute a
decided majority in nearly one-third of the nation's 50 largest cities . . . and
Blacks alone will be the major racial group in at least nine major cities,
notably Detroit, Baltimore, Memphis, Washington, D.C., New Orleans and
Atlanta," according to *Ebony* magazine.[4] But little of the texture of African
American communities appears on newspages produced by a profession 92
percent White. Instead, as numerous studies show, Blacks are reported
mostly as problem people on welfare or drugs or entangled in the law enforcement system.

"The Black images mass produced by them [White decision-makers in
media], however, have been filtered through the racial misconceptions and
fantasies of the dominant White culture, which has tended to deny the
existence of a rich and resilient Black culture of equal worth," write media
scholars Jannette L. Dates and William Barlow.[5]

"By failing to portray the Negro as a matter of routine and in the context
of the total society, the news media have, we believe, contributed to the
Black-White schism in this country," wrote the Kerner Commission in 1968.
"The media report and write from the standpoint of a White man's world,"
they concluded.[6] This can change in the classroom as it is already changing
in the newsroom.

A number of practical steps must be taken in journalism education in order
to respond to the profession's priorities. These include attracting more mi-

norities to journalism; teaching them skills that will help them to compete effectively for internships and at job fairs; and introducing as newsworthy topics and populations heretofore marginalized by mainstream media.

Bringing minorities into journalism education poses a number of problems. Minorities have not generally perceived the profession as a viable option, in part because of the absence of minority journalist role models. According to ASNE, less than 5 percent of all journalists are African American, only about 2 percent are Latino, 1 percent are Asian American and less than .03 percent are Native American.[7] This scarcity also exists in journalism education, where barely 5 percent of all journalism professors are minorities: 4 percent are Black, less than .02 percent are Latino.[8]

Further, journalism education assumes that students have middle-class resources. Once enrolled in classes, most minority students find themselves limited by economics. Few can afford to volunteer hours of unpaid work at a campus daily. Nor are they likely to own their own computers. As a result, minority students have less opportunity to publish, locking them out of competitions and job opportunities requiring clips—published samples of reporting or editing. Standard news-writing and editing courses seldom include minority issues or cover their minority communities. In short, for minorities, journalism education can be an alienating experience.

LABORATORY PUBLICATIONS

A classroom laboratory publication provides a response to these obstacles and an experience in pluralization. Although much of the success of such a venture requires standard journalism skills, specialized knowledge and sensitivity on the part of the professor to the target community are central to the quality of the course. There are obvious advantages to having such a course taught by a minority faculty member, but any professor knowledgeable about and sensitive to minority and class issues can offer it. (Faculty who teach courses that seek to address minority issues or to integrate the curriculum will find essential both the 1947 Hutchins Commission Report—which defined the social responsibility of journalism in a democracy—and Chapter 15 of the 1968 Kerner Commission Report, which addresses racism in media.)[9]

At the University of Texas at Austin, such a laboratory publication course has had significant success. Community Journalism, established in 1988, gives students the opportunity to publish *Tejas*, a quarterly magazine tabloid designed to address a specific community—in this case, campus Latinos.[10] (It is important to note that publications with a minority perspective are *not* alternative press. To label them as such implies that minorities are alternative citizens.)

These flexible publications allow the exploration of changing definitions of newsworthiness. They permit students to polish skills that will make them competent journalists. As a result, the news industry benefits from the value added by these new perspectives.

Obviously, the target community may be defined in any number of ways or within various categories. At UT-Austin, Latino students requested assistance in learning how to cover their own communities and how to provide a voice for other Latinos.

ADVANTAGES

A laboratory publication provides several solid educational experiences. At the same time, through such a course, journalism education can respond to the three critical components—recruitment, relevant experience and news redefinition—required to open access to and contribute toward the success of minorities interested in a journalism career.

Students gain an attractive arena within which to explore the field. Hands-on experience and a finished product offer tangible results, as opposed to the delayed gratification of classroom activities aimed at some future newsroom use. In community-defined publications, students find an opportunity to write about subjects familiar to them for media that consider these topics to be of central—rather than marginal—interest. Clearly, content will often differ from that in mainstream campus publications.

Early editions of the UT laboratory publication *Tejas*, for instance, covered mounting racial tensions on campus, highlighted Hispanic role models, analyzed social conditions and reported on the university's failure to reach its own integration goals.

"Texas—one of 19 states charged by the federal government in 1983 with failing to effectively integrate its student bodies and faculties—had the most severe disparities," wrote student reporter Ana Garza in 1989. She said of the UT-Austin campus, which has a faculty of 2,300, "Faculty figures included 30 Afro-Americans, 66 Hispanics and 7 Native Americans. The increases [from 1983 to 1989] were negligible."[11] In "Decade Harsh for Hispanics Despite Hoopla," Priscilla Martinez provided a 1989 socioeconomic index of Latinos.[12]

A freshman survival guide became a special summer edition that year. But as the publication matured and student enrollment increased, coverage became more sophisticated and the topics more complex. The students eventually reported on organized faculty resistance to affirmative action, a controversial multicultural survey and the accreditation process. Faculty teaching laboratory publication courses must be prepared to help students cover such issues responsibly.

Because the publication is taught as a course, it is a legitimate learning experience. Faculty teach journalism ethics and educational standards which contribute to the quality of the finished product.

Most important, the class gives students a chance to acquire clips, making it possible for them to apply for internships and jobs.

Beyond providing practical experience, such a publication fosters an environment that empowers its staffers and stimulates self-esteem. This is especially important for groups that historically have been marginalized or disenfranchised. As journalists, these individuals acquire a legitimacy that previously had been denied them. Their formal role and institutional connection as student journalists give them the right to interview, question and confront people and institutions that previously could dismiss them.

Producing a community publication also benefits future employers. The content of a publication aimed at a minority readership defines newsworthy topics rarely seen in mainstream media. This has the advantage both of informing a legitimate constituency and of exploring the expansion of news definitions and news-gathering practices. In addition, the community publication also introduces models for future coverage to journalism practice and education.

STUDENT RESPONSE

A laboratory publication course best attracts minorities to explore journalism if it is cross-listed with ethnic studies departments. Because the profession has low minority participation, students cannot easily find role models in the field. Further, since minority communities are seldom covered by mainstream media, often students do not perceive the profession as one that is open to them.

At the University of Texas at Austin, the Latino Community Journalism course is cross-listed with Mexican American Studies as an elective. Thus, students who have never considered journalism viable, and consequently have never looked into related courses, find the class listed within more familiar selections. As a result, newcomers sign up for the class. During its first semester, all students were Latinos, including three economics majors, one journalism major, one government major, one English major, one graduate student in history and a second-year law student. All took the course for at least two semesters.

Within two years, students taking the course included Asian Americans, African Americans and nonminority students, the majority of whom were either journalism majors at the time or who soon changed their career objectives to journalism. The content of the paper the class produced reflected the newsroom diversity.

Attracted by the expanded definition of newsworthiness, a growing number of students who said that they felt marginalized or alienated by other print media and class offerings, enrolled in this laboratory publication. These included several honors students, one of whom graduated with the department's top award, Outstanding Journalism Student of 1991.

Almost all of these students had attempted to work on the campus daily, but said that they left in frustration. Their experiences are part of a national pattern of low minority participation in campus media.

Among the reasons for minority flight from traditional college publications are newsroom racism, marginalization of minority student news and issues, ignorance, and personal financial hardship. Because campus dailies ignore minority communities on campus, say a number of minority students, they are forced to cover a reality they do not share. Too often they are assigned to cover lecture series, art exhibits or other events that rarely include minority representation. Even interviews with significant individuals rarely include people concerned with minority agendas or issues. The students say that covering such stories just feels dishonest and alienating.

Clearly some new, innovative means must be found to draw these minority students into journalism. By creating a laboratory publication that targets a special community, journalism educators provide a new option that defines the field as relevant to the student. This linkage is critical in attracting newcomers to the profession.

FINDING JOBS

As noted above, by participating in the laboratory publication, students acquire clips that they can use to apply for internships and jobs. However, networking assistance on behalf of these students is another critical role for journalism professors. Unless these publications are used as springboards into the journalism competitive track, the course provides a truncated exercise.

Coordinated with informed placement efforts, the course opens opportunities for minority students. With a little effort, these students can move into high visibility for editors searching for future journalists.

The teaching of a laboratory publication is standard course work requiring basic journalism educational skills and special expertise. However, professors must remember that minority students' earlier educational experiences may have been in economically deprived schools with overworked teachers in underfunded, overcrowded classrooms where little time was spent on developing writing skills. Or the students may have had teachers who saw them through the grids of stereotype as people who could not learn to write. In either case, minority college students often feel insecure about writing. So coaching methods, like those developed at the Poynter Institute for Media Studies, may be necessary.[13] One-on-one interaction between editor and writer in a collaborative editing process that balances empathy and respect underpins all the editing techniques described in *Coaching Writers* by Roy Peter Clark and Don Fry of Poynter. Of particular note is the section titled "Coaching for Diversity," which addresses working with minority writers.

The news industry believes that expanding the field to include journalists representative of a diverse society will only improve the profession. Clearly, since 85 percent of entry-level reporters hold journalism degrees, it is the responsibility of journalism education to place itself on the cutting edge of this process. The academy has greater wherewithal to address the related intellectual and skills needs than does the employer. Indeed, a parity goal within the academy that is supportive of the ASNE target is appropriate.

A laboratory publication course is but one of many ways to pluralize the classroom. It can address any minority community that is part or accessible to the campus where the course is taught. The concept is limited only by the imagination, innovativeness and experience of the professor.

NOTES

Some of the ideas in this chapter are excerpted from the author's book on integrating the news product, forthcoming from the University of Texas Press, Austin, in 1994.

1. Task Force on Minorities in the Newspaper Business, *Cornerstone for Growth: How Minorities Are Vital to the Future of Newspapers* (Reston, VA: Task Force on Minorities in the Newspaper Business, 1990), p. 6.

2. American Society of Newspaper Editors, *Report of the ASNE Committee on Minorities*, 4 April 1978: "Leaders among minority journalists have urged the industry to set a goal of minority employment by the year 2000 equivalent to the percentage of minority persons within the national population. This committee believes this is a fair and attainable goal."

3. American Society of Newspaper Editors, annual newsroom census report, April 1991.

4. "The Biggest Secret of Race Relations: The New White Minority" (editorial), *Ebony*, April 1989, p. 84. These projections are supported by 1990 Census data and demographic projections widely circulated.

5. Jannette L. Dates and William Barlow, eds., *Split Image: African Americans in the Mass Media* (Washington, DC: Howard University Press, 1990).

6. *Report of the National Advisory Commission on Civil Disorders* (Washington, DC: U.S. Government Printing Office, 1968), Chapter 15.

7. ASNE, 1991 newsroom census.

8. Lee Becker, "Survey of Journalism and Mass Communications Graduates, 1990," Survey Report, School of Journalism, Ohio State University, 1991.

9. The Hutchins Commission, headed by Chicago University chancellor Robert Hutchins, addressed the matter of race relations in the United States. Particularly useful are the five mandates of a democratic press: (1) providing a truthful, comprehensive and intelligent account of the day's events in a context that gives them meaning; (2) providing a forum for the exchange of comment and criticism; (3) projecting a representative picture of the constituent groups in the society; (4) presenting and clarifying the goals and values of the society; and (5) offering full access to the day's intelligence. The National Advisory Commission on Civil Disorders, known as the Kerner Commission, addressed the role of media in race relations and in contributing to racial tensions that led to the riots in 1967.

10. The course was first taught as an independent study and then listed in the course catalog as J352.

11. Ana Garza, "Texas Five-Year Plan Falls Short of Desired Goals," *Tejas* 1, no. 3 (1989), 1.

12. Priscilla Martinez, "Decade Harsh for Hispanics Despite Hoopla," *Tejas* 1, no. 4 (1989), 1.

13. This method is described in detail in Roy Peter Clark and Don Fry, *Coaching Writers: Editors and Reporters Working Together* (New York: St. Martin's, 1992).

BIBLIOGRAPHY

Carolyn Martindale

INTRODUCING MULTICULTURAL PERSPECTIVES

Aufderheide, Patricia. "Cross-Cultural Film Studies: Seeing Inside Out." *Journalism Educator* 46 (Summer 1991), 31–41.

Bramlett-Solomon, Sharon. "Bringing Cultural Sensitivity into Reporting Classrooms." *Journalism Educator* 44 (Summer 1989), 28.

Cohen, Jeremy, Matthew Lombard and Rosalind M. Pierson. "Developing a Multicultural Mass Communication Course." *Journalism Educator* 47 (Summer 1992), 3–12.

de Uriarte, Mercedes Lynn. "Texas Course Features Barrio as Story Source." *Journalism Educator* 43 (Summer 1988), 78–79.

Escalante, Virginia. "The Bilingual Community Newspaper as a Publication Option: Implementation, Organization, Advantages and Pitfalls." *Southwestern Journal of Minorities and Media* 1 (Fall/Winter 1990), 25–31. Texas Tech University, Box 4710, Lubbock, TX 79409–7392.

Martindale, Carolyn. "Infusing Cultural Diversity into Communication Courses." *Journalism Educator* 45 (Winter 1991), 34–38.

———. "Sensitizing Students to Racial Coverage." *Journalism Educator* 43 (Summer 1988), 79–81.

Miller, Debra. "Multicultural Communications: Sensitizing Public Relations Students to Multicultural Society." Paper presented at the Association for Education in Journalism and Mass Communication convention, Montreal, August 1992.

Mollenkott, Virginia. "Awareness of Diversity: A Classroom Exercise." *Transformations* 2 (Winter 1991), 15–18.

Moriarty, Sandra E., and Lisa Rohe. "Cultural Palettes: An Exercise in Sensitivity for Designers." *Journalism Educator* 46 (Winter 1992), 32–37.

1989 Guide to Multicultural Resources. Praxis Publications, P.O. Box 9869, Madison, WI 53715. Telephone 608–244–5633.

Stoner, Kevin R., Felecia Jones and Pamela J. Creedon. "Addressing Cultural Issues in Classes: The Five Ws and D for Diversity." *Southwestern Journal of Minorities and Media* 1 (Fall 1990), 11–24. Texas Tech University, Box 4710, Lubbock, TX 79409–7392.

PAST NEWS COVERAGE OF PEOPLE OF COLOR AND WOMEN

Black Pols/White Press. This video uses Chicago mayor Harold Washington's experiences with the press to illustrate problems that often arise between Black politicians and the media. PBS Video, 1320 Braddock Place, Alexandria, VA 22314–1698. Telephone 1–800–344–3337.

Drugs in Black and White. This film explores the media's role in promoting the stereotype that America's drug problem is primarily a Black problem. Coronet Films, 108 Wilmot Road, Deerfield, IL 60015.

Entman, Robert M. "Blacks in the News: Television, Modern Racism and Cultural Change." *Journalism Quarterly* 69 (Summer 1992), 341–361.

History and Memory. Focusing on the internment of Japanese Americans during World War II, this film examines the rewriting of history through media representations. Electronic Arts Intermix, 536 Broadway, 9th Floor, New York, NY 10012. Telephone 212–966–4605.

Johnson, Kirk A. "Black and White in Boston." *Columbia Journalism Review* 26 (May/June 1987), 50–52.

Martindale, Carolyn. *The White Press and Black America.* Westport, CT: Greenwood Press, 1986.

New Directions for News. A 1983 study of major newspapers' coverage of issues concerning women, published by the Women's Studies Program and Policy Center, George Washington University, 2025 Eye St. NW, Room 212, Washington, DC 20052.

Race Against Prime Time. This excellent film analyzes media coverage of the 1980 Miami race riots. Resolution, Inc./California Newsreel, 149 9th St. #420, San Francisco, CA 94103. Telephone 415–621–6196.

Rubin, Bernard, ed. *Small Voices and Great Trumpets: Minorities and the Media.* New York: Praeger, 1980.

Shaw, David. Series of nine articles on news coverage of African Americans published 11–14 December 1990, Los Angeles *Times*.

Smith, Erna. *What Color Is the News?* 1990. Copies from New California Alliance, 82 2nd St. #300, San Francisco, CA 94105.

Wilson, Clint, and Félix Gutiérrez. *Minorities and Media: Diversity and the End of Mass Communication.* Beverly Hills, CA: Sage, 1985.

PORTRAYALS OF MINORITIES AND WOMEN IN ENTERTAINMENT MEDIA

Bataille, Gretchen, and Charles Silet, eds. *The Pretend Indians: Images of Native Americans in the Movies.* Ames: Iowa State University Press, 1980.

Bogle, Donald. *Toms, Coons, Mulattoes, Mammies, and Bucks: An Interpretive History of Blacks in American Films*. New York: Continuum, 1989.

Color Adjustment. An update of the Emmy-winning *Ethnic Notions*. Both films explore the portrayal of minorities in the media and trace the roots of racial stereotypes. California Newsreel, 149 9th St. #420, San Francisco, CA 94103. Telephone 415–621–6196.

Dates, Jannette L., and William Barlow, eds. *Split Image: African Americans in the Mass Media*. Washington, DC: Howard University Press, 1990.

Gandy, Oscar H., Jr., and Paula W. Matabane. "Television and Social Perceptions among African Americans and Hispanics." In Molefi Kete Asante and William B. Gudykunst, eds., *Handbook of International and Intercultural Communication*. Newbury Park, CA: Sage, 1989.

MacDonald, Fred. *Blacks and White TV: Afro-Americans in Television since 1948*. Chicago: Nelson-Hall, 1983.

Miller, Randall. *The Kaleidoscopic Lens: How Hollywood Views Ethnic Groups*. Englewood, NJ: Jerome Ozer, 1980.

Murphy, Sharon. "American Indians and the Media: Neglect and Stereotype." *Journalism History* 6 (Summer 1979), 39–43.

Slaying the Dragon. This acclaimed documentary examines the portrayal of Asian women in movies. Asian Cinevision, 32 E. Broadway, New York, NY 10002.

Steenland, Sally. *Unequal Picture: Black, Hispanic, Asian and Native American Characters on Television*. Washington, DC: National Commission on Working Women on Wider Opportunities for Women, 1989.

Still Killing Us Softly. An update of *Killing Us Softly*. Both films are powerful examinations of portrayals of women in advertising. Cambridge Documentary Films Inc., P.O. Box 385, Cambridge, MA 02139. Telephone 617–354–3677.

Stroman, Carolyn, Bishetta Merritt and Paula Matabane. "Twenty Years after Kerner: The Portrayal of African Americans on Prime-Time Television." *Howard Journal of Communications* 2 (Winter 1989–90), 44–56.

Subervi-Vélez, Federico A. "Media." In Nicolás Kanellos, ed., *The Hispanic American Almanac*. Detroit: Gale Research, 1993.

U.S. Commission on Civil Rights. *Window Dressing on the Set: Women and Minorities in Television*. Washington, DC: USCCR, 1977; also *Window Dressing on the Set: An Update*. Washington, DC: USCCR, 1979.

Woll, Allen, and Randall M. Miller, eds. *Ethnic and Racial Images in American Film and Television: Historical Essays and Bibliography*. New York: Garland, 1987.

HISTORIES OF MINORITY MEDIA AND WOMEN JOURNALISTS

The American Experience/Ida B. Wells: A Passion for Justice. This film explores the investigative reporting techniques and crusading spirit of this 19th century African American women editor. PBS Video, 1320 Braddock Place, Alexandria, VA 22314–1698. Telephone 1–800–344–3337.

Belford, Barbara. *Brilliant Bylines: A Bibliographical Anthology of Notable Newspaperwomen in America*. New York: Columbia University Press, 1986.

Cortés, Carlos. "The Mexican-American Press." In Sally M. Miller, ed., *The Ethnic Press in the United States: A Historical Analysis and Handbook*. Westport, CT: Greenwood Press, 1987. This book also includes chapters on the Puerto Rican press and the Chinese American, Japanese American and Filipino American presses.

Dorothea Lange. A 13-minute overview of the works of this outstanding photographer of the Depression. Films for the Humanities and Sciences, P.O. Box 2053, Princeton, NJ 08543-2053.

Littlefield, Daniel F., Jr., and James W. Parins. *American Indian and Alaska Native Newspapers and Periodicals 1826–1924.* Westport, CT: Greenwood Press, 1984. See also works by same title covering the years 1925–1970 and 1971–1985, both published in 1986.

Marzolf, Marion. *Up from the Footnote: A History of Women Journalists.* New York: Hastings House, 1977.

Murphy, James E., and Sharon E. Murphy. *Let My People Know: American Indian Journalism, 1828–1978.* Norman: University of Oklahoma Press, 1981.

Wilson, Clint C., II. *Black Journalists in Paradox: Historical Perspectives and Current Dilemmas.* Westport, CT: Greenwood Press, 1991.

Wolseley, Roland E. *The Black Press, USA.* Ames: Iowa University Press, 1990.

Slide collections on African American, Hispanic and Native American presses are available from Vis-Com Inc., P.O. Box 6182, Minneapolis, MN 55406.

Also available are many excellent biographies and autobiographies of women journalists and journalists of color.

MOVIES TO REVIEW

African Americans: *Glory, A Soldier's Story, The Color Purple, Raisin in the Sun, School Daze, Lady Sings the Blues, Do the Right Thing, Jungle Fever, Boyz 'n' the Hood, Hollywood Shuffle, To Sleep with Anger, A Gathering of Old Men, A Rage in Harlem, Malcolm X.*

Asian Americans: *Alamo Bay, Mississippi Masala, Dim Sum, Farewell to Manzanar.*

Hispanics: *La Bamba, The Milagro Beanfield War, The Mambo Kings, Break of Dawn, El Norte, Salt of the Earth.* (The latter film can be rented from Instructional Video, P.O. Box 21, Maumee, OH 43537.)

Native Americans: *Dances with Wolves, Last of the Mohicans, In the Spirit of Crazy Horse, Powwow Highway, Black Robe, Renegade, Thunder Heart.*

Women Journalists: *Double Exposure* (about photojournalist Margaret Bourke-White), *Reds* (about socialist journalist Louise Bryant), *The China Syndrome, Absence of Malice, Broadcast News, His Girl Friday.*

COPY-EDITING AND REPORTING

Asian American Handbook. A 1991 revision and update of *Asian Pacific Americans: A Handbook on How to Cover and Portray Our Nation's Fastest Growing Minority Group.* National Conference of Christians and Jews, Asian American Journalists Association, Association of Asian Pacific American Artists. Available for $18 from National Conference of Christians and Jews, 360 N. Michigan Ave., Chicago, IL 60601.

Guidelines for Bias-Free Publishing. New York: McGraw-Hill, 1984.

Izard, Ralph S., and Marilyn S. Greenwald. "In Search of Cultural Diversity." In

Public Affairs Reporting: The Citizens' News. 2nd ed. Dubuque, IA: William C. Brown, 1991.

Johnson, Mary, and Susan Elkins. *Reporting on Disability: Approaches and Issues.* 1989. Avocado Press, 1974A Douglass Blvd., Louisville, KY 40205.

Miller, C., and K. Swift. *The Handbook of Nonsexist Writing.* 2nd ed. New York: Harper and Row, 1988.

Pickens, Judy E., ed. *Without Bias: A Guidebook for Nondiscriminatory Communication.* 2nd ed. New York: John Wiley and Sons, 1982.

ARTICLES ON MINORITY AND WOMEN JOURNALISTS

Barrow, Lionel C., Jr. Review of R.J.M. Blackett's *Thomas Morris Chester, Black Civil War Correspondent. Journalism Quarterly* 67 (Winter 1990), p. 1121.

Brower, William. "The Black War Correspondents." *Media History Digest* 1 (Fall 1980), 46–55.

Brown, Charles B. "A Woman's Odyssey: The War Correspondence of Anna Benjamin." *Journalism Quarterly* (Autumn 1969), pp. 522–530.

Gutiérrez, Félix. "Spanish-Language Media in America: Background, Resources, History." *Journalism History* 4 (Summer 1977), 34–41. (This issue is devoted to the Hispanic press.)

Henry, Susan. "Margaret Draper: Colonial Printer Who Challenged the Patriots." *Journalism History* 1 (Winter 1974–75), 141–144.

———. "Reporting 'Deeply and at First Hand': Helen Campbell in the 19th-Century Slums." *Journalism History* 11 (Spring/Summer 1984), 18–25.

Hubbell, Sue. "Polly Pry Did Not Just Report the News; She *Made* It." *Smithsonian,* January 1991.

Jones, Douglas C. "Teresa Dean: Lady Correspondent among the Sioux Indians." *Journalism Quarterly* 49 (1972), 656–662.

Luebke, Barbara. "Elias Boudinott, Indian Editor: Editorial Columns from the *Cherokee Phoenix.*" *Journalism History* 6 (Summer 1979), 48–53.

Moore, Deedee. "Shooting Straight: The Many Worlds of Gordon Parks." *Smithsonian,* April 1989, pp. 66–77.

Murphy, Sharon. "Neglected Pioneers: 19th Century Native American Newspapers." *Journalism History* 4 (Autumn 1977), 79–82.

Pierce, Paula. "Frances Benjamin Johnston: Mother of American Photojournalism." *Media History Digest* 5 (Winter 1985), 54–64.

Stevens, Summer E., and Owen V. Johnson. "From Black Politics to Black Community: Harry C. Smith and the Cleveland *Gazette.*" *Journalism Quarterly* 67 (Winter 1990), 1090–1102.

Streitmatter, Rodger L. "No Taste for Fluff: Ethel L. Payne, African-American Journalist." *Journalism Quarterly* 68 (Autumn 1991), 528–540.

Sullins, William S., and Paul Parsons. "Roscoe Dunjee: Crusading Editor of Oklahoma's *Black Dispatch,* 1915–1955." *Journalism Quarterly* 69 (Spring 1992), 204–213.

Sullivan, Julie. "Another Voice: The Black Cartoonists." *Media History Digest,* 1985, pp. 28–31.

The articles listed here are a sampling of the many to be found in other issues of communications and history periodicals.

HISTORIES OF MINORITY GROUPS

Banks, James A. *Teaching Strategies for Ethnic Education*. 2nd ed. Boston: Allyn and
    Bacon, 1979. Although this is written for teachers of younger students, it
    includes excellent capsule histories of various ethnic groups in the United
    States and an outstanding annotated bibliography.

Black Hills Claim. This film examines the Lakota Sioux efforts to regain control of
    the Black Hills of Dakota. Native American Public Broadcasting Consortium,
    P.O. Box 8311, 1800 N. 33rd St., Lincoln, NE 68501. Telephone 402–472–
    3522.

Black History: Lost/Stolen/Strayed. Narrated by Bill Cosby, this video presents the real
    history of African Americans compared to media images. BFA Educational
    Media, 468 Park Ave., New York, NY 10016.

Dennis, Henry C. *The American Indian: 1492–1976*. 2nd ed. Dobbs Ferry, NY: Oceana
    Publications, 1977.

Fitzpatrick, Joseph P. *Puerto Rican Americans: The Meaning of Migration to the Mainland*.
    Englewood Cliffs, NJ: Prentice-Hall, 1971.

Franklin, John Hope, and Alfred A. Moss, Jr. *From Slavery to Freedom: A History of
    Negro Americans*. 6th ed. New York: McGraw-Hill, 1988.

The Golden Cage: A Story of California's Farm Workers. This documentary examines the
    isolation and living conditions of California farm workers. Filmmakers Library,
    124 E. 40th St., New York, NY 10016. Telephone 212–979–5671.

Home from the Eastern Sea. This film explores the immigration of the Chinese, Japanese
    and Filipinos to America. Filmmakers Library, 124 E. 40th St., New York,
    NY 10016. Telephone 212–979–5671.

Hymowitz, Carol, and Michele Weissman. *A History of Women in America*. New York:
    Bantam, 1978.

Korrol, Virginia E. Sanchez. *From Colonia to Community: The History of Puerto Ricans
    in New York City, 1917–1948*. Westport, CT: Greenwood Press, 1983.

Our Lives in Our Hands. This film examines use of traditional crafts as a means of
    survival by Aroostook Micmac Indians of northern Maine. Documentary Ed-
    ucational Resources, 101 Morse St., Watertown, MA 02172. Telephone 617–
    926–0491.

Samora, Julian, and Patricia Vandel. *A History of the Mexican-American People*. Notre
    Dame, IN: University of Notre Dame Press, 1977.

Sowell, Thomas. *Ethnic America: A History*. New York: Basic Books, 1981.

Takaki, Ronald. *Strangers from a Different Shore*. Boston: Little, Brown, 1990. Tells
    why, when and where Asians came to the United States.

Weber, David. *Foreigners in Their Native Land: Historical Roots of the Mexican Americans*.
    Albuquerque: University of New Mexico Press, 1973.

Who Killed Vincent Chen? This Academy Award–nominated film explores racism in
    working-class America. Filmmakers Library, 124 E. 40th St., New York, NY
    10016. Telephone 212–979–5671.

OTHER RESOURCES

Cornerstone for Growth: How Minorities Are Vital to the Future of Newspapers. Task Force
    on Minorities in the Newspaper Business, Newspaper Center, Box 17407,
    Dulles Airport, Washington, DC 20041.

ERIC database. ERIC makes microfiche copies of scholarly papers presented at the conventions of AEJMC and similar organizations. It is a rich source of unpublished papers on women journalists, journalists of color, minority media, and women editors of temperance, suffragist and abolition newspapers. ERIC Clearinghouse on Reading and Communication Skills, Indiana University, Smith Research Center, Suite 150, 2805 E. 10th St., Bloomington, IN 47408–2698. Telephone 1–800-USE-ERIC.

Lawrence, David, Jr. "Pluralism: It Just Makes Sense." *Minorities in the Newspaper Business* (publication of the American Newspaper Publishers Association Foundation) 5 (Winter 1989), 1.

Minority Professional-in-Residence Program, American Society of Newspaper Editors, P.O. Box 17004, Washington, DC 20041. Through this program journalism educators can arrange to have a minority newsroom professional visit their campus for several days to speak in classes, give workshops and critique student work.

Women and Media Course Outlines. Compiled by Marion Marzolf. This rich collection of bibliographies, assignment ideas and syllabi of courses on women and journalism is available for $10 from Dr. Marion Marzolf, Department of Communication, 2092 Frieze Building, University of Michigan, Ann Arbor, MI 48109–1285.

Teaching Diversity. Compiled by Ted Pease. 1992. This collection of syllabi, bibliographies and other resources for teaching courses on women, people of color and the media is available at cost (about $8) from the Association for Education in Journalism and Mass Communication, University of South Carolina, Columbia, SC 29208–0251. Telephone 803–777–2005.

ORGANIZATIONS OF MINORITY JOURNALISTS

Asian American Journalists Association, 1765 Sutter St., Room 1000, San Francisco, CA 94115.

California Chicano News Media Association, School of Journalism, University of Southern California, Los Angeles, CA 90089–1695.

National Association of Black Journalists, P.O. Box 17212, Washington, DC 20041.

National Association of Hispanic Journalists, National Press Building, Suite 634, Washington, DC 20045.

Native American Press Association, P.O. Box 1734, Boulder, CO 80306–1734.

Native Communications Group, Native American Public Broadcasting Consortium, P.O. Box 83111, Lincoln, NE 68501.

RESOURCES FOR SENSITIZING FACULTY

A Campus of Difference. Workshops on exploring and appreciating cultural differences. Anti-Defamation League. Contact Admire Presentations, Inc., 170 W. 76th St. #101, New York, NY 10023. Telephone 212–580–4128.

Diversity Works. Programs to increase sensitivity toward and to combat discrimination. 201 North Valley Road, Pelham, MA 01002. Telephone 413–256–1868.

Managing Diversity Successfully. Training in respecting diversity and communicating across cultures. Barry Shapiro and Associates, 6757 Armour Dr., Oakland, CA 94611.

Minorities in the College Classroom: Racism in Education. A video designed to sensitize faculty to cultural differences among students and help them enhance the learning environment. Department of Human Relations, Michigan State University, 380 Administration Bldg., East Lansing, MI 48824–1046.

Valuing Diversity. Training and film series on understanding diversity and dealing with prejudice. Copeland Griggs Productions, Inc., 302 23rd Ave., San Francisco, CA 94121. Telephone 415–668–4200.

Additional resources on many of these subjects can be found in the bibliographies at the end of Chapters 11 through 20.

IV PLURALIZING THE STUDENT MEDIA

22 DIVERSIFYING MEDIA COVERAGE

Carolyn Martindale

Pluralizing the coverage and the staffs of student media is an important component of preparing journalism students of all racial and ethnic heritages to report on and work in a multicultural world. Although helping student media staffs diversify is a job that falls primarily on the student media adviser, all communications faculty can help with this endeavor. Faculty who are not advisers can influence the students in their classes who are or will be members of student media staffs by the emphasis they place on diversity and multicultural understanding, by the assignments and projects they give their students, and by the assessments of student and commercial media that they make in class.

Pluralizing the student media is important for a variety of reasons. One has been mentioned by several authors earlier in this book: minority journalism students who have not worked on the student media are at a severe disadvantage when competing for journalism scholarships, internships and jobs, nearly all of which require clippings and publications experience or tapes or other samples of professional work.

Also important is the experience of the White journalism student, who should be learning in class and practicing in student media how to cover people different from herself or himself accurately and sensitively. That student also should be learning how to function in a multicultural workplace, because that's what the newsrooms of the future will be.

Finally, achieving diversity in coverage and staffing is important to the quality of the media product. Having staff members from different backgrounds will give the staff more experiences and input to draw from and more contacts within the university. Such diversity will result in richer, more varied coverage, thereby benefiting all the readers, listeners or viewers in the college community, for whom the lessons of multiculturalism will be reinforced.

Faculty members wanting to encourage the student media toward diversity will need to remember what advisers already know: student media staffs are fiercely protective of their autonomy, and their independence is protected by law. Faculty and advisers alike must attempt to persuade student staffs of the many values—to themselves and their medium—of working toward diversity, and then offer to help provide them with information and ideas that can help them do it.

LEGACY OF MISTRUST

Attracting African American and other minority students to work on a predominantly White newspaper at a predominantly White school or, conversely, attracting White or other racial minority students to work in the media at a predominantly Black school is not easy, however. Any new student is shy about breaking into the close-knit, experienced group in the student newsroom; students from a minority race or ethnic group have the added problem of feeling that they may not be welcome. These students are likely to believe, perhaps with good reason, that the newspaper or other medium has shown itself in the past to be indifferent or even hostile to their minority group.

The situation is exacerbated by the segregated nature of American society. Most college students have grown up in largely segregated neighborhoods and schools, so they have had little opportunity to achieve any knowledge or understanding of, or comfort with, people of other races.

In addition, until the past three decades African Americans and members of other minority groups have been largely invisible in mass circulation media, which are, after all, owned by affluent Whites and produced by and aimed at middle-class Whites. What coverage the media have provided of minority groups has, until recently, been largely negative and often blatantly racist. (It is for these reasons that Black and other minority newspapers and magazines were established, and still remain viable.)

Until the civil rights movement, coverage of Black Americans occupied less than 1 percent of the available news space in most major newspapers, and often 50 to 75 percent of that coverage was crime news. Since the 1960s coverage has improved in many papers; Blacks are more visible, and more coverage is provided of Blacks in terms of everyday life activities, the arts, politics and the kind of community news regularly run about Whites.[1] But many African Americans still claim that Black neighborhoods are portrayed by their community's media exclusively in terms of crime, drugs and poverty.

Black experts are not quoted, they say, even on questions where their expertise is clearly relevant, and the views of average Black persons are not included.[2]

Since college students share the same mix of racial attitudes as their elders, the past tendency of commercial media to ignore the interests and concerns of African Americans and other minorities, and to portray these persons in negative ways, has been exhibited by student media at predominantly White universities also. This has led many generations of minority college students to believe that the student media on their campus are inimical to their interests, and are certainly not places for minority journalism students to obtain publications experience.

COMMITMENT TO CHANGE

Leading commercial papers have been trying for several decades to diversify their staffs, and in just the past decade have begun holding sensitivity sessions for their staffs to try to achieve less biased coverage of minorities. At the end of the 1980s leaders of the Gannett newspapers mandated that any story that could possibly be given a multicultural perspective should be given one.

Unfortunately, that kind of interest in and commitment to diversity has not yet been reflected in the college media, except at a few schools. But it is that kind of action that is needed to make the college publications experience most valuable for White and non-White students alike.

Oddly enough, the best way for predominantly White college media to diversify their staffs is first to diversify their coverage. This may seem like putting the cart before the horse, but it is not. First of all, minority students on campus are likely to have a negative impression of the newspaper's openness to their interests, and the staff must prove, through the coverage they provide, that this is not the case. Otherwise minority students will never begin to trust the paper (or other medium) and be willing to consider working for it.

In addition, it is not necessary to have students of color working for a paper in order for the paper to exhibit diversity in its coverage. The fact is that White students can, and should be required to, learn how to cover stories about other groups accurately and sensitively, just as minority reporters are routinely expected to do.

Thus the best way to pluralize a student newspaper's staff and coverage is to sensitize and inform the present staff. This should lead to more diversified coverage, which in turn should lead to greater credibility among minority readers on campus and may perhaps attract some new minority staffers to the paper.

PROVIDING INFORMATION

An effective way to begin this undertaking is to seek information and ideas for stories from minority staff, faculty and students on campus. This action can be undertaken by journalism faculty members as well as by media advisers. Faculty members can inform students in their classes through guest speakers, while advisers can hold mandatory training sessions for student staff members.

In both cases, the aim is to give students information about minority student populations on their campus and perhaps also in the community. At the same time, the speakers who can help provide this information should be asked for story ideas, which can be used by the campus media or by teachers of reporting and feature-writing classes. Possible speakers include:

- A member of the minority or multicultural student services staff who can provide demographic information about the various minority student populations on campus, explain the nature of minority student organizations, and provide names and phone numbers of their presidents, so that journalism students can begin to compile a list of sources to contact for information later. This speaker can also be asked to explain how the student newspaper is perceived by minority students.

- The university's affirmative action officer or a personnel administrator who can explain the number and backgrounds of minority faculty and staff members, and who can provide names and phone extensions for some of these persons who would be good sources on various subjects.

- Minority reporters from local commercial media who can discuss their own experiences and their perceptions of media portrayal of minorities.

- Reporters from local minority newspapers or broadcasting stations who can discuss their paper or station, its accomplishments and problems, and the role it fills in the community.

- A history or Black Studies faculty member who can explain the experiences of African Americans and/or other minority groups in the United States.

- A sociology or psychology faculty member who can explain the role racism and prejudice play in a society and the function they perform.

- A psychology or drama faculty person who can lead role-playing sessions to help students experience discrimination and who also can teach them how to defuse hostility.

- A minority faculty member who can discuss commercial media portrayal of members of his or her minority group in news coverage, entertainment or advertising.

Projects the class or the staff could undertake include analyzing the newspaper's past coverage of minority persons, groups and interests on campus and assessing the quality of that coverage. The class or staff also could brainstorm for story ideas, and the faculty member teaching a writing class could make sure these stories get covered as part of the work required for the course. The stories could be offered to the student paper or station.

Faculty members not connected with the student media can take several other actions to try to encourage diversity in the media. One is to contact the editors and reporters to praise stories they admire or to point out deficiencies in coverage. Another is to encourage talented minority students to consider working for the student media. Faculty also should remember that student media need photographers, artists, ad salespersons and other personnel as well as reporters.

All journalism faculty also can try to insure that minority professional journalists are among the reporters invited to serve as guest speakers for classes or at Journalism Days, as workshop leaders for the student media and for Press Days, as professionals-in-residence, as judges for writing competitions and as honorees at journalism banquets.

IDEAS FOR ADVISERS

Faculty who serve as advisers to student media have additional avenues for encouraging pluralism in the media. One is to suggest that the student editors explain to the persons appearing as speakers at the sensitivity sessions, and to other campus minority faculty, staff and students, that they are trying to improve their coverage of people of color and would welcome story ideas and guest opinion columns and new staff members.

The adviser also could help the staff hold a publicity clinic for student organizations, maybe with written invitations to minority student groups. At this clinic the staff members could explain what kind of news and features the paper will run and what it will not cover, what the deadlines are, guidelines the groups can use in preparing copy and taking photos, ad rates and deadlines, the names of editors in charge of various kinds of stories, what the word limitations and other requirements are for letters to the editor, opinion columns, and other material submitted. The editor also could explain the paper's quest for story ideas, guest editorials and staff members.

Although the main purpose of the publicity clinic would be to make it easier for all student groups, and especially minority organizations, to get their news into the paper or on the air, an equally important goal is establishing communications between the staffers and minority groups. The clinic should help both the staffers and the minority students put faces and names to each other's organization.

The publicity clinic could be combined with an open house at the newspaper office or the station, at which the paper's or station's operation could be explained. Alternatively, an open house could be held at a different time. Again, the event would be open to all, but special efforts could be made to invite the participation of minority students and organizations.

Another method of opening lines of communication between the student media staff and people of color on campus would be for the staff to host a story idea or coverage suggestions session with interested minority students, both individuals and organizations. Someone from the university's student services staff could serve as an impartial moderator, to keep the discussion focused on what minority students would like to see in the paper, on suggestions for story subjects and issues, and on what the newspaper *could* do, rather than on what it has done wrong in the past.

Some complaints probably will be voiced at such a session, and that is by no means undesirable. But the adviser and moderator need to avoid at all costs allowing a faceoff to develop between the student staff and minority groups. The idea of this session is to promote dialogue and open lines of communication, suggest story ideas and perhaps wake up student media staffers to minority student attitudes about the paper.

KEEPING MINORITY STAFFERS

Retaining minority students on the staff often is as difficult as recruiting them in the first place. The key to retaining new staff members—of any race—is providing them with whatever additional training they may need, plus a mentor from among the present staff members.

The training is very important and should not be left to an already harried copy editor. Some person on the staff should have specific responsibility for contacting walk-ins, or students who come to the paper volunteering to write. These volunteers may not be journalism students, in which case they will need extra training. After the volunteer has been given an assignment and has turned in a story, the staff person should go over the story with the volunteer assessing its strong and weak points and helping the student to improve it.

The volunteer's mentor, a different person, should be a current staff member who can serve as a sort of big brother or big sister, teaching the newcomer how the publication operates and what is expected of staff members. Another form of mentoring is pairing an inexperienced reporter with a seasoned one on specific stories, so that the new staffer can begin to see how the job is done. Conversely, a new minority staff member can act as a mentor for the more seasoned reporter when the story they are covering is a multicultural one.

The adviser can encourage the staff to take seriously any minority staff member's criticisms and suggestions for coverage, instead of labeling the person the staff militant. The staff should be encouraged to try to *value* different viewpoints, not fear them—that's what diversity is all about.

It is important that the newsroom environment be free of prejudice in any form. The adviser and editor can cooperate in ensuring that the staff members recognize that no racist, sexist or ethnic jokes, remarks, or posters will be allowed in the newsroom. This prejudice-free atmosphere in the newsroom should be an outgrowth of sensitizing the staff, and should become a reality well before minority students are sought for the staff.

GOING THE SECOND MILE

Another action an adviser can take is to insure that providing diversified coverage and attempting to pluralize the staff is written into the student editors' job descriptions, so that all are aware that diversity is a goal, just as accuracy and meeting deadlines are. When interviews are held with candidates for editorships for the upcoming year, questioners should attempt to ascertain each candidate's feelings about trying to pluralize the media's staff and coverage.

In addition, rewards should be provided for multicultural coverage and pluralizing efforts, perhaps through awards at year-end banquets, or notations, in students' department file that forms the basis for subsequent job recommendations.

Advisers also can suggest to the staff that they might want to survey students, including a sample of minority students, periodically to see what they like and don't like about the paper and what kinds of stories they would like to see more often.

In addition, advisers could suggest that the paper follow the example of some commercial newspapers and set up an advisory board of minority students, faculty and staff to monitor coverage, answer questions and suggest story ideas and sources. If the editors fight such an idea, they may be willing to set up a committee of present staffers who could pay the same kind of attention to the nature of the paper's minority coverage and make suggestions for improvement.

The adviser also could set up a mentoring situation between members of the media staff and a high school publication at a minority institution with inadequate staffing or limited financial resources to produce the school newspaper. Despite their busy schedules, many college student staffers are very willing to visit a high school paper to lead a workshop in a topic like editorial writing or layout. The students may even be willing to provide help on a continuing basis by "adopting" a school newspaper for a year.

PREPARING FOR CRITICISM

Both advisers and faculty members should be aware that a media staff's initial efforts to pluralize its coverage may be met with suspicion and hostility by students of color because of the paper's past record of indifference to minority interests. It may require more sensitive and diverse coverage for half a year or more before minority students begin to trust the sincerity of the editors' efforts and before journalism students of color will begin to consider working for the paper.

In addition, faculty members and advisers should remember that they and their students won't always get it right. When prejudice is as deeply ingrained in a culture as it is in ours, it also is present in every individual—of every race—to some degree. Even if all reporters and editors are committed to accurate multicultural coverage, they may slip up in some way and run something that is racist, or that is perceived as being racist.

It is important that they not see this as a negation of all their previous efforts. Instead, they should examine the situation and insure that such a problem will not recur, make an apology if called for, and renew their efforts to provide better multicultural coverage.

They also should realize that being called a racist is not the ultimate insult, much as it stings when a staff has been trying particularly hard to provide more sensitive and diverse coverage. In such racially conscious and polarized times as ours, racism, like beauty, is sometimes in the eye of the beholder. Charges of racism probably are inevitable for a media staff that attempts more than the blandest and most positive of multicultural coverage.

Also, faculty and advisers should try to help student staffers not to become discouraged if their pluralizing efforts result in *more* criticism and complaints from minority students and groups than their previous coverage did. The increased criticisms may well be a reflection of minority students' new awareness that this year's newspaper staffers are interested in doing a better job of covering minorities and are open to hearing about what they are doing wrong. The minority students' complaints may be part of what civil rights leaders referred to in the 1960s as "the revolution of rising expectations."

Finally, faculty, advisers and student staffers should remember that pluralizing a paper's coverage and staff is not a job that can be accomplished in one year, or even several. All they can do is make a commitment to begin.

NOTES

1. See Carolyn Martindale, *The White Press and Black America* (Westport, CT: Greenwood Press, 1986); Carolyn Martindale, "Coverage of Black Americans in Four Major Newspapers, 1950–1989," *Newspaper Research Journal* 11 (Summer 1990); Clint Wilson and Félix Gutiérrez, *Minorities and Media: Diversity and the End of Mass Communication* (Newbury Park, CA: Sage, 1985); and Jannette L. Dates and William Barlow, eds., *Split Image: African Americans in the Mass Media* (Washington, DC: Howard University Press, 1990).

2. See Kirk A. Johnson, "Black and White in Boston," *Columbia Journalism Review* 26 (May/June 1987), 50–52.

23 RECRUITING STUDENTS FOR CAMPUS MEDIA

John David Reed

Student media should and can contribute significantly to developing, maintaining and celebrating racial and ethnic diversity on our campuses. Often the only vehicles for campuswide discussion, they are critical to creating the multicultural university environments our diverse society requires. But most student media—usually campus newspapers—have not realized their potential for contributing to efforts to create and nourish campus climates that welcome and enhance pluralism and cross-cultural understanding.

Evidence is abundant. Journalism periodicals regularly report protests over insensitive or nonexistent coverage of minority communities on campus. Pick up a campus newspaper or tune in to a college radio station and look for stories about students or faculty of color, for diversity of news sources, for depth and sensitivity in addressing minority issues. Too often they are lacking. Glance into any campus newsroom and the reason is clear: participation of minority students is limited, as recent studies have concluded.[1] Where students of color and other cultures do not participate, their perspectives are not likely to be found.

Student media whose staffs do not represent the society they are reporting and commenting about cannot effectively achieve their objectives of serving the campus journalistically and providing educational opportunities for both journalism students and student consumers of news. Diversity of staff "yields a superior product," *Wall Street Journal* reporter Carolyn Phillips explained, because "ideas are cross-pollinated, considered more fully and from more points of view. That distillation process, with elements that challenge and balance rather than merely validate, must surely be closer to what the progenitors of a free press had in mind."[2] In addition to improving the newspaper or broadcast product, of course, that process will contribute to a learning environment where, as educator David Nelson has noted, student journalists can "become more multidimensional, sensitive, aware and tolerant members of a larger world."[3] Writing coach Roy Peter Clark has summarized the idea succinctly: "Without diversity, there can be no excellence."[4]

GOOD INTENTIONS NOT GOOD ENOUGH

While college student media may not have embraced the values of having a pluralistic environment, some are beginning to address the issue. Articles examining diversity in college news media are appearing in pedagogical and professional journalism periodicals, and conferences devoted to college journalism are giving significant attention to the issue.[5]

Indicators on campus are positive, too; the percentage of minority student participation in college newsrooms is almost double that of minority staff members in professional newsrooms, and the number of minority students in management positions at college newspapers on campuses with accredited journalism programs was up by 100 percent in 1990–91 over the previous year.[6]

Some journalism educators, student media advisers and student editors, then, have recognized that pluralizing student media is essential to an improved product and a more realistic experience which will provide better professional training for all student journalists and better education for the consumers of those media.

How results can be, and have been, achieved is the subject of this chapter, which will describe ideas, programs and techniques for enhancing diversity, especially in staffing. These have been undertaken by students and advisers who produce college media—primarily newspapers and yearbooks, since they constitute the great majority of student media—or suggested for application by others. Examples have been culled from journalism periodicals, convention seminars, conversations with student editors and faculty advisers, the pages of the college press, and experiences at the author's institution. Suggestions are presented in the context of promoting pluralism in student news media presently staffed with predominantly nonminority students.

Although most ideas are described from the perspective of the media adviser or journalism administrator, they can be adapted as well by student editors and managers of college media. In addition, many of the suggestions about teaching students the values of pluralism can be used effectively in the classroom by teachers whose only contact with the student media is teaching present and future media staffers and consumers in their classes. The many suggestions offered here for recruiting minority students into journalism also will be useful to journalism program administrators and faculty.

While the focus of this chapter is on attracting more minority students to campus media and persuading them to participate, it necessarily devotes considerable attention to the more challenging portion of that process: motivating those media and their predominantly nonminority student staff members to recognize the need to improve the diversity of their staffs, to sensitize the staffers and enhance their cultural awareness, to help them understand the value and essential nature of multicultural perspectives in their professional development and performance. In short, student media must be persuaded to appreciate and even embrace the values represented by pluralism.

BARRIERS TO MINORITY STUDENT PARTICIPATION

Why aren't more minority students participating in student media on our campuses? The reasons they should are plentiful. The most important relates to the educational mission of student media: student media provide experience—resulting in clips, tapes and other tangible signs of participation as well as references who can evaluate the student's record of performance—that can't be duplicated in the classroom and isn't available to most students at professional media. That experience is essential to competing successfully for some scholarships and for virtually all internships and jobs. In sum, as one study about college newspapers concluded, student media "should play a significant role in the development of viable minority candidates who would be better trained to begin work."[7]

In order to provide access for all students to that experience and to improve its value through pluralism, barriers must be overcome. These barriers arise from the traditions, attitudes, realities and images of student media. Some stem from attitudes and perceptions of minority students themselves. They include:

- Failure of predominantly White student media to reach out and invite students of color to participate.
- Perceptions by minority students that those media are elitist and cliquish, creating a climate where they are not welcome.
- Creation of a racist image by student media, which often demonstrate insensitivity toward, or little interest in, minority individuals and groups through news coverage.
- Consequent pressure from minority peers against participation in an organization perceived to be hostile.
- Conflicts created by time demands pitting participation in student media against time needed for work to pay for schooling and time required for good academic performance.

WHERE TO FOCUS RECRUITING EFFORTS

The first step toward eliminating these barriers is to locate students of color who might be interested in participating in student media. Easiest to identify are those students who have indicated an interest in journalism or mass communications through choice of academic discipline or possibly by limited participation in student media. They should be counseled through advising and mentoring about the importance of participation in student media, its effect on job and internship placement, and their role in pluralizing those media.

The next most accessible minority students are those already on campus whose academic interests have not crystallized or lie elsewhere. These students may be identified from lists maintained by the school or found in minority student clubs or in classes in related disciplines such as English, political science and history. Individuals can be contacted by letter or telephone, while groups and classes can be approached through offers to speak about how media operate, potential careers or other related issues. It is especially important to emphasize to these students that college media offer experiences in business, advertising, photography, graphics and production as well as in editorial departments.

Finally, students of color in community colleges, high schools, junior highs and grade schools are potential future staff members for student media, although recruiting them requires greater resources and cooperation. Usually those efforts are undertaken by journalism programs or other academic units. Participation of student media staff members can enhance the effectiveness of such initiatives. Or the recruiting efforts could be undertaken by student media themselves.

Some typical recruiting programs aimed at off-campus persons include summer workshops, outreach programs and campuswide efforts.

Summer workshops. Off-campus recruiting most often is conducted through summer camps and workshops, usually discipline-specific, and involves high school students. The students typically come to campus for a week or two of intensive training in basic print or broadcast journalism. Summer workshops should be supplemented by ongoing projects during the school year, however, since students may be returning to schools that offer limited opportunities for continuing to develop those skills.

Outreach programs. Projects involving teams of faculty and/or student media personnel and offering workshops on site at an area community college or high school during the school year can target schools with significant minority enrollment. A turn-around project, in which students from the target school are brought to the campus to produce an issue of their own school publication or to work as interns on campus media, is especially good since it involves the excitement of hands-on training as well as the campus visit. Students from nearby community colleges and high schools also can be invited to participate in campus media activities as volunteer interns. These workshops are especially beneficial for schools whose limited funding may restrict resources for student media or eliminate them altogether. University student media staff members, minority and nonminority, can be especially effective in working with community college peers as well as high school students.

Campuswide efforts. Recruiting also may be done as a planned portion of a broader campuswide effort or even as a voluntary adjunct to a program not involving journalism. During one two-week high school preparatory program, student media staff members were hired to serve as tutors for minority student participants whose principal journalism class project was to produce a daily workshop newspaper. In another instance, student media staff members volunteered to advise students of color who were preparing a newsletter as part of a precollege summer program for minority students. In a college prep program where no journalism activities were planned, editors at the student newspaper invited the minority high school students from the workshop to visit their newsroom and tutored those who were interested in participating in production of the newspaper as staff interns.

While recruiting students of color and reaching out to invite them to participate is essential to diversifying college media staffs, the benefits of pluralism in student media cannot be achieved through recruiting alone. Dramatic changes in environment must be undertaken simultaneously. The culture of the newsroom must be reshaped, attitudes and perceptions changed, stereotypes struck down, new realities and consequent new images of student media created. If recruiting is to succeed, student media must become environments that welcome diversity.

CHANGING THE CULTURE OF STUDENT MEDIA

The failure of White-dominated college student media to reach out to students of color and invite them to participate creates barriers that may be explained in part by tradition and routine and in part by lack of commitment, lack of knowledge and lack of understanding. Student journalists often are so caught up in trying to get the paper out or stay on the air—in addition to carrying full class loads and attending to the details of their personal lives—that not much time is available for nondeadline duties.

As a result, student media traditionally do little recruiting, formal or informal. Aside from asking a friend or roommate down to the station or paper to help out, recruiting often stops with house ads or flyers posted here and there on campus. As one college editor described it, "They just hold a meeting and take whoever comes. This generally does not result in attracting minorities."[8] More effective recruiting strategies should be implemented, to be sure. But more important, if attitudes are to change and newsroom cultures are to be reshaped, student journalists must understand why those strategies are needed.

Why should college student media embrace pluralism? Because it serves their own educational goals of professional and personal development of student staff members and consumers as well as larger interests.

A commitment to diversity must begin at the top, as editor David Lawrence, Jr., has emphasized. "Progress will be made only when the people in charge embrace the value of a diverse work force and management, then insist on it."[9] Advisers, teachers, student editors and other leaders, then, must undertake to educate and motivate the young journalists who staff student media, to persuade them to buy into commitment, knowledge and understanding of pluralism. Here are some qualities needed and suggestions for how to develop them.

Commitment

Complacency has characterized much of the college press in recent years. A crusading spirit needs to be reinstilled in student journalists. They should be inspired to follow the lead suggested by editor Phil Currie: "One of the key factors in making democracy work in this nation is for groups of varying backgrounds and interests to communicate effectively with and to understand one another better. And the newspaper should play a central role in making that happen."[10]

What to do:

Discuss regularly the First Amendment role of the press in our society, its watchdog function and the concept of the marketplace of ideas. Review the U.S. Supreme Court's landmark decisions on expression.

Examine professional ethical standards, especially accuracy and fairness.

Urge college journalists to re-examine the legacy of their predecessors in the 1960s and 1970s who recognized the great social issues of their time and were energized by them.

Talk about the great issues of our time, especially pluralism in our society: What needs to be done? What is the role of the press? What is the role of student media? Does it have a special responsibility to "do the right thing"?

In that context, consider reporter George Curry's suggested approach to developing pluralism in newspapers: "We need to have an attitude that we would have if we were mobilizing to do a major series. . . . Let's treat this like we're going after a Pulitzer Prize."[11]

Knowledge

College journalists are motivated by professionalism. They want to produce excellent media and through that experience prepare themselves for careers. The values of pluralism in student media relate directly to those two major goals. Students who make the connection will value a culturally diverse newsroom climate.

What to do:

Explore how the quality of the medium and the value of experience on its staff depend on its pluralism. Make the case, along with industry leaders such as Knight-Ridder editor Jackie Thomas and Gannett editor Keith Moyer, that "our newspaper pages must be a diverse sampling of columnists and guest writers, because there's a diverse community out there,"[12] and that "a multi-culturally diverse staff produces a more interesting newspaper, a newspaper that is clearly more in touch with each person in the community."[13]

Share resources such as those listed in the bibliography at the end of Part IV with staffers and faculty. Use them to focus discussion groups.

Explain how a culturally diverse medium will be especially helpful in attracting new staff members to share the workload as well as making new friends among readers.

Emphasize the crucial role pluralistic values play in professional development and preparation for the job market, especially how greater participation by minority students in college media activities will provide a more diverse cultural experience for all students involved.

Point out how socialization can help in development of a "diversity-tolerant personality,"[14] which is crucial to success in our increasingly diverse society.

Note that editors and student leaders have special responsibilities: "Recruiters and hiring editors are beginning to ask job candidates, especially student editors who are white and male, what they've done to diversify their college newspaper staffs."[15]

Understanding

Student journalists share with many of their professional peers the failure to understand the value and essential nature of multicultural perspectives in their professional development and performance. What is needed in college media is largely the same as what is needed in all media: to establish an environment that "not only represents the diversity of the public it serves but also manages that diversity to enable each employee to perform to his or her potential."[16]

What to do:

Implement continuing programs for students and full-time staff members intended to increase awareness of and heighten sensitivity to cultural diversity. Bring in journalists, personnel specialists and others to talk about diversity and about understanding, questioning and reconsidering values.

Infuse multiculturalism into professional training programs by inviting minority journalists to conduct them or including minority sources and examples in materials.

Promote appreciation of individualism and differences by asking professors to talk about contributions of minority journalists and others to American history and by inviting staff members or visitors to share information, especially unique characteristics, about their cultural heritage.

Encourage a professional environment by establishing policies aimed at reducing bias, challenging racial and other stereotypes, and eliminating hurtful behavior.[17] Deal with infractions immediately, on the spot and matter-of-factly.

Set an agenda, articulate a vision and share it with everyone on the staff. In other words, do what Nashville *Tennessean* editor Frank Sutherland suggested: "Define diversity for the newspaper's community and then make sure every staff member knows what the newspaper's goals are."[18]

Give your plans to reshape the cultural climate a high profile by talking frankly and frequently about diversity in our society and in student media and by sharing articles and other information through posting on bulletin boards and circulating them to the staff.

Recognize the vulnerability of all newcomers to the staff and assign them mentors who will be held accountable for seeing to their needs and their development as contributors.

Request a copy of the "ASNE Multicultural Management Guide" from the American Society of Newspaper Editors, P.O. Box 17004, Washington, DC 20041. It is an excellent guide to diversity training.

IMAGES AND REALITIES OF ELITISM AND CLIQUES

Another set of barriers to minority student participation in college media arises out of perceptions, and sometimes realities, that the staffs at those media are elitist and cliquish as well as White-dominated. The staffs at least appear to send the message that outsiders are not welcome.

To some extent those images, sometimes misperceptions, are common to all new students who approach student media. What appears to be elitism results more from lack of common courtesy, poor management or poor judgment, usually a result of time demands. In these cases student journalists are so engrossed in their duties at student media that they fail to take the time to make outsiders feel welcome or to pay much attention to newcomers on the staff. Similarly, what appears to be cliquishness often is simply the expression of camaraderie generated by the intensive work of getting out the next paper or yearbook signature or preparing for the next broadcast.

In too many instances, however, perceptions reflect reality. Too often student media staffs remain, as one person observed, "a closed society that locks out would-be staffers who are different. Hispanics and older students and blacks and handicapped students and physics majors are locked out."[19] In some cases staff members ignore newcomers simply because they're different, or because they're perceived to lack ability or experience or desire. In still others, unintended exclusion may result simply from oversight, from lack of awareness or from insensitivity. Here are some suggestions for correcting these problems.

Changing Images

Examine the physical profile of student media. Does it encourage diversity? Or does the layout encourage formation of cliques, emphasize separateness, discourage interest in differences? Explore with staff members how to rearrange space in student media facilities to create an environment that embraces diversity but emphasizes commonality, that appears to invite participation.

What to do:

Consolidate space to encourage interaction and cooperation among media and among departments within a medium. Create communication and awareness between the newspaper and yearbook staffs, the print and broadcast journalists, the editorial and advertising departments. Emphasize the common goals of all and the need for recognition of different interests and perspectives and for sensitivity to the needs of others.

Establish a common reception area for visitors and outsiders, whether they are greeted in person or by phone. Staff it with students who are interested in personnel services. Train them to provide a warm welcome and personal attention to every newcomer or customer.

Make minority participation visible by making opening up facilities to outsiders. Encourage visitors. Use location of departments to exhibit diversity of participation. Show newcomers, physically, that the environment is a friendly one.

Look for opportunities to create more visibility for practices that emphasize a pluralistic environment. Obtain and display prominently professional periodicals, literature and other resources from minority press groups as well as other sources. Invite minority professionals to speak, consult and otherwise spend time with staff members. Diversify magazines and reading materials available in waiting areas.

Changing Realities

Whether or not a student medium projects a pluralistic image ultimately depends, of course, on the real diversity of its staff. Minority students must be recruited, and the newsroom culture must be reshaped to make them and other newcomers feel welcome, so that they can develop their potential and contribute to the medium.

What to do:

Train staff members in recruiting. Bring in media professionals, invite campus experts to help, visit with other organizations or departments that have achieved diversity in staffing. Seek help from local, state or national minority professional organizations.

Form a multicultural committee of staff members and outsiders if necessary to help identify minority and other students the medium has failed to recruit and serve. Ask them to devise a recruiting program that emphasizes individual and targeted contact. Approach students by major, as described earlier, but seek other opportunities as well. Ask academic advisers to recommend good writers; talk to minority student leaders; meet with minority organizations; offer to organize minority journalism clubs.

Conduct open houses regularly. Issue written invitations, provide refreshments and make the open houses fun.

Encourage students to explain regularly to the campus community, and especially to minority groups, how the student medium operates and how to contact student media leaders. Include such material in open houses, publish or broadcast features, or columns of explanation; pursue opportunities to make presentations to clubs, housing groups and others.

Insist on affirmative action hiring procedures in clerical or production positions that are work-study oriented. Especially important is staffing in reception areas where outsiders gain their initial impressions.

Offer management training for student editors and other leaders in editorial, advertising and other departments where staff members are volunteer and professionally oriented. Teach management for diversity. Help student managers learn to "handle work and people with respect, ability and fairness," as editor John Greenman suggested. He added that minority journalists "want to work for newspapers that are committed to newsrooms as integrated as the communities they serve and that are color blind in the treatment of their staff."[20]

Advise use of periodic evaluations for improvement of skills, even application of standards of competence, and careful attention to suggestions and criticism.

Encourage mentoring by assigning an experienced staff member as a guide and contact for each newcomer. This is the most important element of retention. First, it allows the staff to demonstrate the sincerity of its interest, offers a point of bonding and guards against appearance of unequal treatment. Second, it provides an entrée for the newcomer to learn about the history of the publication or station and its goals, to be introduced to and get to know its managers, and to find out about its requirements for advancement.

Be alert to formation of exclusionary cliques through informal activities such as lunch groups, post-production celebrations, or arranging for traveling companions and roommates during convention trips. Promote social activities that focus on common interests and are designed to bring diverse staff members together.

IMPROVING COVERAGE AND INCREASING SENSITIVITY

Student media whose news coverage and commentary have demonstrated little interest in minority groups and individuals or that have treated them with insensitivity will have erected significant barriers to minority student participation in their activities. Students are not likely to want to associate with a publication or station that seems indifferent or hostile. Adviser Carolyn Martindale, describing a situation at her campus, said the student newspaper had ignored the concerns, activities and interests of minority students for such a long time that these students perceived the paper as being racist.[21] Adviser Vernon C. Thompson, an African American, found that the image of a newspaper that had "all but ignored" minority students carried over to him: "The students simply did not trust anyone working for the newspaper."[22]

Even with no presumption of hostility, the effect is the same. A former minority college journalist described why: "There's a notion that being part of the newspaper as a reporter is foreign because the notion of being part of the paper as a *subject* is foreign."[23] As an editor for *Black Collegian* magazine observed, "If people of color don't believe that the campus paper will serve their interests, they just won't write for it."[24]

The barriers created by lack of attention to a minority community ought to be the easiest to remedy, once a student staff determines to pluralize its medium, because the staff decides what is to be published or broadcast. Adviser Leslie Harriell-Lewis says, "Minority hiring works best when the minorities in the readership area think that your newspaper is doing an adequate job of covering their activities and interests."[25]

Results may not be immediate, however. Adviser Vernon Thompson was surprised at "how long wounds take to heal in an ethnic minority community that had been virtually ignored."[26] A survey of minority student participation in student newspapers made a similar observation: "It takes a history of balanced minority coverage to attract minorities and it takes a diverse and sensitive staff to hold and promote minority staffers."[27]

Here are some approaches for predominantly White staffs interested in creating that track record of improved coverage of minority affairs:

Find out what's been missing; "Stop and listen to minority voices that have an understanding and perspective white editors and reporters don't have," as editor Tim McGuire has suggested.[28]

Survey the campus minority community. Talk to groups, leaders and other individuals of diverse racial and ethnic backgrounds. Ask classmates, roommates and teachers. Form an advisory committee composed of individuals who are interested in enhancing the multicultural climate on the campus. Use those individuals as a sensitivity sounding board.

Conduct a multicultural analysis of news and entertainment in student publications or broadcasts. Are individuals of color routinely included as subjects and sources? Or are they found only in what editor Mary Esther Bullard-Johnson calls "stereotypical 'minority' stories"[29] or in a negative context? Seek out news sources who represent the diversity of academic specialists and other authorities on the campus. In selecting individuals for interviews or photo subjects, be conscientious about making that coverage representative of the campus population.

Establish a beat for diversity issues and maintain it regardless of composition of the staff. Base assignments about minority issues on ability, knowledge and interest, not racial or ethnic heritage. Remember journalist Carolyn Phillips' advice that "A good reporter, sensitive to cultural differences, can tackle any story."[30]

Raid professional journals for ideas applicable to the campus press. Copy articles about improving news coverage; post them and share them. For a start, here are tips from three good ones:

From "Tips for Increasing Minority Coverage": Get out of the office and into the community. Identify hubs of activity for minority students. Tell readers how to share ideas for news coverage. Do your homework. Write not about bureaucracies, but about people who care and who solve problems. Write about people who are helping your campus community. Write about achievements, about underlying issues, about sacrifice, environments and interaction.[31]

From "Reaching Minority Readers": Cultivate sources and contacts outside of the usual power centers, for example, eyewitnesses, clerical employees and student leaders. Redefine good reporting to include cultural diversity. Brainstorm when assignments are made and debrief after an assignment to examine cultural implications of stories. Have reporters and photographers explore the campus community to look for news instead of just covering scheduled events.[32]

From "NEWS 2000 Requires Diversity": Find out where staffers live and work, and develop news sources where they don't. Audit entertainment, campus calendar and other listings to be sure they include multicultural events. Ensure graphic representation of campus diversity by keeping track of how often what groups appear. Create a monthly performance awards system including a diversity category. Rather than waiting for readers to complain, reach out and ask them what they like or don't like. Give coverage of special campus community events a high profile so that those involved will know that their student paper or station is there and cares. Compile a dictionary of offensive terms and avoid them.[33]

Take the lead through the medium's opinion functions in putting pluralism on the campus social and political agenda. Include diverse perspectives and speakers among columnists or in public affairs programming. Ask minority students and others to submit letters or other commentary for publication or airing. Stimulate commentary and discussion through editorial analysis.

Develop a calendar of special events that celebrate the cultural diversity of the campus and plan for extended coverage. Several college newspapers provide a monthlong package of stories during Black History Month, for instance. One daily conducts an essay contest during that month on such topics as contributions of minority Americans, complete with prizes provided by advertisers and other donors.

Consider developing alternate media devoted to coverage of the university's minority community. Minority participation on "mainstream" college newspapers appears to be higher on campuses where alternative minority newspapers are published.[34] One reason may be that those papers provide a more comfortable setting for entry-level experience, which prepares students for moving on to other media.

At Eastern Illinois University, for instance, the campus daily supported development of a minority newspaper by providing production and circulation services and assistance and found the alternative publication to be a significant source of new minority staffing. At the same time the minority papers' presence as well as its staff members gave additional encouragement to the traditional campus paper to fully reflect the diversity of the campus in its own coverage. At the very least, the alternate press provides an outlet for students who don't feel welcome at other campus media.

CHANGING PERCEPTIONS AMONG MINORITY STUDENTS

Perceptions and attitudes of minority students themselves constitute another set of barriers to pluralizing college media. Even where once indifferent student media have undertaken commitments to diversity, participation may be inhibited by a lingering "perception by minority students that they may not be wanted in a predominantly white newsroom."[35] The lack of diversity itself may be a significant barrier, as one student editor observed: "It takes a pretty determined and motivated black journalist to walk into a newsroom of white journalists and make the situation work for him or herself."[36] Advisers agree that "It's hard for a minority student to join a paper where whites have traditionally held the majority of posts."[37] Some of those students work for an alternate minority paper instead, a few find opportunity with local professional media, and too many simply allow themselves to be shut out.

Editor Mervin Aubespin has suggested that the failure of journalism education to integrate the history of minority journalists into the journalism curriculum may contribute to a feeling among minority students that they don't belong. Aubespin concluded that students may "begin to be intimidated by your reinforcement of the belief that African Americans in journalism are something relatively new."[38]

Minority students also may be discouraged from joining the staffs of mostly White college publications and stations because of pressure from peers who see those media as indifferent or hostile. One African American student editor told his adviser that "Other black students on campus sort of shunned him and viewed him as an Uncle Tom because he must have, by definition, sold out to be working for our newspaper."[39] Another adviser reported similar experiences: "Some of the blacks who have worked at our paper tell me they've had to endure pressure from their peers because they worked for the white honky *Northern Star*."[40] Carlos Sanchez, a minority journalist who felt that pressure when he joined his college daily, remembers it as formidable: "Minority students must constantly confront the dilemma of choosing acceptance among their peers—or choosing defiance."[41]

Minority students who appear to lack interest or desire in participating in student media, then, may simply need help or encouragement to overcome these barriers. One African American student leader indicated as much when she told a group of editors on her campus: "Minority students feel they have had doors slammed in their faces so often. It would be wonderful if you were to open the door of your newspaper office and invite us in."[42] Here are some ideas for helping minority students to set old perceptions aside and respond positively to new opportunities:

Explain to all staff members that these barriers exist for minority students *in addition to* the natural apprehensions all students face when they are thrust into unfamiliar environments. Help in dealing with them is not "a freebie," as journalist Carolyn Phillips has pointed out: "Nobody's saying it should be any easier for journalists who are different. It simply shouldn't be any harder."[43]

Provide careful mentoring for minority students beyond that included in training for new staff members. Nonminority students who are "surrounded by role models" may not need additional mentoring, but "customizing advising and nurturing" can make available to minority students resources to help them feel more comfortable in a predominantly White environment.[44] Mentoring should come from student staff members, who are most knowledgeable about the dynamics of the medium itself and about the campus from a journalist's perspective, and from an adviser or journalism teacher who can better counsel students of color about dealing with personal or professional problems, academic performance and career preparation.

Talk frankly and frequently with minority students about the problems they perceive or may experience in a predominantly nonminority student environment. Facilitate regular meetings between them and student managers to discuss comfort levels of the cultural climate at the publication or station.

Form a campus chapter of the National Association of Black Journalists, an affiliate of another national minority journalism organization, or a local club. Such a group "provides support, encourages academic success and promotes minority student involvement," educator Manny Romero notes.[45]

Look to other departments in a student medium to help overcome the impression an all-White newsroom creates. If minority students are present on advertising, business or production staffs, they will demonstrate the medium's diversity even where other departments may still be White-dominated.

Help minority students relate the "pioneering spirit" reporter Frank Santos has mentioned to challenges they may face upon graduation. Santos explained that responsibility to a group of minority students at a jobs fair this way: "When you take an entry-level job, you're going to have to go to a small paper probably. It's probably going to be a mostly white community and you're probably going to feel uncomfortable. But if you're there and the next guy comes, or woman, that person is going to feel a lot more comfortable."[46]

Remind minority students also of the commitment that characterized the careers of minority journalists such as Ida B. Wells. Discuss the implications of their heritage outside of journalism from such pioneers as Rosa Parks. Through seminars, postings and individual discussions, make sure all students are aware of the history of minorities in journalism.

Emphasize the importance of participation in student media to career development and especially preparation for the job market. Post this advice from editor John Greenman: "Newspapers heavily weight college newspaper experience when deciding who will get internships and entry-level jobs. Minority students who don't work on college newspapers are at a disadvantage."[47] The same applies to other media. Stress also how experience in journalism is crucial for developing skills and increasing confidence prior to embarking upon an internship or first job.

GRADES, FINANCES AND SOCIAL LIFE

Competing demands on time available for academic, financial, extracurricular and social activities present additional barriers to participation in college media for some minority students. Many educators would agree that working at a student publication or other medium is what newspaper adviser Cynthia Rawitch calls the "toughest and most time-consuming of the practical experiences."[48] Those conflicts between time required to practice journalism on campus and time needed for studies or to earn money for tuition and expenses may be aggravated by several factors, especially insufficient financial resources, inadequate academic preparation and social isolation. For instance, where students of color comprise a small percentage of the campus population, more time may be needed for developing and maintaining social relationships in which the students can be comfortable. Participation in those social activities becomes more important when opportunities to find other people of color are lacking.

More universal problems are money and grades. Money can be a major determinant in whether a medium can recruit and keep staff members, minority and otherwise. Student media that rely on volunteers or offer only nominal compensation may not fare well in competition with part-time jobs elsewhere that pay minimum wage or better.

Grades are a special concern for students whose financial assistance may depend on academic performance, resulting in pressure to "bypass extracurricular activities that might interfere with studies."[49] Students whose high school and elementary school programs failed to prepare them fully for college work often need tutors or other academic assistance.

While those factors are not unique to students of color and may or may not be aggravated for them, they are certain to hinder efforts to diversify student media. Here are some suggestions for addressing these effects:

Help students learn how to manage time and money more effectively. Call on experts on campus to provide handouts and other materials. Ask them to conduct seminars. Work with students to create daily, weekly and semester-long schedules and to create financial budgets.

Provide personal attention. The earlier academic or financial problems can be identified, the better the chances of minimizing their effect. More money is available on campus at the beginning of a term, and more time remains on the classwork calendar.

Recognize how devastating financial problems can be and redouble efforts to alleviate them. Earning money takes up time needed elsewhere; fretting over it distracts students; lack of it denies them books or other essentials of student life.

Provide paid positions within student media; seek funding from other university resources for the purpose; solicit donations from readers, listeners, viewers and other recipients of student media services. Develop a "friends" organization similar to those relied on by public broadcasting stations. Persuade related academic departments to offer aid to students engaged in related activity in student media.

Seek financial assistance for staffers at student media from sources outside the institution. Tap local media, alumni, community organizations, professional groups.

Urge students to seek, and help them to pursue, scholarships and other financial assistance available through university or discipline-related resources. The school's financial aid office should provide a general listing of scholarships, for instance. The Dow Jones Newspaper Fund can provide a complete listing of journalism scholarships.

Teach students about and encourage freelancing, especially of stories they've done for campus media that may be of interest elsewhere. Educator Manny Romero points out that "initiative pays. Both the student's pocketbook and clip file will benefit through regular submissions to the local paper, wire services, a metro daily or regional magazines."[50]

Schedule academic support seminars for student media staff members; set up study groups and peer support and employ other techniques designed to improve academic performance. Become an expert in academic advising. Create an academic profile for all staff members and monitor progress.

Urge student managers to encourage class attendance and other good academic habits as a service to the student medium, lest they lose the services of students who are dismissed academically.

If a student must drop out of school for financial or academic reasons, encourage him or her to continue gaining media experience, even if only as a part-time volunteer at a hometown radio station or newspaper. Allow such students who remain in the area to work on student media as interns.

COMMITMENT TO PLURALISM

The suggestions included in this chapter are more than any one student media adviser—or even two advisers—could possibly implement, but they provide a smorgasbord of ideas from which advisers can choose those that seem most workable for their own situations. They also perhaps can inspire advisers, teachers and student media personnel to a better understanding of the many actions they can undertake to encourage pluralism in the college media and the many benefits to be gained from such diversity. Among these are a better education for student journalists, a better news product for the campus community and a better preparation for students, faculty and advisers for living in a more multicultural America.

Journalism educator Ted Pease, in urging the nation's newspaper industry to undertake a more aggressive commitment to achieving diversity, describes some other values of such a commitment: "the moral rightness of expanding the diversity of voices in our nation's newspapers . . . the democratic ideal on which the nation was founded . . . [and] the pragmatic, market-driven perspective."[51]

Those reasons for adopting the values of pluralism also will serve the educational interests of college journalists. Using those guideposts, they can learn how doing the right thing will enhance their personal development and how producing student media that contribute to the "democratic ideal" and acknowledge the "market-driven perspective" is essential to professional preparation.

NOTES

1. See Barbara J. Hipsman and Stanley T. Wearden, "Peering Down the Pipeline," *Bulletin of the American Society of Newspaper Editors*, April 1991, pp. 27–28, and John Greenman, Barbara Hipsman and Stanley T. Wearden, "College Newspaper Staffs Are Diversifying, but Most Top Editors Still Are White," *Bulletin of the American Society of Newspaper Editors*, April 1990, pp. 13–17, for studies conducted in 1990 and 1989, respectively.

2. Carolyn Phillips, "Better Coverage Comes from a Diverse Newsroom," *College Media Review* 29 (Summer 1990), 9.

3. David Nelson, "Don't Accept Your Own Excuses," *College Media Review* 29 (Summer 1990), 4.

4. "MMP Welcomes New Board Members," *MMP Gazette* (newsletter of the Multicultural Management Program at the University of Missouri School of Journalism) 5 (Winter 1992), 2.

5. For instance, a survey of journalism literature yielded 18 articles relating to

diversity and the student press, all published since 1986 and all but three since 1989. Similarly, the annual fall college media convention hosted by College Media Advisers and the Associated Collegiate Press offered no sessions on the topic in 1987 but has averaged more than six sessions a year since.

6. In 1991 minority staff members at college newspapers on accredited campuses stood at 16.9 percent, while minority staffing in professional newsrooms was 8.72 percent. See Hipsman and Wearden, "Peering Down the Pipeline."

7. Stanley T. Wearden, Barbara J. Hipsman and John Greenman, "Racial Diversity in the College Newsroom," *Newspaper Research Journal*, Summer 1990, p. 85.

8. Scott Jaschik, "How to Recruit Minorities for College Newspapers," *The Morris Memo*, December 1986, p. 3.

9. David Lawrence, Jr., "Pluralism: Good Intentions Are Not Enough," *Knight-Ridder News*, Summer 1990, p. 4.

10. Phil Currie, "NEWS 2000 Requires Diversity," *Editorially Speaking* 46 (March 1992), 1.

11. Curry, quoted in Jeff Henderson, ed., "Miniplenary: Pluralizing the College Media," account of session at the national convention of the Association for Education in Journalism and Mass Communication, Washington, DC, August 1989, in *Leadtime*, AEJMC newspaper division newletter, October 1989, p. 8.

12. Thomas, quoted in Lawrence, "Pluralism," p. 1.

13. Moyer, quoted in Currie, "NEWS 2000," p. 8.

14. Barbara J. Hipsman, Stanley T. Wearden and John Greenman, "The College Newsroom: Still White at the Top," *College Media Review* 29 (Summer 1990), 6.

15. Phillips, "Better Coverage," p. 9.

16. R. Roosevelt Thomas, Jr., "Managing a Diverse Work Force Goes Beyond Affirmative Action," *presstime*, February 1992, p. 35.

17. See Terri Dickerson-Jones, "A Common Sense Guide to Reducing Bias," *Minorities in the Newspaper Business*, June-July 1988, pp. 2–3.

18. Quoted in Currie, "NEWS 2000," p. 2.

19. Phillips, "Better Coverage," p. 9.

20. Quoted in Lawrence, "Pluralism," p. 4.

21. Quoted in Henderson, "Miniplenary," p. 3.

22. Vernon C. Thompson, "Racial Incidents Challenge Campus News Coverage," *Journalism Educator* 44 (Summer 1989), 53.

23. Rick Greenberg, "The College Press: Why Minorities Are Turned Off," *Columbia Journalism Review*, January/February 1987, p. 43.

24. Allan Wolper and Mary Collins, "College Papers Roil Racial Sensitivities," *Washington Journalism Review*, May 1990, p. 43.

25. Quoted in Henderson, "Miniplenary," p. 4.

26. Thompson, "Racial Incidents," p. 53.

27. Hipsman, Wearden and Greenman, "College Newsroom," p. 7.

28. Quoted in "Reaching Minority Readers," *Poynter Report*, Summer 1991, p. 2.

29. Mary Esther Bullard-Johnson, " 'FIX IT,' " *The Quill* 79 (May 1991), p. 41.

30. Phillips, "Better Coverage," p. 9.

31. Karen F. Brown and Roy Peter Clark, "Tips for Increasing Minority Coverage," *The Quill* 81 (July/August 1991), 25.

32. "Reaching Minority Readers," pp. 2–3.

33. Currie, "NEWS 2000," pp. 1–8.

34. Hipsman and Wearden, "Peering Down the Pipeline," p. 28.

35. Greenman, Hipsman and Wearden, "College Newspaper Staffs," p. 15.

36. Ibid., pp. 15–16.

37. Hipsman, Wearden and Greenman, "College Newsroom," p. 7.

38. Mervin Aubespin, "Diversity: We Can Make a Difference," *Journalism and Mass Communication Administrator* 2 (November 1991), 6.

39. Henderson, "Miniplenary," p. 3.

40. Greenman, Hipsman and Wearden, "College Newspaper Staffs," p. 16.

41. Carlos Sanchez, "Pluralizing the Newsroom: Make It a Requirement," *College Media Review* 29 (Summer 1990), 12.

42. Carolyn Martindale, "Inclusivity on the College Newspaper," *Student Press Review*, Fall 1991, p. 13.

43. Phillips, "Better Coverage," p. 9.

44. Wearden, Hipsman and Greenman, "Racial Diversity," p. 93.

45. Manny Romero, "Full Court Press: Attracting Minority Students into College Media," paper presented at the national convention of the Associated Collegiate Press/College Media Advisers, Denver, November 1991, p. 8.

46. Quoted in Henderson, "Miniplenary," p. 6.

47. Quoted in Carolyn Martindale, "Adding New Dimensions to Your Staff... and Its Product," *College Media Review* 29 (Summer 1990), 20.

48. Quoted in Greenman, Hipsman and Wearden, "College Newspaper Staffs," p. 16.

49. Greenberg, "College Press," p. 43.

50. Romero, "Full Court Press," p. 8.

51. Ted Pease, "Ducking the Diversity Issue," *Newspaper Research Journal*, Summer 1990, p. 35.

24 ORGANIZING MINORITY STUDENT JOURNALISTS TO ENHANCE DIVERSITY IN THE COLLEGE NEWSROOM

Sharon Bramlett-Solomon

Although the issue of newsroom diversity is a topic frequently discussed among U.S. news industry managers, the diversity issue has not been widely addressed by the college press. Too many campus editors have made little effort to attract minority students and have shown little concern about diversifying their news staffs.

However, racial diversity is just as important in the college press as in the commercial press. The need for pluralism in the college newsroom is manifested by the dismal fact that the majority of the college press consists of largely all-White newsrooms.[1] Students of color still are not commonly seen in the campus newsroom and are extremely rare in editorship positions.[2]

The figures speak for themselves. A 1989 survey by the American Society of Newspaper Editors (ASNE) of newspapers at the nation's 90 accredited journalism institutions found that 62 percent of the papers had all-White editing and management staffs.[3] The survey showed that minority students constituted about 16.8 percent of the campus newsroom staffs. Of the 90 schools surveyed, only 8 had newspapers run by minority editors, and 4 of these were at predominantly Black colleges.[4]

John Greenman, managing editor of the Akron *Beacon Journal* and former ASNE Minority Committee chairman, feels that minority students are getting shortchanged when they do not get media experience while in college to help prepare them for today's highly competitive journalism job market. He said that when he recruits at regional or national job fairs, the resumes he receives from students of color "rarely show writing experience and never show editorships on the college newspaper."[5]

Greenman emphasized that diversity in the campus press is inextricably linked to diversity in the larger U.S. news industry. The news industry cannot thrive, he said, "until minority students move into editing and managing positions that bond students to the journalism profession."[6]

The ASNE findings indicate the need for greater emphasis on racial diversity among college newspaper staffs. The thesis of this discussion is that minority student participation in the campus media will increase if an organized effort is made to recruit minority staffers.

Organizing minority journalism students can enhance their participation in the campus media and improve campus news coverage of people of color. In fact, racial pluralism in the campus media is essential for more accurate and sensitive coverage of minorities in the college community, as college newspapers that are concerned about staff diversity are more likely to be sensitive to news coverage of people of color.

The need for pluralism in the college press is underscored by a number of current campus trends:

1. Race relations on the college campus today are a major story.
2. Racial tension exists on many on U.S. college campuses.
3. In recent years, confrontations between minority students and campus newspapers have made headlines.
4. Too many college newsrooms remain all-White operations in which little or no effort is made to reach out to the campus minority community.
5. Many students of color do not aggressively go after campus media jobs because of a perception that White students do not want them in the newsroom and do not welcome their participation.
6. Minority students hurt themselves when they do not take advantage of campus media jobs.

On a few college campuses, journalism associations have been formed to encourage campus media pluralism. Organizing such a network is particularly valuable on large, predominantly White college campuses where students of color sometimes feel alienated from the majority student body.

ORGANIZATIONS PROMOTE DIVERSITY

It was concern about the lack of minority student involvement in the campus press three years ago that prompted me to organize minority journalism students at Arizona State University and to serve as their faculty adviser. After listening for two years to complaints from individual students of color about campus press coverage of minorities, and after finding that minority students generally did not apply for campus media jobs, I believed that a minority association was needed to promote campus media opportunities among minority journalism students.

Twelve students attended a meeting called in September 1989 to organize the association. The purpose of the meeting was to discuss why such an organization was needed and to develop its purpose and goals. Every student was given an opportunity to express his or her view of the proposed organization's role and purpose. The students also were asked if they were interested in applying for jobs on the school's newspaper or yearbook staff or at the campus radio station. The students' most frequent sentiment regarding the campus media was that they did not feel welcome to apply for positions at the campus newspaper and radio station.

"Why do you feel unwelcome?" the faculty adviser asked students at the meeting. One African American female student responded this way: "For the most part, the campus press acts like we're not here. When we see little about minorities in the campus press and when we see no minorities in the campus newsroom, we feel we are not wanted there." Most of the minority students in attendance expressed similar views about the campus press.

The result of this meeting was the formation of the Association of AHANA Journalists (AAJ) at Arizona State. AHANA stands for African, Hispanic, Asian and Native Americans. The purpose of the association was articulated as follows:

1. To encourage AHANA student involvement in the campus media.

2. To promote academic excellence among AHANA print and broadcast students.

3. To foster recruiting and retention of AHANA students in the Walter Cronkite School of Journalism and Telecommunication.

4. To provide opportunities for AHANA journalism students to meet and network with local print and broadcast journalists and news executives.

5. To provide a network of shared communication about journalism career opportunities, minority job fairs, scholarships and job internships.

6. To provide a campus resource for media managers who want to locate and recruit AHANA journalism students.

At the first meeting the group also elected officers and defined the role of the faculty adviser. The AAJ faculty adviser's job was (1) to serve as a liaison between AAJ members, the Cronkite School and local media professionals, (2) to provide career and scholarship information, and (3) to insure AAJ continuity from year to year. The 12 students attending the first meeting decided that AAJ meetings would be held monthly.

Twice as many students attended the second AAJ meeting. The meeting featured the editors of the campus newspaper, yearbook and magazine as guest speakers, along with the campus radio station manager. The student media managers were asked to discuss hiring procedures for jobs in their newsrooms and were asked whether or not they had made any special attempts to attract students of color, such as visiting journalism classes to recruit minority students or asking journalism teachers for help in recruiting such students.

All of the campus media were run by White students. While all stated that they wanted staff diversity, none of the student media managers said they had made a special effort to attract minority students. They said they simply "welcome all students to apply." All of the student managers, however, applauded the start of AAJ and said they planned to use AAJ as a resource for recruiting minority staffers.

RESULTS OF ORGANIZING

In the three years since its inception, the AAJ at Arizona State has been a resource for minority journalism students, the Cronkite School and the campus media. AAJ holds monthly meetings in the Cronkite School, operates under a set of bylaws and has 28 dues-paying members (about one-fifth of the 149 AHANA students in the Cronkite School of 1,200 majors).

The association has contributed to a significant increase in the number of students of color holding campus media jobs. The semester after AAJ was organized, the number of minority students in the campus media increased from four to nine. In 1991, for the first time in the history of the campus newspaper, a minority student was selected as editor of the campus newspaper and a cultural diversity beat was started at the paper.

AAJ also has enhanced minority student participation in the campus broadcast media. For the past two years, AAJ members have produced *AHANA News*, a biweekly public affairs program on the campus radio station that features current events, issues and profiles about people of color in the campus community. *AHANA News* gives minority journalism students an opportunity to obtain both on-air and production radio experience.

In addition, campus editors and news managers attend AAJ meetings at the start of each semester to talk about job opportunities and to invite students of color to apply for jobs. AAJ also sponsors multicultural awareness sessions for campus press staffers and for journalism students. Such meetings have opened and enhanced communications between minority journalism students and campus press managers at Arizona State.

In other words, the AAJ at Arizona State is an active and thriving student organization that has been a significant resource for journalism students of color and the student media. Since AAJ's inception, minority students have been much more aggressive in applying for campus media jobs. Minority students are reminded at AAJ meetings that they hurt only themselves when they do not take advantage of campus media opportunities.

Some professional organizations of minority journalists, such as the National Association of Black Journalists and the National Association of Hispanic Journalists, have blamed the slow increase in the number of journalists of color in U.S. newsrooms on the failure of college journalism programs to produce enough minority candidates.[7] Encouraging increased diversity in the college media offers the chance to help solve this problem and promote greater diversity in the media workforce.

Since students of color at most predominantly White colleges generally do not seek campus media jobs because of a perception that they are not wanted there, this perception must be changed. The college press needs to embrace the idea of pluralism and to vastly improve its minority student hiring record.

Minority student involvement in the campus media will increase if an organized effort is made to recruit minority staffers. Campus media jobs can give students of color practical preparation for print and broadcast news jobs and can increase their chances of landing a job after college. Organizing minority journalism students on campus is one way to get more minority students into the campus newsroom and, in the long run, into the news industry.

NOTES

1. Carolyn Martindale, "Promoting Pluralism in the College Press," paper presented at the national convention of the Association for Education in Journalism and Mass Communication, Washington, DC, 11 August 1989, "Minority Employment," *Editor and Publisher*, September 1989, p.6.

2. Martindale, "Promoting Pluralism," p. 4.

3. Allan Wolper and Mary Collins, "College Papers Roil Racial Sensitivities," *Washington Journalism Review*, May 1990, pp. 42–44; Martindale, "Promoting Pluralism," p. 4.

4. Wolper and Collins, "College Papers," p. 43.

5. Martindale, "Promoting Pluralism," p. 8.

6. Wolper and Collins, "College Papers," p. 43.

7. "Minority Employment," p. 8.

BIBLIOGRAPHY

John David Reed

ANPA Foundation. *Recruiting and Retaining Newspaper Minority Employees: How to Do It*. 1986. ANPA (American Newspaper Publishers Association) Foundation, Box 17404, Washington, DC.

ASNE Multicultural Management Guide. American Society of Newspaper Editors, P.O. Box 17004, Washington, DC 20041.

Aubespin, Mervin. "Diversity: We Can Make a Difference." *Journalism and Mass Communication Administrator* 2 (November 1991), 4–7.

Blount, Tom. "Advice for Minorities on How to Get into the Daily Newspaper Business." *Bulletin of the American Society of Newspaper Editors* 736 (November 1991), 26–29.

Brown, Karen F. "Reaching New Audiences by Redefining the News." *Minorities in the Newspaper Business*, Spring 1991, pp. 4–5.

Brown, Karen F., and Roy Peter Clark. "Tips for Increasing Minority Coverage." *The Quill* 81 (July/August 1991), 25.

Bullard-Johnson, Mary Esther. " 'FIX IT.' " *The Quill* 79 (May 1991), 40–41.

Burroughs, Elise S. "Here Are 15 Strategies that Managers from Small Dailies Can Use to Help Diversify Their Work Forces." *Bulletin of the American Society of Newspaper Editors*, April 1990, pp. 6–7.

Conant, Colleen. "Shop Talk: How to Bring Cultural, Racial Diversity to the News Columns." *Scripps Howard News*, December 1990, pp. 15, 20.

Currie, Phil, ed. "NEWS 2000 Requires Diversity." *Editorially Speaking* 46 (March 1992), 1–8, published as an adjunct to *Gannetteer*, March-April 1992.

Dickerson-Jones, Terri. "A Common Sense Guide to Reducing Bias." *Minorities in the Newspaper Business*, June-July 1988, pp. 2–3.

Greenberg, Rick. "The College Press: Why Minorities Are Turned Off." *Columbia Journalism Review*, January/February 1987, p. 43.

Greenman, John, Barbara Hipsman and Stanley T. Wearden. "College Newspaper Staffs Are Diversifying, but Most Top Editors Still Are White." *Bulletin of the American Society of Newspaper Editors*, April 1990, pp. 13–17.

Henderson, Jeff, ed. "Miniplenary: Pluralizing the College Media." transcript excerpts from presentations by George Curry, Leslie Harriell-Lewis, Carolyn Martindale, John David Reed, Carlos Sanchez and Ken Siver at the national convention of the Association for Education in Journalism and Mass Communication, Washington, DC, August 1989. *Leadtime*, AEJMC newspaper division newsletter, October 1989, pp. 3–8.

Hipsman, Barbara J., and Stanley T. Wearden. "Peering Down the Pipeline." *Bulletin of the American Society of Newspaper Editors*, April 1991, 27–28.

Hipsman, Barbara J., Stanley T. Wearden and John Greenman. "The College Newsroom: Still White at the Top." *College Media Review* 29 (Summer 1990), 5–7.

Jaschik, Scott. "How to Recruit Minorities for College Newspapers." *The Morris Memo*, December 1986, p. 3.

Lawrence, David, Jr. "Pluralism: Good Intentions Are Not Enough." *Knight-Ridder News*, Summer 1990, pp. 1–5.

"Managing Diversity: Your Workforce Is Changing. Are You Ready?" *ASNE Multicultural Management Guide*, March 1992.

Martindale, Carolyn. "Adding New Dimensions to Your Staff . . . and Its Product." *College Media Review* 29 (Summer 1990), 17–20.

———. "Coverage Improvement Suggestions." In *The White Press and Black America*. Westport, CT: Greenwood Press, 1986.

———. "Improving Images of African Americans in the Media." Paper presented at the Eastern Communication Association convention, Pittsburgh, April 1991.

———. "Inclusivity on the College Newspaper." *Student Press Review*, Fall 1991, pp. 12–13.

———. "Infusing Cultural Diversity into Communication Courses." *Journalism Educator* 45 (Winter 1991), 34–38.

———. "Promoting Pluralism in the College Press." Paper presented at the national convention of AEJMC, Washington, DC, August 1989.

———. "Sensitizing Students to Racial Coverage." *Journalism Educator* 43 (Summer 1988), 79–81.

"MMP Welcomes New Board Members." *MMP Gazette* (newsletter of the Multicultural Management Program at the University of Missouri School of Journalism) 5 (Winter 1992), 2–3.

Nelson, David. "Don't Accept Your Own Excuses." *College Media Review* 29 (Summer 1990), 4.

Pease, Ted. "Ducking the Diversity Issue." *Newspaper Research Journal*, Summer 1990, pp. 24–37.

Phillips, Carolyn. "Better Coverage Comes from a Diverse Newsroom." *College Media Review* 29 (Summer 1990), 8–10.

"Reaching Minority Readers." *Poynter Report*, Summer 1991, pp. 2–3.

Romero, Manny. "Full Court Press: Attracting Minority Students into College Media." Paper presented at the national convention of the Associated Collegiate Press/College Media Advisers, Denver, November 1991.

Sanchez, Carlos. "Pluralizing the Newsroom: Make It a Requirement." *College Media Review* 29 (Summer 1990), 11–12.

Smith, Ronald. "In the Search for Minority Journalists, the Quest Begins Before College." *The Quill* 79 (May 1991), 25–27.

Thomas, R. Roosevelt, Jr. "Managing a Diverse Work Force Goes Beyond Affirmative Action." *presstime*, February 1992, p. 35.

Thompson, Vernon C. "Racial Incidents Challenge Campus News Coverage." *Journalism Educator* 44 (Summer 1989), 52–55, 61.

Vores, Ibby. "Thriving on Diversity." *Minorities in the Newspaper Business* 5 (Fall 1989), 1–2.

Wearden, Stanley T., Barbara J. Hipsman and John Greenman. "Racial Diversity in the College Newsroom." *Newspaper Research Journal*, Summer 1990, pp. 80–95.

Weinberg, Marilyn. "Getting Students to Resist Bias and Think Objectively." *College Media Review* 29 (Summer 1990), 13–14.

Wolper, Allan, and Mary Collins. "College Papers Roil Racial Sensitivities." *Washington Journalism Review*, May 1990, pp. 42–44.

INDEX

ABOUT THE CONTRIBUTORS

SHARON BRAMLETT-SOLOMON is an associate professor of journalism at Arizona State University, where she has taught since 1986 and has received three awards for teaching, research and service. She is founder and coordinator of the university's association of AHANA journalists and program adviser for the *AHANA News* radio program. A former reporter for the Louisville (KY) *Courier Journal* and the Memphis (TN) *Commerical Appeal*, she is secretary of the Minorities and Communication Division of AEJMC, a member of the AEJMC-American Newspaper Publishers Association Cooperative Committee on Education, and a member of the National Association of Black Journalists.

CARLOS E. CORTÉS is a professor of history at the University of California, Riverside. Among his publications are *Three Perspectives on Ethnicity*, *A Filmic Approach to the Study of Historical Dilemmas* and *Images and Realities of Four World Regions*; he has edited three major book series on Latinos. He is currently working on a three-volume study of the history of the U.S. motion picture treatment of ethnic groups, foreign nations and world cultures. The recipient of two book awards, Cortes has also received his university's Distinguished Teaching Award and has been honored as a humanist and a multicultural trainer.

JOHN M. COWARD teaches journalism and communication at the University of Tulsa. A native of Tennessee, he has been a newspaper reporter and has degrees from East Tennessee State University, the University of Tennessee and the University of Texas. His research interests include Native Americans and the mass media, Western history and literary journalism. He has published scholarly articles on news coverage of the Indian wars and on Horace Greeley's encounters with Native Americans. At Tulsa, he teaches a class in Native Americans and the Popular Imagination, an interdisciplinary study of the image of the Indian from Columbus to the present.

MERCEDES LYNN DE URIARTE, associate professor at the University of Texas at Austin, previously worked at the Los Angeles *Times* for eight years as an Opinion Section editor and a feature writer. She is a media consultant on diversification of the news product for the Austin *American-Statesman*. She is frequently an adjunct faculty member at the Poynter Institute for Media Studies and has received several fellowships, including a Ford and a Fulbright. During 1991–92 she was a research fellow at the Freedom Forum Media Studies Center and wrote a book on integrating the news product, forthcoming in 1994. She is ABD at Yale University, where she earned a master's degree.

VIRGINIA ESCALANTE is an assistant professor in the Journalism Department at the University of Arizona in Tucson. She is instructor for a bilingual community newspaper which trains future journalists to cover minority communities, has taught a graduate seminar in covering ethnic populations and has served as director of a summer journalism workshop for minority high school students. She was a reporter for the Los Angeles *Times*, where she covered predominantly Latino communities for five years and was a member of a Pulitzer Prize–winning team in 1984. Previously, she taught English and Chicano Studies at the high school level.

JOHN F. GREENMAN is associate publisher for Stark/Wayne editions of the Akron (Ohio) *Beacon Journal*. He is a member of the American Society of Newspaper Editors and its Minorities Committee, which he chaired in 1990–91. He is the author or co-author of more than a dozen papers and reports on newsroom diversity, including the census of minorities in college newspaper newsrooms. Greenman joined the *Beacon Journal* in 1985 as executive news editor. He was assistant managing editor for metropolitan news and managing editor for administration before assuming his current position in 1991. Greenman has a master's degree in media studies from Antioch (Ohio) College.

BARBARA J. HIPSMAN is associate professor in the School of Journalism and Mass Communication at Kent State University in Kent, Ohio. She has taught reporting public affairs, mid-level reporting and ethics, and a graduate level specialized reporting class. She previously taught at Bradley University in Peoria, Illinois, and was the statehouse bureau chief for the Belleville *News Democrat*, a medium-sized daily that covers the Illinois–St. Louis metropolitan area. Hipsman's research efforts center on minorities in the college media, translation as it is applied to specialized reporting, and skills tests as a screening tool at American newspapers.

JAMES PHILLIP JETER is an associate professor in the School of Journalism, Media and Graphic Arts and director of university broadcast services at Florida A&M University in Tallahassee. He earned a Ph.D. in communication arts from the University of Wisconsin-Madison. A former head of the Minorities and Communication Division of the Association for Education in Journalism and Mass Communication, he also is active in the Broadcast Education Association. He has served on several site visit teams in connection with journalism and mass communication education accreditation. His research interests include minorities and the mass media, media management, telecommunications policy and radio and television production.

MARILYN KERN-FOXWORTH, an accredited public relations practitioner, is an associate professor in the Department of Journalism at Texas A&M University. The first African American in the nation to receive a doctorate with a concentration in advertising and public relations, she has published numerous articles and has initiated and taught courses on multiracial groups and the mass madia. A former head of the AEJMC Minorities and Communications Division, she received a postdoctoral fellowship from the American Association of University Women in 1991 to complete her forthcoming book *Aunt Jemima, Uncle Ben, and Rastus: Blacks in Advertising Yesterday, Today and Tomorrow.*

CAROLYN MARTINDALE, compiling editor of this book, is the author of *The White Press and Black America*, a study of major newspapers' coverage of African Americans before, during and after the civil rights movement. Published by Greenwood Press in 1986, it was selected by *Choice* as Academic Book of the Year. Director of the journalism program at Youngstown (Ohio) State University, Martindale has been adviser of the student newspaper there for 15 years. She has written numerous articles on press coverage of Black Americans, student press rights, pluralizing the journalism curriculum and diversifying the coverage and staffs of student media.

MARION MARZOLF is a professor in the Department of Communication at the University of Michigan. She offered what was probably the first Women in Media course in the nation in 1971 and has published articles and a book, *Up from the Footnote* (1977), about women in journalism history. Her most recent book, *Civilizing Voices: American Press Criticism 1880–1950*, was published in 1991. She also has published on the Danish immigrant press. She has been associate chair of her department and is currently director of Michigan's Scandinavian Studies Program. She has received a Faculty Achievement Award and the first Outstanding Achievement Award given by AEJMC's Commission on the Status of Women.

TED PEASE, associate director for publications for the Freedom Forum Media Studies Center in New York, is editor of *Media Studies Journal*. He is the former chair of the Journalism Department at St. Michael's College in Vermont and has directed the Midwest Newspaper Workshop for Minorities at Ohio University. He has written numerous research studies on diversity, including "The Newsroom Barometer," a benchmark 1991 survey of 1,328 newspaper journalists on issues of job satisfaction and race. Pease was for four years associate editor of *Newspaper Research Journal* and is an adjunct member of the American Society of Newspaper Editors' Minorities Committee and the newspaper industry's Task Force on Minorities in the Newspaper Business.

JOHN DAVID REED, chair of the Department of Journalism and coordinator of student publications at Eastern Illinois University, has advised the *Daily Eastern News* since 1972. A member and former chair of EIU's Affirmative Action Advisory Committee, he was co-chair of the steering committee for the school's 1990 Task Force on Enhancing Minority Participation. Formerly a reporter for the Chicago *Sun-Times*, he holds a Ph.D. and an M.A. in journalism from Southern Illinois University and the University of Missouri and a B.A. in English from the University of Illinois, where he was a student journalist at the *Daily Illini*.

ROBERT M. RUGGLES is dean of the Florida A&M University School of Journalism, Media and Graphic Arts. In 1974 he began the journalism degree program at FAMU, and in 1982 it received accreditation from the Accrediting Council on Education in Journalism and Mass Communication, the first program at a historically Black college to do so. In 1982 he was made dean of the newly formed School of Journalism, Media and Graphic Arts. He has served on the accrediting council representing the Association of Schools of Journalism and Mass Communication and the Association of Black College Journalism and Mass Communications Programs.

FEDERICO A. SUBERVI-VÉLEZ, Ph.D., University of Wisconsin-Madison, is an associate professor in the Department of Radio-TV-Film at the University of Texas-Austin. He teaches communication and ethnic groups, communication and Latino politics, and ethnic-oriented media institutions. His research interests include political communication, ethnic minority issues in U.S. and Brazilian media, and the mass communication system of Puerto Rico, where he was born. He has been a Fulbright Scholar in Brazil and has received research grants from the Tinker Foundation, the Ford Foundation, the California Policy Seminar, the University of California at Santa Barbara and the University of Texas-Austin.

ALEXIS S. TAN, Ph.D., University of Wisconsin, is professor and director of the Murrow School of Communication at Washington State University. He is the author of *Mass Communication Theories and Research* (2nd ed., 1985) and of more than 40 book chapters and research articles in *Journalism Quarterly*, *Public Opinion Quarterly*, *Journal of Broadcasting*, the *Quarterly Journal of Speech* and *Communication Monographs*. He has taught at the University of the Philippines, Cornell University and Texas Tech University. He is a student of Eastern religions and the martial arts. He is researching the media's socialization effects on cultural minorities in the United States.

ORLANDO L. TAYLOR is dean and graduate professor at the School of Communications at Howard University in Washington, DC. He received his bachelor's degree from Hampton University, his master's degree from Indiana University, and his Ph.D. from the University of Michigan. Dean Taylor has held academic appointments at several other major universities, including Indiana University, Stanford University and the University of Pittsburgh. He has lectured and consulted extensively throughout the nation in a variety of public, professional and academic settings. He is the author of approximately 75 books, articles and monographs on various topics pertaining to communication and culture.

CLINT C. WILSON II, Ed.D., is chair of the Journalism Department in the Howard University School of Communications. He has written for various news organizations, including the Associated Press, Los Angeles *Times*, Washington *Post*, Los Angeles *Herald-Examiner*, Pasadena *Star-News* and Los Angeles *Sentinel*. He is author of *Black Journalists in Paradox: Historical Perspectives and Current Dilemmas* (1991) and co-author, with Félix Gutiérrez, of *Minorities and Media: Diversity and the End of Mass Communication* (1985). His scholarly work on ethnic minorities and mass media has been published in *Journalism Educator*, *Columbia Journalism Review* and *Change* magazine.